LIVING NEXT
TO THE GIANT

LIVING NEXT TO THE GIANT

The Political Economy of Vietnam's
Relations with China under *Doi Moi*

Le Hong Hiep

ISEAS YUSOF ISHAK
INSTITUTE

First published in Singapore in 2017 by
ISEAS Publishing
30 Heng Mui Keng Terrace
Singapore 119614

E-mail: publish@iseas.edu.sg
Website: <http://bookshop.iseas.edu.sg>

The responsibility for facts and opinions in this publication rests exclusively with the author and his interpretations do not necessarily reflect the views or the policy of the publisher or its supporters.

ISEAS Library Cataloguing-in-Publication Data

Le Hong Hiep.
Living Next to the Giant : The Political Economy of Vietnam's Relations with China under *Doi Moi*.
1. Vietnam—Politics and government.
2. Vietnam—Foreign relations—China.
3. China—Foreign relations—Vietnam.
I. Title.
DS556.58 C5L43   2017

ISBN 978-981-4459-63-1 (soft cover)
ISBN 978-981-4459-64-8 (e-book PDF)

Typeset by International Typesetters Pte Ltd
Printed in Singapore by Markono Print Media Pte Ltd

CONTENTS

LIST OF TABLES

LIST OF FIGURES

LIST OF ABBREVIATIONS

ADB	Asian Development Bank
ASEAN	Association of Southeast Asian Nations
CAFTA	China-ASEAN Free Trade Agreement
CMEA	Council for Mutual Economic Assistance
CNOOC	China National Offshore Oil Company
COC	Code of Conduct
CPV	Communist Party of Vietnam
DOC	Declaration on the Conduct of Parties in the South China Sea
DRV	Democratic Republic of Vietnam
EEZ	exclusive economic zone
FDI	foreign direct investment
FTA	free trade agreement
GDP	gross domestic product
GNI	gross national income
GSO	General Statistics Office
IMF	International Monetary Fund
MOF	Ministry of Finance
MOFA	Ministry of Foreign Affairs
MOI	Ministry of Industry
MOIT	Ministry of Industry and Trade
MOLISA	Ministry of Labour, War Invalids and Social Affairs
MPI	Ministry of Planning and Investment
ODA	Official Development Assistance
OECD	Organization for Economic Cooperation and Development
PPP	purchasing power parity
PRC	People's Republic of China

RMB	renminbi
SIPRI	Stockholm International Peace Research Institute
SOE	state-owned enterprise
TPP	Trans-Pacific Partnership
UN	United Nations
UNCLOS	United Nations Convention on the Law of the Sea
UNCTAD	United Nations Conference on Trade and Development
VCG	Vietnam Coast Guard
VEA	Vietnam Energy Association
VFRS	Vietnam Fisheries Resources Surveillance
VPN	Vietnam People's Navy
WB	World Bank
WTO	World Trade Organization

ACKNOWLEDGEMENTS

This book is the revised and updated version of my PhD thesis which I did at the University of New South Wales at the Australian Defence Force Academy (UNSW@ADFA) from 2011 to 2014. It would not have been completed without the support and encouragement of many people.

First of all, I am greatly indebted to Professor Carlyle A. Thayer at the School of Humanities and Social Sciences (HASS) of the UNSW@ ADFA. His exemplary expertise and highly inspiring and responsible supervision made my PhD study an enlightening and enjoyable journey. I would also like to thank Mrs Zubeida Thayer for taking very good care of me and my family during our stay in Canberra.

I owe lots of gratitude to HASS for providing me with great facilities and support during my study. My special thanks go to Professor David Lovell, Head of School, for his kind support from the very beginning of my study. I would also like to thank Professor Craig Stockings, Professor Jian Zhang, Mrs Jo Muggleton, Mrs Bernadette McDermott, Mrs Marilyn Anderson-Smith, Mrs Shirley Ramsay and Mrs Marg McGee for their guidance and support. My thanks also go to Mr Christopher Dawkins at the Academy Library as well as Mrs Elvira Berra and other staff at the Research Student Unit for their kind help during my study.

I am deeply grateful to the Australian Government for granting me with a Prime Minister's Australia Asia Award (under the Endeavour scholarship programme), without which my PhD study would have been impossible in the first place. I would not have won the scholarship without the kind help from Professor William Malley, Dr Do Son Hai and Dr Dao Minh Hong who acted as my referees.

Under the scholarship, I have also received very efficient and timely support from various case managers at Austraining International (now Scope Global), for which I am very grateful.

I would also like to thank Mrs Tran Thanh Thuy, Mrs Pham Thi Hong Lan for their help with data collection, Dr Nguyen Dang Thang for his helpful academic discussions, and Mr Quynh Vu and his family for being our kind and helpful friends since we arrived in Canberra.

This book as well as my PhD study would have been impossible without the support and encouragement of my family. My parents have always been a great source of encouragement for my academic endeavours since I was a little boy. I am thankful to my parents-in-law for their support, and especially my father-in-law for his intellectual inspiration. My wife Nguyen Ngoc Tuong Ngan has always been very supportive, and I am grateful for all the sacrifices that she has made to assist me in completing my study. I would also like to thank my daughter Le Hong Thien Kim for being a little friend of mine whose lovely distractions helped me survive the stress of studying.

Parts of this book draw on journal articles that have been published elsewhere. Chapter 3 is based on "Vietnam's Domestic and Foreign Policy Nexus: Doi Moi Foreign Policy Reform, and Sino-Vietnamese Normalization", *Asian Politics and Policy* 5, no. 3 (2012); Chapter 6 on "Vietnam's South China Sea Disputes with China: The Economic Determinants", *Korean Journal of Defense Analysis* 26, no. 2 (2014); and Chapter 7 on "Vietnam's Hedging Strategy against China since Normalization", *Contemporary Southeast Asia* 35, no. 3 (2013). I thank the editors and publishers for permission to use them in this book.

Last but not least, during the preparation of this book manuscript, I have received generous help from Mr Ng Kok Kiong and Ms Rahilah Yusuf of ISEAS Publishing, for which I am grateful. I would also like to thank three anonymous reviewers for their valuable comments and suggestions that have helped to improve the manuscript.

1

Introduction

China has long been a major source of influence on the evolution of Vietnam as a modern state. This is well illustrated by some researchers' analogy that likens China to a rooster, with Korea as its beak and Vietnam its legs. The analogy, while highlighting the strategic importance of Vietnam towards China's well-being, especially in terms of security, also implies that Vietnam has long been living under the weight of China. In other words, Vietnam is condemned to a "tyranny of geography" (Thayer 2002, p. 271), whereby it has no choice but to learn to share its destiny with China through every twist and turn of its history.

Factors Shaping Vietnam–China Relations

Vietnam has been so much influenced by China that any account of the country's history would be incomplete without referring to its relations with the northern neighbour. Vietnam came under Chinese suzerainty for more than 1,000 years, since the Han dynasty conquered and annexed the country in 111 BC until Vietnam gained its formal independence for the first time in AD 938. Since then until the encroachment of the West in the latter half of the nineteenth century, despite intermittent attempts by China to reoccupy Vietnam, the relationship between the two countries was characterized by the relatively stable coexistence of the two empires with the latter being part of the former's tributary system (see, for example, Woodside 1971). After gaining its independence from colonial powers in 1945, Vietnam seemed to be in a better position to deal with China, but again, the northern neighbour continued to exert tremendous impact on the country, both before and after it was unified under communist control.

The history of interactions between the two countries shows that their relationship has been heavily conditioned by three major factors. The first is the geographical proximity between the two countries. Living next to China brings Vietnam both good and bad fortune. Vietnam, as one of the most sinicized countries in Asia, has benefited from China's immense cultural wealth, which more or less shaped the country's development as a nation-state. On the other hand, geographical proximity turned Vietnam into a convenient target for expansionist designs of Chinese dynasties. While the "China threat" rhetoric is relatively new in the literature on international relations (Yee and Storey 2002, p. 1), Vietnam's discourse on national security has traditionally been dominated by a sense of vulnerability towards threats from the north partly due to the effect of geographical proximity.

The second factor defining Vietnam's relations with China is the "asymmetry", or the great disparity in size and power, between the two countries (Womack 2006). Throughout history, Vietnam has always been the much smaller partner in the dyad, which caused the country to undertake never-ending efforts to protect its sovereignty, territorial integrity and national identity against military and cultural invasions from China. Typically, Vietnam has been willing to offer nominal deference to China for the sake of peace and internal development, and to stand up against the northern threat whenever China forcefully imposed its will on the country.

The third major factor shaping Vietnam's relations with China is the internal political and socio-economic development of each country. While geographical proximity and power asymmetry can be seen as long-term constants, domestic developments shape more visible transformations in bilateral relations over shorter periods of time.

History shows that since gaining its independence from China in 938, Vietnam has enjoyed more peace and less intervention from the North in times when China was embroiled in domestic turmoil or faced with foreign intervention. At the same time, Vietnam tended to be more vulnerable to Chinese interference during periods when the country itself was weak or divided.

Over the past three decades, bilateral relations have also undergone significant transformations as both countries pursued their own modernization programmes, which, in turn, have become a major source of influence on their foreign policy in general and their bilateral relations in particular.

On the part of Vietnam, the adoption of *Doi Moi* (Renovation) policy in 1986 has gone down in the country's history as a major landmark. Economic reforms have not only transformed the defunct command economy into a market-based one, but also informed transformations in its international relations. On one hand, *Doi Moi* demanded that the country switch to a more open foreign policy conducive to its domestic economic development. At the same time, a stronger economy and an enhanced international status have strengthened Vietnam's bargaining power and provided it with more options in dealing with other countries. On the other hand, growing economic interdependence and international integration, while providing a cushion for Vietnam's potential conflicts with its foreign partners, have also exposed the country to new security threats and foreign policy challenges.

Under *Doi Moi*, Vietnam's relations with China have been greatly transformed. By 1986, the relationship between the two countries was still in stalemate with Vietnam considering China as "the most dangerous and immediate enemy."[1] But soon after Vietnam adopted *Doi Moi*, bilateral relations started to improve and the two countries officially normalized their relations in 1991. After this watershed, bilateral ties were further consolidated, and a "comprehensive strategic partnership" was established in 2008. Nevertheless, the two countries are still facing a wide range of challenges that may threaten to destabilize their future relations. The most notable problems include competing claims in the South China Sea, Vietnam's security concerns regarding China's rise, renewed nationalism in both countries, and a web of increasingly interdependent yet potentially problematic economic relations. The two countries' prospects of democratization also make the trajectory of their relationship even more complex and unpredictable.

In sum, *Doi Moi* has generated significant and far-reaching impacts on Vietnam's external relations, especially with China. Yet, so far there has been no major research in either Vietnamese or English that addresses this issue. This book seeks to fill the gap by examining the interactions between political and economic factors under *Doi Moi* that have shaped bilateral relations since the late 1980s.

Doi Moi and Bilateral Relations

Doi Moi, while originally being an initiative of the Communist Party of Vietnam (CPV) to remedy its sinking legitimacy at home, eventually led to enormous changes in Vietnam's foreign policy in general and its China policy in particular. Following the adoption of *Doi Moi*, Vietnam made great efforts to normalize its relations with China, which it achieved in 1991. With a view to creating a more peaceful regional environment conducive to its domestic reforms, Vietnam also sought to settle its territorial disputes with China by concluding bilateral treaties on land border demarcation and Tonkin Gulf delimitation. Economic exchanges have also been strengthened to provide a stronger economic foundation for political relations. Under *Doi Moi*, bilateral relations entered a more stable and peaceful stage, which is described as "mature asymmetry" (Womack 2006). Yet, *Doi Moi* has also generated new challenges for Hanoi's relations with Beijing. New frictions in economic realms have emerged, while the two countries' quest for territorial sovereignty, maritime entitlements and economic interests in the South China Sea has also added further tension to their relationship.

Nevertheless, *Doi Moi* and the accompanying economic and foreign policy reforms have brought Vietnam newfound opportunities to develop a multi-level, omni-directional hedging strategy against China. Hanoi has accordingly strengthened economic ties and engagement mechanisms to maintain a stable and peaceful relationship with Beijing. At the same time, it has employed hard and soft balancing measures to counter China's growing power, especially Beijing's increasing assertiveness in the South China Sea.

When it comes to future bilateral relations, it should be noted that sustained socio-economic development will make democratization increasingly likely in both countries, which may bear implications for their ties. However, even when both countries have become democracies, their relations will not likely enjoy the "perpetual peace" that Immanuel Karl and contemporary democratic peace proponents predict, especially if the South China Sea disputes persist due to their complex nature. In that case, nationalism, historical distrust and rivalry in the South China Sea will continue to constrain future bilateral relations no matter who are the rulers in Hanoi and Beijing.

Based on primary as well as secondary sources of data, the book will provide in-depth analyses of the above-mentioned issues and their implications. It will analyse two important case studies to illustrate how the interaction between economic and political considerations under *Doi Moi* has shaped Vietnam's China policy and bilateral relations since normalization. One will focus on bilateral economic ties and their political implications, and the other on how Vietnam's economic development under *Doi Moi* has contributed to the dynamics of bilateral rivalry in the South China Sea.

The first case study is selected due to the rising importance of economic exchanges as a source of both bilateral cooperation and tension. Under *Doi Moi*, Vietnam is faced with the challenge of how to secure economic ties with China to facilitate domestic development while trying to mitigate any negative implications that deepened economic exchanges may generate for the country. As such, Vietnam's perception of and reaction to the possible merits and problems presented by deepened economic ties will contribute to how its relationship with Beijing is shaped.

Meanwhile, the case of the South China Sea disputes is selected for three reasons. First, the disputes now remain the most outstanding issue that threatens to destabilize Vietnam's relations with China. Second, over the last three decades, the dynamics of the disputes have been greatly transformed by both countries' political and economic developments, including those under Vietnam's *Doi Moi*. Third, given the complex nature of the disputes, they are likely to persist and bear important implications for future bilateral relations. Therefore, studying bilateral disputes in the South China Sea along with the growing economic ties between the two countries will provide us with useful insights into how the complex relationship between Vietnam and China has evolved since normalization.

It should be noted that, this book, as its title suggests, is an investigation of Vietnam's China policy and its relations with China under *Doi Moi*, not a comprehensive survey of bilateral relations. Accordingly, the book will mainly analyse drivers of Vietnam's relations with China as viewed from the Vietnamese side, and will use mainly Vietnamese and English sources.

Structure of the Book

Apart from the Introduction (Chapter 1) and Conclusion (Chapter 9), the book is composed of seven main chapters.

Chapter 2 lays out the historical context of Vietnam–China relations. Specifically, it will examine how bilateral ties developed through history until the 1980s. It will first examine the adverse effects of the hard "tyranny of geography" on Vietnam by providing an overview of how and why China had been a source of security threat to the country in the past. Next, it will discuss the effects of the soft "tyranny of geography", or how China had been influencing Vietnam culturally and economically. Finally, the chapter will look into the traditional structure of bilateral relations and the way Vietnam adapted itself to co-exist with China through the Sino-centric tributary system.

Chapter 3 focuses on Vietnam's adoption of *Doi Moi* and its implications for the normalization of Sino-Vietnamese relations. After providing an overview of the literature on the domestic–foreign policy nexus, the chapter will examine how transformations in Vietnam's foreign policy in the late 1980s and early 1990s were driven by the CPV's domestic agenda of economic reform and regime maintenance. Finally, the chapter will investigate the connection between Vietnam's adoption of *Doi Moi* and its quest for normalized relations with China.

Chapter 4 seeks to provide an overview of Vietnam–China relations since normalization. The chapter will start by reviewing Vietnam's economic development under *Doi Moi* and analysing the important role that foreign economic exchanges, including those with China, have played in this process. The chapter will then examine the evolution of Vietnam's relations with China since normalization. It will first discuss progress regarding the solution of bilateral territorial disputes, followed by an analysis of how the two countries have consolidated their political relations over the past two decades. Finally, the chapter will briefly discuss the development of bilateral economic ties and their contribution to Vietnam's overall relations with China.

Drawing on the initial analyses offered in Chapter 4, Chapter 5 will further investigate the development of bilateral economic relations since normalization and its political implications as the first case study of the book. The chapter will specifically examine four key aspects of bilateral economic exchanges, namely, Chinese aid and preferential export buyer's credits for Vietnam, project contracting, bilateral trade, and investment relations. The chapter will therefore analyse how economic and political factors have interacted to shape the trajectory of bilateral ties since normalization.

Chapter 6 will analyse the second case study, which illustrates how Vietnam's economic considerations under *Doi Moi* have contributed to the dynamics of bilateral disputes in the South China Sea. The chapter will first offer a background overview of the disputes and how they have presented themselves as the most serious irritant to bilateral relations. It will then briefly analyse Vietnam's geo-strategic and economic drivers in the disputes. Finally, the chapter will examine the role of economic factors in the shaping of Vietnam's strategy towards the disputes over the past two decades.

Chapter 7 will examine Vietnam's hedging strategy against China since normalization. The strategy is composed of four major components, namely economic pragmatism, direct engagement, hard balancing, and soft balancing, all of which are premised upon the economic and diplomatic successes that Vietnam has achieved under *Doi Moi*. The chapter will first provide an overview of the hedging strategy. It will then analyse the rationale and foundations of the strategy in the Vietnamese context. Finally, the chapter will investigate how the strategy has been developed and operationalized by Vietnam since bilateral normalization.

Chapter 8 will look into future political prospects of Vietnam and China and investigate their implications for bilateral relations. The chapter will start by discussing the theoretical link between socio-economic development and democratization as proposed by modernization theory. It will then apply these theoretical assumptions to both Vietnam and China and evaluate the prospects for democratization in each country. Finally, the chapter will conclude by assessing four scenarios in which democratization in both countries may happen and their implications for future bilateral relations.

NOTE

1. This was officially enshrined in the 1980 Constitution of Vietnam and was not dropped until August 1988.

2

The Historical Context of Vietnam–China Relations

Introduction

The popular Vietnamese legend "My Chau – Trong Thuy" has it that after defeating the last Hung King in what is now northern Vietnam, Thuc Phan ascended to the throne under the royal name of An Duong Vuong and renamed the nation from Van Lang to Au Lac, which he ruled from 257 BC to 207 BC. Seeking to establish a new capital, he decided to build a spiral, shell-shaped citadel at Co Loa but found the construction extremely difficult to complete, as every time it was near completion, the citadel would be undone at night by evil spirits. It was only with the assistance of Saint Kim Quy (Golden Turtle) that the citadel was finally completed. In order to help him protect the citadel from enemies, the Saint also offered him one of his claws to make the trigger of a magic crossbow, which was capable of hitting a thousand enemies with just a single shot.

From 217 BC to 207 BC, Trieu Da (Zhao Tuo), who was ruling what is now China's Guangdong and Guangxi provinces, made numerous attempts to invade and conquer Au Lac but never succeeded due to

An Duong Vuong's defence tactics, especially with the help of the magic crossbow. In order to find out the secret behind his foe's invincibility, Trieu Da decided to devise a plot. He pretended to negotiate a peace treaty with Au Lac and proposed marriage between An Duong Vuong's daughter, Princess My Chau and his son Trong Thuy (Zhong Shi), to which An Duong Vuong carelessly agreed. It was not before long that Trieu Da learned through My Chau about An Duong Vuong's magic crossbow. He then told his son Trong Thuy to steal and replace the crossbow with a fake one. Now in possession of the magic weapon, Trieu Da launched a new attack on An Duong Vuong and Co Loa soon fell into Trieu Da's hands. An Duong Vuong took My Chau on horseback and fled away to the southern seashore. With the enemy pursuing right behind, An Duong Vuong was desperate and prayed to Saint Kim Quy for help. Replying to his words, the Saint appeared and told him that "The enemy is sitting right behind you!". Waking up to reality and angered by his own daughter's betrayal, An Duong Vuong drew his sword out and beheaded My Chau before jumping into the sea. Following the victory over An Duong Vuong, Trieu Da annexed Au Lac territory to his own and created the state of Nam Viet (Nanyue), proclaiming himself emperor of the Trieu (Zhao) dynasty (207 BC to 111 BC).

The legend, while remaining a mythical account of an ancient episode of Vietnam's history and its early interactions with Chinese states, encapsulates the essence of Vietnam's traditional perception of China: one of distrust and animosity, reinforced by China's repeated invasions and overwhelming influence over the country. The "tyranny of geography", as Thayer (2002, p. 271) puts it, has left Vietnam with no option but to learn to share its destiny with the northern giant. In effect, defending its own national identity, independence and territorial integrity against the northern threat has been deeply entrenched in Vietnam's perception of itself and its relationship with China.

The history of Vietnam's relations with China, however, is not characterized by constant military animosity or cultural friction only. In fact, geographical proximity has also enabled Vietnam to benefit from the cultural wealth of China, one of the world's major cradles of civilization. Through more than 2,000 years of interactions, Vietnam has selectively borrowed from China a wide range of cultural and social norms, administrative institutions, and even a significant portion of its language (see, most notably, Lam 1987, pp. 1–40; Lieberman 2003, pp. 338–456; Vien 1993, pp. 123–38; Woodside 1971). Chinese cultural influence has actually turned Vietnam into the most sinicized country in Southeast Asia, where Indian cultural radiation is better established and more widespread. As a result, a more balanced account of Vietnam–China relations should take into consideration not only the antagonistic rivalry perpetuated by the "tyranny of geography", but also the resilient symbiosis made possible by the geographical proximity between the two countries.

The Hard "Tyranny of Geography"

The legend of My Chau and Trong Thuy is perhaps the earliest record of the official interactions between what are now the two modern states of Vietnam and China. The mythical nature of the story does not totally undermine its historical value, which is supported by archaeological discoveries as well as ancient historical annals. In fact, Trieu Da's invasion of Au Lac marked the beginning of the millennium-long Chinese domination over Vietnam,[1] which ended only after Ngo Quyen defeated the Southern Han army on the Bach Dang estuary in 938 and established the indigenous Ngo dynasty one year later. Since then until the Western intervention in both countries in the nineteenth century, Vietnam and China existed as a dyad of "unequal empires" with Vietnam as a unit in China's tributary system. And despite its failure to reassert a long-term domination over Vietnam, China continued to pose a formidable security threat to the country through its repeated invasions and interventions.

After 1858, France replaced China as the main source of influence on Vietnam. It step by step annexed the country into its territory through a series of unequal treaties. The French advance, however, did not go unchallenged. A number of resistance movements were launched by Vietnamese patriots against France, and King Tu Duc in 1882 even appealed to the Qing court for military assistance in the fight against France in Tonkin.[2] The Qing court accordingly sent to Vietnam 10,000 troops who took up positions to the northwest of Hanoi (Vien 1993, p. 149). It was unclear whether the Qing court wanted to help Vietnam maintain its independence as a preventive measure against possible French invasions into southern China, or to seize the opportunity to re-establish its control over Tonkin.[3] Nevertheless, France eventually

established its colonial control over entire Vietnam after the conclusion
of the Harmand Treaty (also known as the Treaty of Hue, signed
on 25 August 1883) by which a French protectorate over Annam and
Tonkin was recognized by the Nguyen court.[4] However, it was not
until the conclusion of the Treaty of Tianjin (9 June 1885), which
officially ended the Sino-France War (1884–85), that French control
over Vietnam became firmly established and no longer challenged
by China.[5] France subsequently signed two conventions with Qing
China in 1887 and 1895 to settle the Sino-Vietnamese border. The two
conventions later served as the foundation for negotiations between
Vietnam and China over their land border demarcation in the 1990s
(Thao 2000, pp. 87–88).

After more than seven decades of direct rule over entire Vietnam,
the French colonial regime finally collapsed in March 1945 when the
Japanese overthrew the French to take over Vietnam. The Japanese
rule was short-lived as the communist-led August Revolution broke
out five months later, resulting in the proclamation of the Democratic
Republic of Vietnam (DRV) on 2 September 1945. The newly
independent Vietnam, however, was facing grave threats as France
sought to reimpose its rule over the country. After a number of failed
diplomatic attempts, the First Indochina War finally broke out in late
1946 between France and Vietnamese forces led by Viet Minh. The
war raged on until the French were defeated at the decisive battle of
Dien Bien Phu in May 1954, which led to the conclusion of the Geneva
Accords a few months later. During the war, Viet Minh received critical
moral and material support from China, which then also came under
communist rule after the People's Republic of China was proclaimed
in October 1949. China continued to support the DRV in the Second
Indochina War between the DRV and the United States. Chinese sources
estimate that China provided the DRV with approximately $20 billion
worth of economic and military aid during the 1949–75 period (Du and
Zhao 1988, p. 109, cited in Khoo 2011, p. 1).

Unlike previous chapters in bilateral relations, during the 1950s
and early 1960s China was generally perceived by Vietnamese leaders
as a friendly and helpful neighbour rather than a long-standing threat
to the country. President Ho Chi Minh even hailed the bilateral
relationship during this period as "close as lips and teeth", and that
Chinese and Vietnamese communists were "comrades plus brothers".
It seemed that the shared communist ideology in particular had provided

a common ground for bilateral relations to flourish during this period. However, as it later turned out, it was the two countries' pragmatic considerations in terms of national interests that brought the two countries into a *de facto* alliance. While Vietnam needed Chinese assistance to pursue its own fight for independence and unification, China also wanted to use Vietnam in its strategic calculations, especially vis-à-vis other great powers. Therefore, as the two countries' national interests began to diverge, bilateral relations inevitably suffered as a consequence.

Bilateral ties began to deteriorate from 1968 due to the said reason. While Hanoi wanted to accelerate its war efforts and forge a closer relationship with the Soviet Union, Beijing wanted Hanoi to pursue a protracted war and not to tilt towards Moscow at the expense of Beijing. Before the Tet Offensive in 1968, China also obstructed Vietnam from entering into peace negotiations with the United States (MOFA 1979, pp. 50–55; Zhai 1997), allegedly with a view to keeping Vietnam divided indefinitely (MOFA 1979, p. 38). Moreover, when China took moves to foster closer relations with the United States in the early 1970s, bilateral relations turned sour as Vietnam felt betrayed by China and that China was negotiating with the United States behind its back (MOFA 1979, pp. 55–67; L.-H. T. Nguyen 2006, pp. 18–25). In January 1974, China took advantage of Vietnam's internal situation to forcefully seize the western part of the Paracel islands which was then held by Republic of Vietnam forces (Lo 1989, pp. 53–83).[6] The Chinese invasion of the Paracels caused Vietnam to be increasingly suspicious of China's real intentions towards Vietnam and contributed to the further downward spiral in bilateral relations (MOFA 1979).

In the wake of Vietnam's reunification in 1975, the split between the two countries soon became open. Border skirmishes, the fleeing of the Hoa (ethnic Chinese) people out of Vietnam, Vietnam's drift towards the Soviet Union, and China's support for the Khmer Rouge regime's hostile activities against Vietnam all added to the growing tension between the two countries. At the climax of the crisis in bilateral relations, Vietnam entered into a *de facto* alliance with the Soviet Union and sent troops into Cambodia to remove the Khmer Rouge regime in late 1978. In response, in a visit to Washington D.C. in January 1979, Deng Xiaoping implied that China would take military actions against Vietnam and that China would "teach Vietnam a lesson" (K.C. Chen, 1987, p. 92; Zhang, 2010, p. 24). On 17 February 1979, China launched an all-out military invasion into the northern border of Vietnam and caused substantial devastation to the Vietnamese towns that it seized along the border area before withdrawing its troops on 16 March 1979. The brief yet bloody war left both sides with substantial casualties[7] and a deep scar in their already volatile and distrustful relationship.

For Vietnam, however, the war against China was not over even after China withdrew its troops out of the country. As former U.S. National Security Advisor Zbigniew Brzezinski remarked after his meeting with Deng Xiaoping in early 1979 that "China said they will teach Vietnam a lesson, I say it will be an entire curriculum" (*Vietnamnet* 2011), Vietnam continued to suffer from Chinese hostility in the 1980s. Apart from maintaining its incessant shelling and armed harassments in a "phony war" along the Sino-Vietnamese border (Thayer 1987), China also pursued the policy of isolating Vietnam diplomatically and providing aid to the Khmer Rouge in their guerrilla war against Vietnamese forces with a view to "bleeding Vietnam white". On the part of Vietnam, the war again highlighted the permanent security threat that China had long posed to Vietnam and deepened anti-Chinese sentiments within the country. In the preamble to Vietnam's 1980 Constitution, the defeat of Chinese "expansionists" and "hegemonists" was mentioned as a source of national pride but the resentful anti-Chinese connotation was obvious.[8] Nevertheless, Vietnam soon realized that it could not afford a hostile relationship with China. In effect, Vietnam's attempts to break down its diplomatic isolation and to pursue peaceful domestic development during the 1980s were largely unsuccessful due to Chinese obstruction.[9] Bilateral relations during the 1980s testify to the fact that due to power asymmetry, either a good or a bad bilateral relationship means much more for Vietnam than for China.

As summarized in Table 2.1, the history of traditional Vietnam–China relations may be condensed into one major point: China has long presented itself as a major source of security threat to Vietnam. Between 938 and 1991, when the two countries normalized their relations, China invaded Vietnam ten times. Such a long history of Chinese expansionism has been responsible for Vietnam's natural tendency to distrust China as well as the popular anti-Chinese sentiments among its population.

TABLE 2.1
China as a Security Threat to Vietnam

Chinese states	Form of Threat	Year/ Period
Zhao (207–111 BC)	Invade and direct rule	179 BC –111 BC
Han (206 BC–AD 220)	Direct rule	111 BC – AD 39, AD 43–220
Eastern Wu (222–280)	Direct rule	220–280
(Three Kingdoms period — 220–280)		
Jin (256–420)	Direct rule	280–420
Song, Qi, Liang	Direct rule	420–544
(Southern and Northern Dynasties Period — 420–589)		
Sui (589–618)	Invade and direct rule	602–618
Tang (618–907)	Direct rule	618–907
Later Liang, Southern Han	Direct rule	907–938
(5 Dynasties and 10 Kingdoms Period — 907–960)		
Song (960–1279)	Invade	980–981, 1076–1077
Mongol — Yuan (1271–1368)	Invade	1285, 1287
Ming (1368–1644)	Invade and direct rule	1407–1427
Qing (1644–1911)	Invade	1788
	Intervention	1882–1885
People's Republic of China	Invade and occupy territory	1956, 1974, 1988
	Invade	1979

Source: Author's own compilation.

History has also shown that the "tyranny of geography" does not leave Vietnam with many options in its dealing with China. It not only forces Vietnam to live under a permanent military threat, but also intervenes to dictate the course of development of Vietnam's identity as a nation-state. However, while the hard "tyranny of geography", which involves the military and security aspects, presents Vietnam with the image of China as a threatening and long-standing enemy, the soft form of the "tyranny of geography", which involves the cultural and economic facets of bilateral relations, causes Vietnam to perceive China as a less intimidating neighbour, and sometimes even as a favourable and convenient source of cultural learning and economic well-being.

The Soft "Tyranny of Geography"

Chinese Cultural Influence on Vietnam

Vietnam is arguably the most sinicized country in Southeast Asia, where Indian influence was more pronounced in most parts of the region in the pre-colonial era. This is a distinctive result of the intense interactions between Vietnam and China for more than 2,000 years. However, the Vietnamese absorption of Chinese culture is neither a straightforward process nor an inescapable outcome of geographical proximity. It is much more nuanced. In fact, Chinese cultural influence forms only one layer of Vietnam's cultural identity. The most important and substantial elements of the country's cultural identity still rests with indigenous norms, customs, and practices, while cultural borrowings from Southeast Asia and the West form yet another layer (Them 1999, Chapter 1).

Two distinct features characterize the Vietnamese absorption of Chinese cultural elements over the past 2,000 years. First, Vietnam has been willing to borrow culturally from China as long as it was a voluntary, internal process rather than a forceful imposition from the north. Second, Vietnam's borrowing from China is a selective process — most Chinese influences are filtered and adapted to fit local needs. So the "sinicization" of Vietnam could also be understood as the "Vietnamization" of Chinese elements. At the core of Vietnamese society and culture is still the overwhelming presence of its indigenous cultural and social values and norms, which shape Vietnam's national identity and guide its perception of, and relations with, China.

The fact that Vietnam successfully preserved its cultural identity to finally win its independence after more than a millennium living under Chinese rule was, by any measure or standard, a spectacular achievement. It signified Vietnam's vigorous national consciousness and its enduring resistance against unwarranted foreign influence. During the era of Chinese domination, a consistent policy of cultural assimilation was undertaken by Chinese dynasties with a view to both integrating the southern domain into the northern empire and implementing the *mission civilisatrice*. However, these efforts ended up with limited success. For example, the Han Chinese who were sent into Vietnam not only failed to assimilate Vietnamese people but, on the contrary, eventually became Vietnamized and even fought against Chinese domination for Vietnam's independence.[10] During the era of Chinese domination, the penetration of Confucianism as the most significant symbol of Chinese cultural assimilation of the country was also superficial. In even the most sinicized regions, Confucianism was present only at the top hierarchy of the society, while the peasantry, who was virtually beyond the reach of Chinese norms, retained many of their indigenous traditional habits (Lieberman 2003, p. 340). As such, the most significant impact that a millennium of Chinese domination left on Vietnam was perhaps the establishment of a feudal system on which the Vietnamese state and society were organized and further developed into later centuries.

Chinese failure to culturally assimilate Vietnam can be explained on a number of accounts. First, long before the period of Chinese domination, the Vietnamese had developed a range of distinctive indigenous cultural traits of Southeast Asian origin that endured for the centuries to come, even in the face of China's strict policy of assimilation. These indigenous cultural traits include, among others, tattooing, cockfighting, betel-chewing, building stilt houses, practising multiform spirit cults (Lieberman 2003, p. 347; Whitmore 1986, p. 122), teeth blackening, or allowing women to maintain a significant level of autonomy (Whitmore 1984, p. 300). Vietnam's cultural borrowings from Southeast Asia also increased when Vietnam, following its independence, deepened its interactions with other Southeast Asian counterparts, such as the Cham, Khmer and Siam empires. For example, Vietnam under the Tran dynasty showed interest in and intensified its borrowing of Cham music, choreography and architecture (Lieberman 2003, p. 362).

On the other hand, the firmly established indigenous cultural identity not only enabled the country to survive Chinese cultural assimilation but also reinforced Vietnam's national consciousness and the aspiration to build a totally independent state. For example, when Vietnamese Confucian scholars pressed for more Chinese-style reforms, Emperor Tran Minh Tong (1320–57) declared in the 1320s that "Our country has its own definite principles [of laws]. The Northern and Southern countries [China and Vietnam] are different. If we adopt the plan of the pale-faced [Confucian] students, disorder will immediately follow" (N.H. Nguyen, Ta and Tran 1987, p. 14).

In sum, Vietnam's efforts to preserve its indigenous cultural identity obviously became a strong force driving its relentless struggle against Chinese attempts to conquer and assimilate the country. However, while China's forceful attempts to impose its cultural norms and practices on Vietnam met with fierce resistance, Vietnamese rulers also viewed China as a model with certain relevant values that could help Vietnamese society thrive. Vietnam therefore began to borrow culturally from China in a voluntary and conscious manner as long as it was in Vietnam's self-interest and not an imposed process by China.

A particular example is the spread of Confucianism into Vietnam. Confucianism was introduced into Vietnam during the era of Chinese domination. However, it did not gain a foothold and become influential until Vietnam won its independence from China and began to treat Confucianism as a tool of nation-building rather than a cultural legacy imposed by the north. Accordingly, the Ly dynasty built the Temple of Literature in 1070 to worship Confucius and established the Imperial Academy six years later to educate Vietnamese nobles and bureaucrats along Confucian lines. By the fourteenth century, Confucian scholars had become an increasingly powerful force under the Tran court at the expense of Buddhist monks. By the time the Le dynasty came to power in the fifteenth century, Confucianism was enthusiastically embraced as the ideological framework on which the Vietnamese state and society operated (Ba 2006, pp. 89–100; Lieberman 2003, pp. 377–83; Them 1999, p. 47). Sinicization persisted until the Nguyen dynasty, Vietnam's last feudal dynasty. According to Them (1999, pp. 264–65), the different statuses of Confucianism in Vietnamese society in the two eras of Chinese domination and Vietnamese independence was determined by the way Confucianism was cultivated into the country. During the age of Chinese domination, as Confucianism was forcefully imposed on Vietnamese people as a means of colonization and assimilation, it invited resistance from Vietnamese people. Meanwhile, during the age of national independence, Vietnamese dynasties voluntarily imported Confucianism for the purpose of nation-building and social management, thereby gradually absorbing the ideology into Vietnam's cultural foundation.

Vietnam's willingness to absorb Chinese cultural values, such as Confucianism, to a certain extent embodies one of the key ironies in Vietnamese history that despite Vietnam's persistent struggle to preserve its national identity and to maintain political independence from China, the country eventually sought to borrow and localize a significant portion of Chinese culture and administrative practices. Such a paradox was made possible by two major factors. First, despite the expansionist propensity of Chinese dynasties, it was undeniable that many Chinese values, norms and practices were valuable to Vietnamese rulers, especially with regard to their nation-building and power maintenance efforts. Second, India, China's only comparable competitor as a source of cultural influence, was much more distant to Vietnam than China. Moreover, its cultural radiation into Vietnam through Southeast Asian countries was hindered by Vietnam's antagonistic rivalry with its indic neighbours such as the Cham, Khmer, and Siamese empires. Therefore, Vietnam's intense interactions with China due to geographical proximity turned China into a convenient source of cultural borrowing for the country.

The second outstanding feature of Vietnamese absorption of Chinese cultural elements was its deliberate endeavour to filter and adapt the imported elements to best fit local needs. Lieberman (2003, p. 341) observes that Vietnamese rulers, like their East Asian counterparts, tended to consider Chinese culture and civilization as "the common property of all civilized people and which they internalized to the point that their alien origins became irrelevant". However, this does not mean Vietnam made a wholesale import of whatever they were looking for without making alterations to suit its local conditions. The so-called "Chinese model" was therefore the reflection of China through the eyes of Vietnamese, of what considered by Vietnamese as universal yet locally desirable values.

There are a number of examples that can substantiate the above observation. For instance, Them (1999) points out five major changes that Vietnamese made to Confucianism over time to make it conform with local socio-economic conditions and cultural traditions. These major changes are summarized in Table 2.2.

As discussed above, the alterations that the Vietnamese made to the imported ideology obviously reflected their adherence to indigenous cultural values. For example, Vietnamese people's matriarchal traditions, thus their respect for women's role and rights, should have been the rationale behind the second difference. The Vietnamese traditional recognition of women's roles and rights were even codified in a number of Vietnam's legal codes. The Hong Duc Code in the fifteenth century under the Le dynasty, for example, provided that women could possess their own property and share equally with men in inheritance, and in case the family had no son, the whole family fortune would be inherited by the daughters. Another provision even allowed the wife to repudiate her husband if the latter had abandoned her for a certain period of time (Vien 1993, p. 72; Woodside 1971, p. 45). Therefore, although a substantial portion of the Hong Duc Code was borrowed from the Tang Code, these progressive provisions were unique to the Hong Duc Code and showed no Chinese influence.

Another classic example that illustrates Vietnam's filtering and adaptation of Chinese borrowings to fit its local conditions is the Nguyen dynasty's basic administrative plan. Vietnam's borrowings from the Chinese administrative system, as Woodside (1971, p. 81) observes, "exhibited the usual variegated patterns of acculturation in which some institutions and objects spread rapidly from one society to another, some spread more slowly, and some do not spread at all or are rejected". Specifically, Woodside pinpoints a significant number of differences between the Nguyen civil government and that of the Qing court, the model on which the Nguyen system was built. These differences range from the structure of the central civil administration to the way civil service examinations were held. Most of the alterations were made to match Vietnam's smaller, less complex administrative bureaucracy as well as its limited resources. These adaptations therefore show that contrary to "the little China fallacy" endorsed by Frenchmen (Lieberman 2003, p. 338), Vietnam in the nineteenth century maintained a largely distinct cultural and social system, where Chinese influences served only as the background on which the Vietnamese national identity was consolidated and developed through creative adaptations.

TABLE 2.2
Major Differences between Chinese and Vietnamese Confucianism

Elements	Chinese Confucianism	Vietnamese Confucianism
Stability	Emphasis on internal stability (Confucianism as a tool to control society and maintain power for rulers)	Emphasis on both internal and external stability, and stability for both the royal dynasties and the lay people
Women's role and rights	No or little recognition of women's social role and rights	Higher recognition of women's roles and rights
Loyalty to rulers	Emphasis on loyalty to rulers only	Emphasis on both loyalty to rulers and patriotism/ nationalism
Role of literatis	Literatis are equally or less important than military generals	Literatis are generally more important and better respected than generals
Attitude towards merchants	Merchants are respected	Merchants are disdained

Source: Adapted from Them (1999, pp. 267–271)

Since the late nineteenth century, Chinese cultural influence on Vietnam began to wane as France established its colonial rule over the country. The sinicization of Vietnam symbolically faded away in 1918 with the abolition of all civil service examinations which tested candidates' knowledge on Confucian classics and skills in prose and poetry writing using both Han and Nom characters (D.H. Nguyen 1987, p. 22). More than 2,000 years of interactions, however, has left Vietnam with a multitude of Chinese cultural influences that could not be undone overnight.

Traditional Economic Relations

In addition to cultural influences, economic ties form another major aspect of the soft "tyranny of geography" that Vietnam has been subject to during its long-standing relations with China. Unlike the current era of economic globalization that has been brought about by technological advances in transport and communications over the past century, pre-modern Vietnam and China were largely autarkic economies in which foreign exchanges played an insignificant role. Therefore, although China was considered the world's largest and most advanced economy until the nineteenth century (Dahlman and Aubert 2001, p. 1), its economic impact on Vietnam's internal development was rather limited. China's most significant economic impact on Vietnam as well as other countries in the pre-modern world was perhaps generated through its international trading activities (see, for example, Curtin 1984). In the case of Vietnam, the lack of reliable data prevents us from reconstructing a comprehensive picture of Vietnam's traditional trade relations with China. However, sporadic historical accounts tend to confirm that China was a major trade partner of Vietnam and trade was the most important source of Chinese economic influence on the country. Other sources of Chinese economic influence came from the transfer of technologies and the immigration of ethnic Han people into Vietnam.

Archaeological evidence shows that Vietnam started foreign exchanges with China and other Southeast Asian states more than 2,000 years ago. Various objects such as weapons, durable prestige goods of Chinese origin, including those of the Warring States Period (fifth to third century BC), have been discovered in tombs in Vietnam, while Dong Son bronze drums have also been found in southern China and elsewhere in Southeast Asia (see, for example, Manguin 1993, p. 255; Mariko, Manh and Hoang 2001; H.P. Ray 1989, p. 54; K.W. Taylor 1983, p. 4; Vien 1993, p. 14). Although the origin of bronze drums (including Dong Son ones) used to be a controversial topic between Vietnamese and Chinese archaeologists during the 1980s when both groups tried to prove that the earliest bronze drums originated in their respective country (Han 1998), the fact that a large number of bronze drums of various types have been found in both northern Vietnam and southern China suggests that exchanges between what are now modern Vietnam and China possibly took place many centuries before Vietnam came under Chinese suzerainty.

After Chinese dynasties successfully established their direct rule over Vietnam, economic exchanges between the two countries were distorted by Chinese colonial policies, which involved both cultural assimilation and economic exploitation. During the Han rule, for example, the Han exploited the local population through both tribute to the imperial court in China as well as taxes, duties and corvée to the local colonial administration and military apparatus. The tribute comprised valuable tropical products such as ivory, pearls, sandalwood, tropical fruits, and other valuable commodities such as handicrafts items, fabrics, gold or silver engraving, and mother-of-pearl inlay works. Meanwhile, in addition to such taxes as head tax or land tax that each inhabitant had to pay, the colonial administration also forced the population to provide corvée for building public works such as canals, roads and citadels (Vien 1993, p. 21). The colonial administrations of subsequent Chinese dynasties implemented the same exploitative policies, leading to the eruption of numerous local insurrections against the Chinese colonial rule during the first millennium.

After Vietnam gained its independence from China in the tenth century, trade between the two countries was conducted via both tribute missions and regular merchants. The main goal of Vietnamese dynasties in sending tribute missions to China was to show their deference to the northern courts with a hope of maintaining peace with the northern neighbour. However, another important task of tribute missions was to conduct trade. During the Song reign (960–1279), for example, Vietnam sent more tribute missions to China than any other country in the Nan-hai (South China Sea) region (Shiro 1998, p. 9).[11] Apart from offering Chinese emperors with gifts, for which they were also paid, the missions also sold various regional products. Historical records show that the tribute missions from Vietnam normally made some profit from their trip. For example, in 1022, official gifts and merchandise evaluated at 1,682 strings of cash presented by the Vietnamese envoys were paid 2,000 strings of cash, while in 1028, the Vietnamese mission received a return gift of 4,000 strings of cash for a tribute worth approximately 3,060 strings of cash (Bielenstein 2005, p. 35; Shiro 1998, pp. 7–9). The practice of tributary trade was maintained well until the nineteenth century. The Vietnamese goods that Nguyen envoys took to China helped them trade for essential Chinese products that could hardly be obtained in Vietnam, such as ginseng, drugs, and books (Woodside 1971, p. 114).

Tributary trade with China, however, was relatively insignificant due to both the infrequency of envoys as well as the limited amount of products that each envoy could take with them. Therefore, non-tributary or regular trade became the main method for goods to be exchanged between the two countries. Regular trade, however, was strictly monitored by both imperial courts and heavily influenced by each country's political conditions. A typical example on the part of China was the order by northern Song (960–1127) to limit trade by Dai Viet merchants to only two sea ports at Lien-chou and Ch'in Chou and its prohibition of Chinese junks from sailing to a number of foreign countries, including Dai Viet. Meanwhile, in the wake of Mongol-Yuan invasions, Dai Viet responded by tightening its control on Chinese merchants. Accordingly, Dai Viet under the Tran dynasty banned foreign merchant junks from entering deep into its territory because the government was concerned about Chinese spies. Chinese merchants were therefore allowed to trade only at the port of Van Don, which lies off the north-eastern coast of the country. This restriction was later relaxed by the Le dynasty during the fifteenth century, but even then Chinese merchants were allowed to access only nine border ports and market towns (Shiro 1998, pp. 10, 20). Nevertheless, in a number of cases, economic considerations in terms of trading benefits appeared to be the driving force behind a number of political decisions by both Vietnamese and Chinese governments. A number of studies suggest that one goal of the Ming invasion of Vietnam in 1407 was to gain control of the Vietnamese emporia, especially when Dai Viet ports played an important role in relaying trade items from Southeast Asian countries to China and vice versa. Similarly, in expanding to the west and south in the fifteenth century, Dai Viet under the Le dynasty also aimed at seizing Champa's profitable trade with China and to set up a Ming-style tributary trade system (Lieberman 2003, p. 383).

As a neighbour of a big economy, Vietnam did benefit from China economically in a number of ways. First, China was an important trade partner of Vietnam. After Vietnam gained its independence from China, despite Vietnam's tight control on the border, bilateral trade relations were further developed. Vietnam soon joined the Chinese overseas trade network. Major Vietnamese trade centres such as Van Don (fifteenth century), Pho Hien (sixteenth century), Hoi An (seventeenth century) and Sai Gon – Cho Lon (eighteenth to nineteenth century) became the emporia where most of the trade between the two countries took place. These trade centres also acted as the connecting points where goods from China were forwarded to other countries in the region and vice versa.

China provided Vietnam with many essential trade items, especially bullion for domestic circulation. For example, before Japanese and Western bullion was tapped, Vietnam was heavily dependent on Chinese bullion. As mine output in China plummeted in the mid-1400s leading to a coin shortage in China and throughout East Asia, Dai Viet economy suffered heavily as a consequence. It was only when China's shortage eased and more cash was imported from the north in late 1400s that the situation improved (Whitmore 1983). In the late seventeenth and eighteenth centuries, Vietnam suffered from another bullion shortage. This time, the opening of Chinese mines along the Yunnan and Guangxi border again helped relieve the pressure on the Vietnamese economy (Lieberman 2003, p. 436).

China was also an essential source for Vietnam to import numerous regular items. Nguyen rulers in the 1800s considered China as "a limitless cornucopia" from which they sought to import various goods. However, in order to avoid entering into too close a relationship with China which might weaken Vietnam's independence, the Nguyen administration chose instead to import indirectly through Chinese middlemen who resided permanently in Vietnam. The imported goods would include both essential and exotic items as well as locally available ones, such as silks, fresh and dried fruits, teas, drugs, incense, paper, and even bamboo chairs, bricks and tiles (Woodside 1971, pp. 274–75).

At the same time, geographical proximity also turned China into a convenient export market for Vietnam. However, as mentioned above, trade restrictions imposed by both Chinese and Vietnamese dynasties sometimes created obstacles to Vietnamese exports to China and vice versa. Moreover, the importance of China as an export market for Vietnam was inconsistent throughout history. During the early seventeenth century, for example, Japan was much more important for Dang Trong's (South Vietnam)[12] exports than China was. Only after the Japanese Tokugawa imposed restrictions on foreign exchanges in the 1630s did China begin to replace Japan as Dang Trong's most important export market (Hai 2008, p. 3; Lieberman 2003, p. 415; Woodside 1995, pp. 162–63). Similarly, in Dang Ngoai (North Vietnam), falling Japanese demand was compensated by Chinese demand, turning the eighteenth century into a "Chinese century" in Dang Ngoai no less than in Dang Trong or Siam (Lieberman 2003, p. 435).

Although Vietnam's foreign trade in general and its trade with China in particular were impressive during certain historical periods, its importance for Vietnam's internal development should not be overstated. In reality, as an agrarian and largely self-sufficient economy, Vietnam was more dependent on internal rather than external resources for its development. In the heyday of foreign trade in Dang Trong before the prosperous port of Hoi An declined, for example, most of the Nguyen government's revenue still came from domestic sources rather than foreign trade (Lieberman 2003, p. 417). The rather limited role of foreign trade in Vietnam's economy during this era was related to its rulers' perception of foreign exchanges. For example, harbouring suspicion towards foreign traders for fear of military invasion as well as cultural and religious contamination, the Nguyen government in the nineteenth century restricted foreign trade to just a few ports, imposed heavy duties, and prohibited the export of basic Vietnamese commodities such as rice, silk and metals used for imperial coinage (Woodside 1971, p. 264).

Apart from strict government regulations, low demands and difficult transport conditions might be another set of problems that constrained the significance of Vietnam's trade with China. Some studies suggest that in the early 1800s, there were about 300 Chinese junks a year visiting the ports of central and south Vietnam, while

Hoi An at its height received only seventy to eighty junks annually (Lieberman 2003, p. 435). Such a small volume of trade with China could hardly make a significant difference to the country's economy. Moreover, as the majority of imports from China were consumer goods[13] rather than input materials or machineries, trade with China mainly met the consumption demands of a small segment of the population. Therefore, foreign trade could hardly make any significant contribution to the productivity of the economy as it is the case in Vietnam's modern economy today.

Another economic benefit that Vietnam might have gained through its interactions with China was the transfer of technologies. The transfer of Chinese technologies into Vietnam was first and foremost a side-effect of the Chinese immigration into the country. Chinese immigrants normally brought with them Chinese traditional handicrafts such as ceramics, paper and ink making, printing, weaving, etc. After holding a monopoly on these handicrafts for some time, they gradually transferred the techniques to Vietnamese partners and helped to expand the manufacturing base of the Vietnamese economy (Hai 1998, p. 25; Hai and Duong 1998, Chapters 6, 7 and 8). This was confirmed by British explorer William Dampier who reported in 1690 that Ming refugees had introduced to the Vietnamese "many useful arts, of which they were wholly ignorant before" (cited in Lieberman 2003, p. 437). By the seventeenth century, while European technologies transformed Vietnam's arms manufactures, Chinese techniques were dominant in the mining, printing, papermaking, sugar-processing, and some textile processing industries (Lieberman 2003, p. 437). In addition, some scholars have argued that the transfer of Chinese gunpowder technology contributed significantly to Vietnam's successful conquest of the Cham Empire in 1471 (Sun 2003), thereby eliminating an irritant source of threats to the country and paving the way for its further advance into the southern territory.

Chinese immigrants not only helped introduce new technologies into Vietnam but also contributed to its economy in various ways. The migration of ethnic Han people into Vietnam initially resulted from the policy of Chinese dynasties to assimilate the country, but later was mainly driven by violence and chaos within Chinese society. According to Hai (1998, p. 17), the influx of Chinese refugees into Vietnam surged during the Three Kingdoms Period (220–280) and the

Five Dynasties and Ten Kingdoms Period (907–960). After Vietnam gained its independence in 938, this pattern continued with Chinese immigrants into Vietnam increasing considerably during the conflict-prone interregnums between dynasties. In addition to fleeing China as political émigrés, Chinese immigrants also went to Vietnam to pursue wealth as merchants and then decided to settle in the country. Chinese historical records of the Song dynasty notes that "people from Fujian and Guangdong have pursued commerce in Jiaozhi [northern Vietnam] and some have even stayed there to work". The Song court later had no other options but to accept the reality and legalize the practice, which allowed their family members to accompany them to Vietnam (Clark 1991, p. 124).

After settling in Vietnam, Chinese immigrants played a significant role in the development of the local economy. For example, Chinese immigrants from the sixteenth century afterwards helped reclaim the new lands in South Vietnam, especially in the Mekong Delta (T. Li 1998, p. 33). An outstanding example was the reclamation and establishment of the town of Ha Tien in early eighteenth century by Mac Cuu (Mo Jiu), an émigré from Guangdong (Cooke and Li 2004, pp. 23, 62). The influx of Chinese immigrants and the economic wealth they generated helped strengthen the southern economy and consolidate the Nguyen lords' power base there.

In addition, Chinese immigrants, with their commercial skills, entrepreneurship as well as extensive linkages to China and elsewhere, also played a significant role in expanding Vietnam's foreign trade. For example, Chinese traders were the main agents in the rise of Hoi An as a commercial hub of the South China Sea economy in the seventeenth century after Japanese traders withdrew from the city. During this period, trade junks run by Chinese merchants from both Dang Trong and Dang Ngoai became the main channel through which Vietnamese products were exported. As Dang Trong expanded further south, Chinese traders followed the footprints of Nguyen lords and further expanded their presence. When the trade hub of Cu Lao Pho (in modern Bien Hoa) was destroyed by Tay Son troops in 1788, Chinese traders moved their business to Sai Gon in the late eighteenth century. They built a number of major markets, include Cho Lon and Binh Tay, and helped turn Sai Gon – Cho Lon into a prosperous trading centre of South Vietnam (Hai 2008).

Chinese immigrants, however, did not always present a favourable image to the Vietnamese people. In some circumstances, they even became a nuisance for the government. In an interesting case that holds striking resemblance to the problem of illegal Chinese workers in major Chinese-run projects in the early twenty-first century Vietnam,[14] Chinese miners in Thai Nguyen province in the 1830s were viewed as a source of antagonism by local government and residents. In a memorial to the court in 1834, Nguyen Cong Tru, then a high-ranking provincial official, described Chinese miners in northern provinces as troublemakers who, among other things, owed debts, provoked quarrels, and went beyond the local government's control. Nguyen Cong Tru's request to deport them to China, however, was turned down by Emperor Minh Mang under the excuse that Vietnam's mining industry was dependent on Chinese miners due to a shortage in local mining artisans (Woodside 1971, pp. 277–78).

The problem of Chinese miners in northern Vietnam was directly linked to another issue that highlighted the initial signs of economic interdependence between Vietnam and China. Vietnam in the early nineteenth century experienced a high rate of inflation mainly due to the rise in silver price. By the late 1830s, the price of one silver tael had increased three times within twenty years. The rise of silver price, however, was not an issue of entirely domestic origin. An important contributing factor was China's overwhelming demand for the precious metal due to the exhaustion of China's silver mines as well as its need for silver to pay for opium imports from Britain after the first Opium War broke out in 1839. China's high demand for silver therefore led Chinese merchants to accumulate and illegally export Vietnamese silver to China. Silver therefore became scarcer and its short supply drove inflation in Vietnam to rise even higher, causing severe economic problems for the Hue court (Woodside 1971, pp. 278–79).

The case of silver price in Vietnam in the 1830s and 1840s pointed not only to the significant role that Chinese merchants played in Vietnamese economy during that time but also the economic vulnerability that Vietnam had been exposed towards China's domestic developments. It is also another example showing how geographical proximity to China has presented Vietnam with both positive and negative economic fortunes.

The Sino-centric Tributary System and Vietnam's "Peace Diplomacy" Towards China

Geopolitical conditions leave Vietnam with little choice in dealing with China. In fact, Vietnam is entrapped in a long-standing dilemma. In the past, it had to unflaggingly struggle for its own survival and national identity in the face of a more powerful and inherently expansionist China. As such, China was perceived as a permanent security threat that the country had to keep an eye on. At the same time, China's cultural wealth and trade opportunities turned it into a benign neighbour, even an attractive model, in the eyes of many Vietnamese elites. Therefore, Vietnam gradually developed a dual perception of China which, in turn, informed its traditional attitude and behaviour towards the northern neighbour.

Vietnam's dual perception of China, however, does not mean that Vietnam treated the "China threat" and the "China opportunity" equally. History shows that Vietnam always considered its national survival and political autonomy as its top priority, and would sacrifice any potential benefits from a submissive relationship with China to protect its survival. It is this powerful mentality that underlay the emergence of Vietnam as an independent state after more than a millennium of Chinese domination as well as its successful resistance against China's repeated attempts to reconquer the country since then. Vietnam's realist, pragmatic tradition of handling China therefore turned the "China threat" into the prevailing theme in its traditional perception of the northern neighbour, which was further reinforced by the long-standing asymmetry of national power between the two countries.

A close look at the material capabilities of both Vietnam and China throughout history shows that Vietnam has always been the junior partner in its relationship with China although the level of asymmetry has not always ben the same. Among the four basic components of material capabilities, namely territory, population, military capabilities and economic capacity,[15] territory and population are the two factors that show the most visible difference. In fact, China had been the largest country in the world until the modern age and its population also accounted for one-third of the global total for a long period of history (Cao and Sun 2011, p. vii). Meanwhile, when Vietnam gained its independence in the tenth century, its territory was restricted to the Red River delta and the modern provinces of Thanh Hoa, Nghe An and Ha Tinh. Vietnamese dynasties later succeeded in expanding into the North West and the South[16] but its territory remained a fraction of China's. Table 2.3 compares the territory of China and Vietnam at various points in history.

As shown in Table 2.3, the greatest territorial disparity between Vietnam and China was recorded during the Mongol-Yuan dynasty when China was over ninety-three times larger than Vietnam. In the subsequent centuries, the disparity tended to decrease. A number of events in both countries helped to account for this. In Vietnam, the Le dynasty under Le Thanh Tong defeated the Cham Empire and annexed most of its territory in 1471. In the seventeenth and eighteenth century, the Nguyen lords under the pressure of the Trinh family were successful in expanding further south and eventually established their sovereignty over Vietnam's modern southeast region and the Mekong Delta. Vietnam's territory further expanded under the Nguyen dynasty as the Central Highland was annexed in the 1830s and the 1895 Franco-China Convention formally brought part of Vietnam's northwestern tip into its current territory. Therefore, within 500 years from the fourteenth century to the nineteenth century,

TABLE 2.3
Territory of China and Vietnam at Various Points in History
(in approx. '000 km²)

| Year | China | | Vietnam | | China/Vietnam |
	Regime	Area	Regime	Area	
980	Song	3,100	Early Le	68	45.6
1310	Mongol-Yuan	11,000	Tran	118	93.2
1450	Ming	6,500	Le	118	55.1
1790	Qing	14,700	Tây Sơn	266	55.3
1860	Qing	13,400	Nguyen	321	41.7
1976	PRC	9,640	SRV	331	29.1

Source: Data on China is based on Turchin, Hall and Adams (2006, pp. 222–23) and Taagepera (1997, pp. 492–502); data on Vietnam is author's own estimate based on GSO (2011, pp. 55–56) and the history of Vietnamese territorial changes charted in Anh (1964) and Đau (1999).

Vietnamese territory almost tripled. Meanwhile, the decline of the Qing dynasty led to the shrinking of China's territory in the nineteenth century. Nevertheless, by the twentieth century when the boundaries of both countries became stable, China was still twenty-nine times larger than Vietnam, and Vietnam is now even smaller than China's border province of Yunnan.[17]

Due to its much larger territory, China has also been dominating Vietnam in terms of population. Table 2.4 depicts the disparity between the two countries' population at various points in history. During the premodern era, when technological advances were limited, human resources were arguably the most essential forces driving a country's economic and military power. The large population not only turned China into an economy of unprecedented scale but also enabled it to sustain a colossal army. For example, the standing army of the Ming dynasty consisted of up to 1 million troops (Ebrey, Walthall and Palais 2006, p. 271), which was roughly equal to two-thirds of the whole Vietnamese population in the late fourteenth century. By 1820, with 381 million people, China had already been the most populous country in the world, accounting for approximately 36.6 per cent of the world's total population (Maddison 2003).

TABLE 2.4
Population of China and Vietnam at Various Points in History
(in approx. million people)

Year	China		Vietnam		China/Vietnam
	Regime	Population	Regime	Population	
1014	Song	60	Ly	1.6	37.5
1103	Song	123	Ly	2	61.5
1393	Ming	61	Tran	1.5	40.7
1751	Qing	207	Le	6.3	32.9
1820	Qing	381	Nguyen	6.6	57.7
1870	Qing	358	Nguyen	10.5	34.1
1913	ROC	437	Nguyen	19.3	22.6
1976	PRC	931	SRV	49.3	18.9
2000	PRC	1,264	SRV	78.5	16.1

Source: Data on China from 1014 to 1751 is based on Durand (1960, p. 249), data on Vietnam from 1014 to 1751 is adapted from Lieberman (2003, p. 420), data on both China and Vietnam from 1820 to 2000 is based on Maddison (2003, pp. 155, 160–68).

The power asymmetry obviously had a latent yet enduring effect on both Vietnam and China's perception of the relationship. Accordingly, Vietnam tended to pay excessive attention to China, while China tended to neglect Vietnam (Womack 2006, pp. 80–84). The politics of over-attention versus inattention therefore became yet another overarching feature of Sino-Vietnamese relationship. China tended to pay limited attention to Vietnam as it had too many relationships to take care of and Vietnam was perceived as being too small to cause any significant harm to China. Meanwhile, Vietnam's over-sensitiveness towards China could be explained by at least four major reasons. First, as the junior partner in the dyad, Vietnam was much more vulnerable to China than China was to Vietnam. Second, Vietnam's particular geographical conditions with a long coastline to the east and high mountain ranges to the west[18] restricted its external interaction mainly to the northern and southern neighbours. However, as China was much more powerful and influential than Vietnam's southern neighbours, it was natural for Vietnam to pay greater attention to China. Third, more than 1,000 years of Chinese domination had left Vietnam with inherent suspicion of China. Finally, as Vietnamese Confucian elites generally viewed China as a cultural and social model to follow, they paid close attention to developments within the northern neighbour.

Due to this long-standing power asymmetry, Vietnam's traditional strategy has been to seek peace and accommodation with China. Accordingly, Vietnamese rulers tended to avoid wars and confrontation with China whenever possible. In cases where wars did break out, after defeating Chinese forces, Vietnamese rulers normally took measures to save China's face or even to appease the latter to avoid renewed hostilities. In 1077, for example, after defeating the Song army, Ly rulers proposed to cede five border districts to China. After several years, however, they managed to win them back. In 1427, upon crushing the Ming army, Le Loi offered food supplies, horses and boats for the defeated army to get back to China. Later, he also returned to China tens of thousands of Chinese war prisoners and weapons at the Ming dynasty's request (Institute of History 2001b, pp. 271–73). Similarly, in 1789, after driving the Qing army out of the country, Nguyen Hue offered generous treatment toward thousands of Qing troops left in the country and buried properly the remains of the fallen ones. He also sent tributes and a petition to the Qing court to apologize for the attack on Chinese troops (Loi 2000, p. 179; Man-Cheong 2004, p. 189).

Vietnam's "peace diplomacy" towards China also led to the country's acceptance of the Sino-centric tributary system that governed bilateral interactions since Vietnam gained its independence until the late nineteenth century. The system essentially involved Vietnam's acknowledgement of China's superiority and China's acknowledgement of Vietnam's autonomy. The tributary relations started in 973 when Dinh Tien Hoang, the first emperor of independent Vietnam, sent tributes to China. The Song court conferred him the title of King of Giao Chi, and China acknowledged Vietnam as an independent country for the first time in history (Loi 2000, p. 198). Since then Vietnamese courts maintained the practice of sending tributary missions to China, many of which were to request investiture for new rulers. In a sense, Vietnam's acceptance of the Sino-centric tributary system became a symbol of the power asymmetry between the two countries.

The frequency of Vietnamese tributary missions to China and Chinese attitude towards the investiture of Vietnamese rulers in particular reflected domestic conditions of each country as well as the shifts in their power balance. For example, as Table 2.5 shows, Vietnam frequently sent tributary missions to the Northern Song (960–1126). However, after the Song lost control of northern China to the Jin dynasty and had to retreat south of Yangzi River in 1127, the number of Vietnamese tributary missions sent to the Southern Song (1127–1276) decreased remarkably. A plausible explanation for the decrease is that Vietnam perceived Southern Song as a weak state while Vietnam itself enjoyed a considerable growth in power under the Ly and Tran dynasties. Similarly, when the Ming dynasty was still powerful, it normally delayed or even refused the investiture of Le rulers.[19] However, in the 1640s, the Ming dynasty became much more generous in conferring royal titles to Le rulers. This change of attitude was possibly related to the fact that the Ming dynasty was in decline and came under attack by the Manchus in the 1640s, while in Vietnam the Le dynasty showed signs of resurgence against the backdrop of the Mac family's sinking power (Loi 2000, p. 207).

Vietnam's willingness to embrace the Sino-centric tributary system therefore did not imply its intention to submit to the Chinese power.

TABLE 2.5
Number of Vietnamese Tributary Missions to the Northern and Southern Song

Northern Song		Southern Song	
967–986	10	1127–1146	4
987–1006	7	1147–1166	5
1007–1026	11	1167–1186	5
1027–1046	11	1187–1206	2
1047–1066	7	1207–1226	0
1067–1086	8	1227–1246	2
1087–1106	3	1247–1266	3
1107–1126	2	1267–1276	2
Total	59	Total	23

Source: Bielenstein (2005), p. 34.

As Womack (2006, p. 118) puts it, "deference to China was not the same as submission". In fact, Vietnam undertook an independent course of development in the domestic context and even established a Vietnam-centric tributary system in its relations with weaker neighbours.[20] Vietnam also accepted the Sino-centric tributary system for the benefits that it expected to gain through cultural and economic exchanges with China. In the face of China's overwhelming power, the nominal deference that Vietnam paid to Chinese courts was a minimal cost that it could afford in exchange for peace, stability and autonomous development. For example, the peaceful relationship with China for more than 300 years from 1427 to 1788, which was achieved mostly through the tributary system, played an essential part in Vietnam's nation building process. It was during this critical period that Vietnam had the opportunity to consolidate its power and expand southward to eventually establish the current shape of its territory. Therefore, the acceptance of China's tributary system can be seen as Vietnam's strategy to neutralize the negative effects of its power asymmetry vis-à-vis China.

Conclusion

Vietnam's traditional perception of China is characterized first and foremost by the deep-rooted distrust and animosity resulting from China's millennium-long domination and repeated invasions of the country. As such, Vietnam has always viewed China as a major source of security threats on which it has to keep a wary eye. Such a perception, however, is also accompanied by the view of China as a source of rather benign influence in terms of cultural borrowings and economic exchanges.

The voluntary absorption of Chinese norms and values became an essential tool for Vietnam's nation-building ever since the country gained its independence from China in the tenth century. Vietnamese elites selectively borrowed certain Chinese cultural elements and governance practices as they saw fit to help lay the cultural and social foundations for their rule as well as the country's development. The selective borrowing of Chinese norms and values therefore allowed Vietnam to preserve its national identity while benefiting the most from China's vast cultural wealth.

Meanwhile, geographical proximity also enabled Vietnam to benefit economically from China through trade, technological transfer, and, to a lesser extent, the migration of ethnic Han people into the country. Despite certain problems emanating from China's economic influence, Vietnam largely found its economic ties with China beneficial rather than threatening. Nevertheless, transport and communications difficulties as well as the inward-looking tendency of both economies put a constraint on the scope and depth of their traditional economic ties. China's economic influence on Vietnam was therefore rather limited and superficial. Vietnam's domestic development was still mainly determined by its internal conditions rather than external economic interactions.

Vietnam's dual perception of China moulded through historical experiences and the long-standing power asymmetry between the two countries are the two major factors underlying Vietnam's traditional China strategy, which is composed of Vietnam's peace diplomacy towards the northern neighbour and its acceptance of the Sino-centric tributary system. In pursuing this strategy, Vietnam expected to maintain a peaceful relationship with China, thereby minimizing the adverse effect of power asymmetry on the country. In effect, when it comes to the structure of bilateral relations, power asymmetry proves to be the single most important factor that defines the way the two countries interacted with each other. It is also a constant variable that turns China into a permanent security threat for Vietnam. However, as history has shown, power asymmetry did not always drive the bilateral relations into conflict and instability. For most of the pre-colonial era, Vietnam's pursuit of peace diplomacy and its acceptance of the Sino-centric tributary system tended to make bilateral relations relatively peaceful and stable.

NOTES

1. Vietnam's contemporary official position considers the Trieu as an extraneous dynasty and hence Trieu Da a foreign invader rather than a national unifier. This view was first adopted by North Vietnamese historians after the Democratic Republic of Vietnam was established in 1945 and became the official historical view of the country following its unification in 1975. However, most of traditional Vietnamese historical records consider Trieu Da as a legitimate emperor of Vietnam. Such evaluation of Trieu Da was adopted by celebrated Vietnamese historians such as Le Van Huu (thirteenth century) and Ngo Si Lien (sixteenth century). This view went unchallenged until Ngo Thi Si, an eighteenth century scholar, argued that Trieu Da was a Chinese invader and thus he should not be deemed a legitimate emperor of Vietnam.

2. In 1834, King Minh Mang divided Vietnam into three regions, namely Bac Ky (from Ninh Binh northward), Trung Ky (from Thanh Hoa down to Binh Thuan), and Nam Ky (from Bien Hoa southward). The French then named the three regions as Tonkin, Annam, and Cochinchina, respectively.

3. However, according to historian Tran Trong Kim (1971, p. 299), China decided to send troops into Tonkin with a long-term vision of occupying the region.

4. The French had earlier turned Cochinchina into a colony in 1867.

5. The treaty provided for China's withdrawal of its troops out of Tonkin and recognition of the French protectorate over Annam and Tonkin. Thereby, China had practically abandoned its own claims to suzerainty over Vietnam.

6. Taking advantage of the French withdrawal of troops from Vietnam following the Geneva Conference, China sent troops to occupy the eastern part of the Paracels in 1956.

7. The actual numbers of casualties on both sides are still contested. However, Western sources estimate as many as 26,000 PLA troops were killed in action and another 37,000 wounded. Meanwhile, 30,000 and 32,000 Vietnamese troops were killed and wounded, respectively. See Chen (1987, pp. 113–14), Zhang (2005, pp. 866–67).

8. Paragraph ten of the preamble of Vietnam's 1980 Constitution reads:

> Having just emerged out of the 30-year-long war of liberation, our people sincerely longed for peace to rebuild the Nation, but we had to rise up again to fight the Chinese expansionist invaders and their lackeys in Cambodia. Inheriting and promoting the glorious tradition of the Nation, our people and army have achieved resounding victories in the two national defense wars against the Cambodian reactionaries on the southwestern border and the Chinese hegemonists on the northern border, thereby successfully defending our national sovereignty, independence, unity and territorial integrity.

This paragraph was excluded from the 1992 Constitution.

9. This is also a major rationale for Vietnam's attempts to normalize its relations with China in the late 1980s, which will be examined in Chapter 3.

10. For example, Ly Bi, who led the armed insurrection against China in 542, was of Chinese origin (Institute of History 2001a, p. 328).

11. Song dynasty sources recorded seventy-six missions from Vietnam, but Vietnamese sources like *Dai Viet su ky toan thu* and *Dai Viet su luoc* recorded six more missions.

12. Dang Trong and Dang Ngoai refer to South and North Vietnam respectively during the seventeenth and eighteenth centuries when the country was divided between Trinh and Nguyen war lords. After Mac Dang Dung usurped power from the Le Dynasty in 1527, the Mac family was challenged by a coalition between the Nguyen and Trinh families who wished to restore the Le Dynasty. Fighting between the two sides raged until 1592 when the Trinh–Nguyen coalition finally captured the capital, drove the Mac into the northern hills, and restored the Le dynasty. However, the Trinh–Nguyen alliance soon split along regional lines. In order to escape persecution by the more powerful Trinh family, the Nguyen lords fled to the south of the country. Open war between the two camps broke out in 1627 and persisted until a peace deal was struck in 1673. Accordingly, the two sides agreed to take the Gianh River as their dividing line, which remained stable until 1774. Therefore, during this episode, the Le Dynasty continued to exist but only nominally, while real power was in the hand of the Trinh and Nguyen families, who ruled Dang Ngoai (the North) and Dang Trong (the South), respectively.

13. For more details on consumer imports, see Li (1998, p. 86), Woodside (1995, p. 166).

14. Vietnamnet reported in June 2009 that 200 Chinese workers attacked local residents in Nghi Son, Thanh Hoa province, where a cement plant was being constructed by Chinese contractors. See Vietnamnet (2009).

15. See, for example, Ferris (1973), Russett (1972), Singer (1980), and especially Cline (1977).

16. For a history of Vietnamese territorial expansion, see Anh (1964) and Dau (1999).

17. Yunnan's area in 2011 is 394,000 km².
18. In Lieberman's (2003, p. 338) words, Vietnam is "the least coherent territory in the world".
19. For example, until his death in 1533, Le Loi, the founder of the Le dynasty, still had not been conferred the title of King of An Nam by the Ming court although he had requested it.
20. For example, in 1815, Emperor Gia Long published a list of Vietnam's thirteen vassals, including Luang Prabang, Vientiane, Burma, France, England, Tran Ninh (eastern Laos), and two countries which Vietnamese called "Water Haven" and "Fire Haven" (in modern Vietnam's Central Highlands) (Woodside, 1971, p. 237).

3

Vietnam's *Doi Moi* and Its Quest for Normalized Relations with China

Introduction

After Vietnam was reunified in 1975, the CPV enthusiastically embarked on a new project: transforming the country along the socialist path. There was a widespread sense of optimism among communist leaders that the war-torn country would soon recover and prosper through a socialist transformation. However, the new task turned out to be far more challenging than they had imagined. The country's economic performance in the first ten years after reunification shows that Vietnam "won a war but lost the peace" (Kolko 1995, p. 351), with economic failures causing the people's living standards to deteriorate dramatically after 1975. The situation got even worse after Vietnam was forced to engage in two costly armed conflicts, one against the Khmer Rouge and the other against China. Sustaining war efforts put excessive strains on the already war-torn economy and contributed to the outbreak of a socio-economic crisis in the mid-1980s, causing a sharp decline in the CPV's legitimacy. Against this backdrop, the CPV decided to adopt the

Doi Moi (Renovation) policy at its sixth national congress in late 1986, with a view to reforming the national economy before the socio-economic crisis could threaten the regime's survival.

In order to implement *Doi Moi*, the CPV started to introduce within a short period of time a series of new policies, which included developing a multi-sector market-based economy, renovating the economic structure, stabilizing the socio-economic environment, promoting science and technology, and opening up the country's foreign relations. It should be noted that by 1986, hostile relations with China and Vietnam's engagement in the Cambodian conflict were still destabilizing Vietnam's immediate external environment, which was unfavourable for its economic development. Disengaging from the Cambodian quagmire and especially normalizing relations with China emerged as Vietnam's top foreign policy priorities.

Focusing on Vietnam's domestic–foreign policy nexus, the current chapter will look into the link between Vietnam's adoption of *Doi Moi* and transformations in its China policy in the late 1980s and early 1990s. The chapter argues that during this period, changes in Vietnam's foreign policy in general and its China policy in particular originated first and foremost from the CPV's domestic agenda of promoting economic reform and protecting the regime's survival. As the CPV considered hostile relations with China as detrimental to both its economic reform and regime security, it gave renewed emphasis to improving relations with China. The CPV's desire to achieve normalization with China became even stronger after the collapse of communism in Eastern Europe, which deepened the CPV's concerns about regime security. Against this backdrop, Vietnam made a number of important concessions to China regarding the Cambodian issue in order to accelerate the normalization process, which eventually concluded in late 1991.

The chapter seeks to contribute to the literature on modern Sino-Vietnamese relations by employing the domestic–foreign policy nexus as the main analytical framework to account for changes in Vietnam's China policy in the late 1980s and early 1990s. As such, the chapter is not meant to undermine alternative explanations of transformations in bilateral relations during this critical period. Rather, it seeks to deepen the understanding of such transformations through a new approach. In addition, the chapter will also make extensive use of former Vietnamese Deputy Foreign Minister Tran Quang Co's unpublished memoir

"Hoi uc va suy nghi: 1975–1991" [Memoir and Reflections: 1975–1991], a valuable source that has hardly been tapped by researchers of Sino–Vietnamese relations, to provide new insights into the normalization process between the two countries.

The Domestic–Foreign Policy Nexus in Vietnam's Political Context

How domestic factors shape a state's foreign policy has been widely studied by political scientists and foreign policy analysts. The existing body of literature on the topic mention at least five major domestic determinants of a state's foreign policy, namely domestic political situation, electoral cycles, the government's accountability to the legislature and domestic constituencies, public opinion, and economic interests (see, for example, Brule and Mintz 2006; Holsti 1991; Jack S. Levy 1989; Jack S. Levy and Vakili 1992; Maoz, 1998; R. A. Miller, 1995; Mintz & DeRouen, 2010; Morgan & Anderson, 1999; Putnam, 1988; J.L. Ray 1995; Russett 1993; Smith 1996).

Domestic political situation is undoubtedly an important factor that foreign policymakers need to take into account when making their decisions. A popular argument that highlights the impact of domestic political situation on a state's foreign policy can be found in the Diversionary War Theory. The theory posits that state leaders may turn to foreign adventures, including instigating wars or escalating existing conflicts, in order to distract the population from domestic problems, or to promote domestic political support for themselves (see, for example, Levy 1989; Levy and Vakili 1992; Meernik and Waterman 1996; R.A. Miller 1995, 1999; Morgan and Anderson 1999; Morgan and Bickers 1992; Morgan and Campbell 1991; Smith 1996). The theory originated from the "in-group/out-group hypothesis" initially developed by German sociologist Georg Simmel (1898) and later expanded by Lewis Coser (1956). The theory posits that a common external threat can help reduce conflict and increase cohesion within a group. Despite the fact that certain recent quantitative studies tend to nullify the theory, its central argument has enjoyed wide acceptance as well as support in various case studies (Morgan and Anderson 1999). For example, in examining the Diversionary War Theory literature, Levy (1989) found that the outbreak of nearly every war during the two centuries prior to 1989 had been attributed by some scholars to state leaders' wish to enhance their domestic standing.

Another important factor in domestic politics that shapes state leaders' foreign policy decisions is electoral cycles. As the incumbent leaders' political survival is subject to voters' support, they tend to choose foreign policies that make voters happy rather than unhappy (Mintz and DeRouen 2010). Research by Gaubatz (1991) finds that just before elections, leaders tend to avoid major wars with high casualties which may diminish their popularity and hence their chance to be re-elected. Meanwhile, another study by Smith (1996) indicates governments that are assured of re-election or have no prospects of re-election tend to make unbiased foreign policy decisions. However, if a government perceives election results to be affected by voters' evaluation of foreign policy outcomes, it is likely to favour violent, adventurous foreign policy projects.

The fact that incumbent governments tend to pay more attention to voters' opinion prior to elections does not mean that they are not accountable to their domestic constituencies for their foreign policy decisions after election time. A third domestic factor influencing foreign policy, the role of domestic constituencies especially regarding the negotiation of international treaties, is demonstrated by the two-level game model developed by Robert Putnam (1988). The two-level game model highlights the interactive process in which governments have to undertake negotiations on international treaties at both international and domestic levels simultaneously. As important international treaties normally need to be ratified by the legislature to be effective for the country in question, a government, while working to reach an agreement with foreign partners at the international negotiation (Level I), will also have to try to get the agreement accepted by the legislature at the domestic negotiation (Level II). This two-level negotiation process "tends to slide the negotiators of both camps into an imbroglio where they have to conciliate intense domestic pressure with international pulls and pushes" (Boukhars 2001). The negotiation at the domestic level is particularly important in cases where the government in question does not enjoy a majority in the legislature that can help it get international treaties ratified with ease.

The fourth major domestic determinant of a state's foreign policies is public opinion. Specifically, public opinion may encourage a state to use force, to escalate or terminate a particular conflict that it is involved in, or to pursue other foreign policy decisions. David Brule and Alex Mintz (2006), for example, find that U.S. presidents tend to refrain from using force when they face high opposition to foreign military intervention, and are likely to use force when public support for such actions reaches above 50 per cent. The power of public opinion is also a major factor supporting the institutional logic of the Democratic Peace Theory, which states that democratic states never go to war with each other (see, for example, Maoz 1998; Mesquita et al., 1999; Oneal and Russett, 1999; J.L. Ray 1995; Russett 1993; Weart 1998). According to this logic, political elites in democracies are accountable to a wide range of social groups, and they therefore pay attention to what these groups' opinions may be, especially regarding the matter of war and peace. As domestic groups have various reasons to oppose wars, such as the costs of wars in terms of casualties and material loss, the disruption of international trade and investment, or the view of war as morally unacceptable if waged against other liberal states, leaders in democracies tend to be discouraged from pursuing war efforts against other democracies. War casualties, in particular, have a strong influence on public opinion, and thus public support for war efforts, whether they are against a democracy or non-democracy. For example, an experiment conducted by Scott Gartner (2008, cited in Mintz and DeRouen 2010, p. 132) demonstrates that support for the war in Iraq declined when images of war casualties were shown to subjects of the experiment. Meanwhile, several quantitative studies of the Diversionary War Theory also find that U.S. presidents are less likely to use force when the country has already engaged in a major war due to public concern over casualties (DeRouen Jr. 2001).

The final domestic factor that helps shape a state's foreign policy is its economic interests. Studies on the origin of wars throughout history, for example, have identified economic interests as one of the main rationales for wars. These economic interests are diverse, ranging from establishing monopolies over trade routes, expanding foreign markets, to securing access to strategic resources. An important work by Holsti (1991) identifies economic interests to be a major cause of interstate wars, especially during the periods of 1648–1814 (between Westphalia and the Congress of Vienna) and 1918–41 (between the two World Wars). Economic issues, for example, accounted for the outbreak of almost 50 per cent of international conflicts during the 1648–1814 period

(Holsti 1991, p. 316). Since the end of World War II, although economic interests have become less important as a cause of international conflicts, they remain a significant factor that influences the decisions of foreign policy makers around the world. The 1991 Gulf War, for example, was marketed to the American public by the first Bush administration as a war about jobs, oil, and national economic security (Mintz and DeRouen 2010, p. 130). Recent research (Brautigam 2009, 2010; Rotberg 2008; Tull 2006; Zafar 2007) also finds that economic interests, such as securing access to energy resources, have been a key determinant of China's policy towards African nations. In addition, unlike previous historical periods, economic interests nowadays tend to promote the endurance of peace rather than the proliferation of wars. For example, although there are still debates around the pacifying effect of economic interdependence, a significant thread in the literature on the topic argues that economic interdependence does discourage countries from engaging in armed conflicts with each other mainly for fear of losing the welfare gains associated with the economic relationship, especially in terms of trade and investment (Domke 1988; Gartzke, Li and Boehmer 2001; Gasiorowski and Polachek 1982; Maoz 2009; Oneal et al. 1996; Oneal and Ray 1997; Oneal and Russett 1997; Polachek 1980, 1992; Polachek and McDonald 1992).

In sum, five major domestic determinants of a state's foreign policies include the domestic political situation, electoral cycles, the government's accountability to the legislature and domestic constituencies, public opinion, and economic interests. However, while all of these factors are influential in liberal democracies, such factors as electoral cycles, the government's accountability to the legislature and domestic constituencies, and public opinion, have a much more limited role in the foreign policy-making of authoritarian states.

The limited influence of these three domestic factors on the foreign policy-making of authoritarian states derives from these states' particular political nature and power structure. In authoritarian states, as there is no free and competitive election, electoral cycles barely have any influence on the government's foreign policy decisions. Similarly, as the whole political system is controlled by the authoritarian regime, the legislature and domestic constituencies do not have the necessary independence and power to either effectively oversee the government's negotiation of international treaties, or to hold it accountable for its foreign policy decisions. The lack of press freedom and the government's ability to manipulate information also constrain the influence of public opinion on foreign policies of authoritarian states.

As an authoritarian state, Vietnam also shares the above-mentioned characteristics of the domestic–foreign policy nexus. Table 3.1 summarizes the relevance and significance of domestic factors' influence on its foreign policy-making.

Three out of the five factors, namely electoral cycles, accountability to the legislature and domestic constituencies, and public opinion, barely have any influence on Vietnam's foreign policy-making due to above-mentioned reasons. However, it should be noted that although the CPV's foreign policy-making is not affected by electoral cycles, the Party tends to pursue foreign policies that help enhance its international legitimacy and consolidate its rule at home. In the same vein, it will also shy away from any foreign policy that may have negative implications for its rule. The Party's wish to use foreign policy as a tool for sustaining its power, as demonstrated in the final section, also partly accounts for its leadership's anxiety to achieve normalization with China in order to, among other things, "safeguard socialism", code-words for protecting its rule.

Meanwhile, just like state leaders around the world, Vietnam's communist leaders are also tempted to use diversionary tactics whenever appropriate to divert public attention from internal problems or to improve their domestic political standing. However, diversionary foreign policies became irrelevant for Vietnam after it launched *Doi Moi*

TABLE 3.1
The Relevance and Significance of Domestic Factors to Vietnam's Foreign Policy-making

Domestic Factors	Relevance	Significance
Domestic political conditions (diversionary tactics)	Yes	No
Electoral cycles	No	N/A
Accountability to the legislature and domestic constituencies	No	N/A
Public opinion	No	N/A
Economic interests	Yes	Yes

Source: Author's own compilation.

in 1986. As a peaceful regional environment has become essential for its economic reform, it is not in the interest of the CPV to initiate military hostilities with foreign countries just to relieve domestic pressures. Instead, as the sole ruling party, the CPV has other tools at its disposal to control the domestic situation without harming its foreign relations and dampening its economic reform efforts. Therefore, although diversionary tactics remain a foreign policy choice for Vietnam, it is a remote possibility that the CPV will ever have to resort to them.

Finally, unlike the other domestic factors, economic interests play an important role in the formulation of Vietnam's foreign policy. As argued in the next section, foreign policy changes that Vietnam has pursued since the late 1980s originated first and foremost from the CPV's wish to facilitate its economic reform under *Doi Moi*. Economic interests have been able to play a significant role in the formulation of Vietnam's foreign policy because economic interests exist and matter to a country's government regardless of the type of its political regime. Promoting economic interests through foreign policies serves the interest of not only the Vietnamese people but also the CPV itself, as robust economic development helps the Party enhance its performance-based legitimacy and strengthen its rule.

In sum, out of the five major domestic determinants of a state's foreign policy, only economic interests have been an important source of influence on Vietnam's foreign policy-making. Due to the authoritarian nature of Vietnam's political regime, the other four factors are either irrelevant or insignificant in their influence. It should also be noted that while electoral cycles do not have a role in Vietnam's foreign policy-making, the CPV's wish to maintain and strengthen its rule instead has a significant impact on the country's foreign policy decisions. The following two sections will further illuminate these points.

Doi Moi and Vietnam's Foreign Policy Reform

By 1986, economic failures had been the most important reason behind the CPV's falling legitimacy which threatened the Party's political survival. The CPV's official adoption of *Doi Moi* at its sixth national congress in December 1986 therefore could be seen as an effort by the Party to switch to the performance-based legitimation mode to sustain its rule. Accordingly, the Party began to rely on the improvement of the country's socio-economic performance as the single most important source of its political legitimacy (Hiep 2012). The adoption of *Doi Moi*, however, did not solve the CPV's legitimacy crisis overnight. While struggling to change the country's economic model to a market-based one, the Party also faced the arduous challenge of reforming its foreign policy in order to help the country break out of international diplomatic isolation and facilitate its domestic economic transformation.

Following the sixth congress, the CPV sought to change its foreign policy to achieve three critical objectives: to get Vietnam out of international isolation and economic embargo; to create a peaceful external environment conducive to the country's internal development; and to pave the way for its international economic integration. The CPV also sought to open up and diversify the country's external economic relations in order to take advantage of foreign resources, such as markets, capital and technologies, to boost the domestic economic reform.

Towards these ends, the CPV began to step up its efforts in retuning the country's foreign policy after the sixth congress. However, the process was actually launched earlier than that. Before the sixth congress was convened, the CPV Politburo had passed Resolution no. 32 dated 9 July 1986. The Resolution, entitled "The solution to the Cambodian issue must preserve the Cambodian revolutionary gains and solidarity among three Indochinese countries", sought to articulate changes to Vietnam's foreign policy against the background of the country's prolonged international isolation due to its military engagement in Cambodia.

The top foreign policy objective identified by the Resolution was to "combine the strength of the nation with that of the time; take advantage of favourable international conditions to build socialism and defend the nation; *proactively create a stable environment to focus on economic development*" [emphasis added] (Nam 2006, p. 26).[1] Accordingly, the Resolution stated that Vietnam should seek to peacefully coexist with China, ASEAN and the United States, and to help turn Southeast Asia into a region of peace, stability and cooperation. On the Cambodian issue, however, the Resolution emphasized that Vietnam should look for a solution which would preserve the revolutionary gains of Cambodia and reinforce the Indochinese tri-national alliance.

The Resolution was remarkable in that it considered the country's foreign policy as both an agent and a target of change. On the one hand, the CPV wished to use its foreign policy as a tool to change the regional and international environment into a peaceful and stable one favourable for its economic reform. On the other hand, such a change would be impossible without Vietnam first making changes to its foreign policy itself. An overhaul to the country's foreign policy therefore became necessary. However, as shown by the above points, changes introduced by Resolution no. 32 were not radical enough, especially regarding the Cambodian issue, to bring about meaningful improvements in the country's external relations. The CPV's goals of preserving the "revolutionary gains" in Cambodia and reinforcing the Indochinese alliance were at odds with its objective of improving relations with China, ASEAN and the United States.

Meanwhile, the CPV's foreign policy introduced in the sixth congress' official documents a few months later remained heavily ideology-based and did not bring about major breakthroughs. Therefore, it was no surprise that no major advance in Vietnam's foreign relations was made within the first few years after the sixth congress. In the meantime, improvements in the country's economic conditions were modest. Inflation remained as high as 700 per cent in 1988, causing the macroeconomic environment to stay unstable. Vietnam continued to be heavily dependent on Council for Mutual Economic Assistance (CMEA) member countries for its external trade, while foreign investors remained hesitant in pouring money into the country.[2] The enduring economic plight therefore forced the CPV leadership to speed up its foreign policy reforms to help the country get out of the Cambodian quagmire and break out of its international isolation, thereby facilitating the economic reform at home.

It was against this backdrop that in 1987, the CPV Politburo secretly adopted Resolution no. 2 which sought to bring about more radical strategic modifications to the country's national security policy and foreign policy posture.[3] According to Thayer (1994*b*), who was the first scholar to develop a detailed account of the classified document by dissecting commentaries in Vietnamese military journals and newspapers that made reference to it in the 1989–90 period, the Resolution aimed to redefine the national defence policy to suit the post-war conditions. At the same time, the resolution also established new roles for the military in economic activities as well as new responsibilities for the national defence industry. In light of the unfolding economic reform under *Doi Moi*, the Resolution also decided that

Vietnam would completely withdraw its forces out of Cambodia and Laos, and reduce the size of its standing army to save resources for economic development efforts (Thayer 1994b, pp. 14–17).

Soon after that, the CPV Politburo adopted Resolution no. 13 dated 20 May 1988 on "Tasks and foreign policy in the new situation". As revealed by the title, the Resolution assessed new developments in domestic and international conditions, thereby outlining new directions for the country's foreign policy. With the general theme of "maintaining peace, developing the economy", the Resolution stressed that the top objectives of Vietnam's foreign policy would be to assist stabilizing the political system and to facilitate the country's economic renovation. Towards these ends, the Resolution laid down the policy of getting "more friends, fewer enemies" *(them ban bot thu)* and diversifying the country's foreign relations on the principle of national independence, equal sovereignty and mutual benefits. The Resolution also set specific foreign policy tasks for the country, which included actively contributing to a solution of the Cambodian issue; normalizing relations with China; improving relations with ASEAN; expanding ties with Japan, western and northern European countries; and step by step achieving normalization with the United States (Nam 2006, p. 27). The Resolution has since been considered a landmark in the renovation of the CPV's foreign policy thinking and a foundation on which the country's policy of diversifying and multilateralizing foreign relations was later developed by the Party (Hung 2006, p. 14; Nam 2006, p. 27).

At its seventh congress in 1991, the CPV reaffirmed the overall foreign policy objective of maintaining peace and expanding its foreign relations to facilitate domestic development. In the *Strategy for Socio-economic Stabilization and Development up to the Year 2000*, which was also adopted by the congress, the CPV declared that Vietnam would "diversify and multilateralize economic relations with all countries and economic organizations". The prevalent theme of promoting economic development and opening up the country's foreign policy at the seventh congress confirmed that *Doi Moi* had become an irreversible process.

More importantly, it was at the seventh congress that the CPV officially departed from its traditional ideology-based foreign policy-making in favour of a more pragmatic approach. Accordingly, it officially stated that Vietnam wished "to be friend with all countries in the world community" (CPV 2010, p. 403) and sought "equal and mutually beneficial cooperation with all countries based on the principles of peaceful co-existence and regardless of differences in socio-political regimes" (ibid., p. 351). This was the culmination of a series of changes in the CPV's world view, through which the Party leadership gradually shifted from the view of world politics as an arena of struggle between the two camps of imperialism and socialism, to the view that all countries were interdependent and therefore amenable to peaceful co-existence (Porter 1990). The worldwide retreat of communism also reinforced Vietnam's determination to abandon the ideology-based approach to foreign policy-making. The pragmatic approach to foreign policy-making was then maintained and further developed by the CPV in its subsequent congresses.

In other words, modifications to Vietnam's foreign policy since the late 1980s, as demonstrated by the above analysis of the CPV's major foreign policy documents during this period, originated first and foremost from the launch of *Doi Moi* which made it compulsory for Vietnam to change its foreign policy to facilitate its economic reform. That said, in retrospect, there were at least two other factors that may also have contributed to the reform process of Vietnam's foreign policy.

First, in the 1980s, changes in the international conditions began to influence the CPV's world view, its perception of national interests as well as its definition of "friends" *(ban)* and "enemies" *(thu)*. By the late 1980s, the rapprochement between China, its main antagonist, and the Soviet Union, its most important ally, put Vietnam in a foreign policy dilemma. While continuing to consider relations with the Soviet Union as the "cornerstone" of its foreign policy, Vietnam could no longer afford to be reliant on the Soviet Union as a patron that could effectively help protect its national interests in the international arena. At the same time, the renewed detente between the Soviet Union and the United States which resulted in the Malta summit in 1989 had *de facto* lifted the Iron Curtain and put an end to the Cold War. The development caused the CPV to assume that "dialogue and cooperation" *(doi thoai va hop tac)* rather than "confrontation" *(doi dau)* had become the mainstream of international relations. The CPV therefore perceived it as a window of opportunity to settle differences with other countries through dialogue and cooperation. The retuning of the country's foreign policy towards openness, diversification and multilateralization therefore became necessary.

At the same time, changes in Vietnam's foreign policy in the late 1980s also resulted from the CPV's process of "renovation of thinking" *(doi moi tu duy)*. The importance of renovation in the CPV's strategic thinking to the country's developments in general and its foreign relations in particular was well echoed in a comment made by then General Secretary Nguyen Van Linh at the seventh congress:

> An issue of paramount importance is to continue renovating the thinking and elevate the Party's intellectual capacity to a new level of development. It is now than ever before that should our Party wish to lead the renovation cause toward success, it has to enhance its intellectual capability and implementation capacity, which ranges from the identification and full understanding of the developmental laws of our society and the Party itself, to the understanding of the world and the time, of friends, allies and enemies (CPV 2010, pp. 385–86).

Accordingly, the transformations of the CPV's world view, the abandonment of ideology-based foreign policy-making, or the adoption of the dialogue and cooperation over confrontation are the cases in point showing evolutions in the CPV's perception of international conditions, its interests as well as its approaches to managing international relations. However, neither were the changes in the CPV's foreign policy-thinking happening in a vacuum, nor were they a process initiated entirely by the CPV only. The country's economic renovation under *Doi Moi* and developments in international politics, as mentioned above, were important factors that shaped changes in the CPV's foreign policy-thinking and reinforced its inclination toward a more open foreign policy.

In sum, Vietnam undertook major changes to its foreign policy in the late 1980s. By 1991, its foreign policy had become much more open, with the key foreign policy objectives being diversifying and multilateralizing the country's foreign relations. The most important factor that drove all these changes was the country's economic reform under *Doi Moi*. The CPV sought to revise its foreign policy in order to create a favourable external environment and to take advantage of foreign resources for the promotion of its domestic economic development. As such, economic interests became the most significant domestic determinant that underlay Vietnam's foreign policy reform during this critical episode of the country's history.

Vietnam's Quest for Normalization with China

Despite the CPV's efforts in the late 1980s to change the country's foreign policy and break out of international isolation, its achievements until the seventh congress were limited. By June 1991, Vietnam's relations with the ASEAN states, China, the United States, and major international institutions such as the WB and IMF, had not been normalized. In particular, although Vietnam laid great emphasis on normalizing relations with China, its efforts in this regard met with limited results and it was not until November 1991 that the two countries finally normalized their relations.

At least by 1988, the most important thrust behind Vietnam's efforts to normalize relations with China had been the fact that a hostile Sino-Vietnamese relationship caused Vietnam to suffer from an unstable regional environment unfavourable for its economic reform under *Doi Moi*. Bilaterally, China continued to conduct warlike activities, mainly in terms of shelling and "land-grabbing", against Vietnamese border districts during the 1980s. Major Chinese military harassments along the Vietnamese border took place in July 1980, May 1981, April 1983, April 1984, June 1985, and December 1986/January 1987 (see, for example, Thayer 1987). Shelling was used as the main method in China's "war of sabotage" against Vietnam. For example, it was reported that China had fired about 250,000 artillery and mortar shells into Vietnamese territory in the first half of 1986. Meanwhile, starting in May 1985, China also began to feed plastic mines into rivers which flowed into Vietnam, causing 100 mine explosions in various Vietnamese provinces (ibid., pp. 21–24). At the same time, China continued to use the Cambodian issue to drain Vietnam economically and isolate the country politically. Therefore, if Vietnam could not improve its relations with China, the country would face enormous difficulties in promoting its domestic economic reform under *Doi Moi*.

Since 1989, as communist regimes began to collapse one after another in Eastern Europe, deepened regime security concerns among the CPV leadership also added another important driving force to Vietnam's quest for normalization with China. Vietnamese leaders accordingly sought to mend bilateral relations as quickly as possible so that the two communist parties could join hands to protect their regimes. Therefore, while economic interests in terms of promoting the economic reform under *Doi Moi* served as the original trigger of Vietnam's quest for normalization with China, it was the CPV's desire to maintain its rule amidst developments in Eastern Europe that helped accelerate the process. Evidence from the bilateral normalization process in the late 1980s and early 1990s substantiate these observations.

Although Vietnam's quest for normalization with China was particularly stepped up after the adoption of *Doi Moi*, the process, especially on the part of Vietnam, effectively started right after the end of the Sino-Vietnamese border war in 1979. From 18 April to 18 May 1979, Vietnam and China conducted the first round of negotiation in Ha Noi, followed by the second round in Beijing from 28 June 1979 to 6 March 1980. However, the first two rounds of negotiation did not yield any result, and China unilaterally cut off the negotiation. From 1980 until late 1988 when China finally agreed to reopen talks with Vietnam on normalization, Vietnam sent China about twenty letters and diplomatic notes requesting resumption of negotiation, all were ignored or turned down by China (Co 2003, p. 36).

The central obstacle to the normalization of bilateral relations was Vietnam's military occupation of Cambodia. Initially, China demanded Vietnam to withdraw completely from Cambodia, promising that as soon as Vietnam withdrew the first batch of its troops, China would be prepared to start negotiation with Vietnam on normalization (Loi 2006, p. 405). In 1985, however, when Vietnam declared that it would complete troop withdrawal out of Cambodia by 1990, China complained that the 1990 deadline was too distant and did not show Vietnam's goodwill. Soon afterwards, sensing that Vietnam's complete withdrawal from Cambodia would be inevitable, China raised its conditions for normalization by adding that Vietnam must agree to include the Khmer Rouge in any political solution of the Cambodian issue and stop referring to their past genocidal crimes (Co 2003, pp. 33–36).

By 1986, Vietnam's response to China's escalating conditions for normalization had been inconsistent. On the one hand, Vietnam spared every effort to improve relations with China by any relevant measure, including gradually withdrawing its troops from Cambodia since as early as 1982. As Vietnam moved closer to economic reform, its interest in achieving normalization with China deepened. Addressing the CMEA summit in Moscow on 10 November 1986, CPV General Secretary Truong Chinh declared that Vietnam was "ready to conduct negotiations with China *at any level, any time, any place and without any precondition*" [emphasis added] (CPV 2006a, p. 300). The same offer was repeated in the Political Report of the CPV's sixth congress one month later. To show its goodwill, the CPV also decided at the sixth congress to drop its reference to China as "the most direct and dangerous enemy" out of the Party's Constitution (Co 2003, p. 155; Thayer 1987, p. 25). On the other hand, Vietnam appeared resistant to a number of China's conditions, especially regarding the Khmer Rouge and intra-Cambodian issues. In Resolution no. 32 of July 1986, for example, the CPV maintained the objective of "preserving revolutionary gains" in Cambodia, which implied no compromise with the Khmer Rouge.

Nevertheless, following the adoption of *Doi Moi*, Vietnam began to accelerate its efforts to normalize its relations with China. In April 1987, the Foreign Ministry decided to establish an internal research group code-named CP87 and headed by Deputy Foreign Minister Tran Quang Co. CP87's key mandate was to study and make recommendations regarding the normalization with China and the resolution of the Cambodian issue (Co 2003, p. 29). In May 1988, the CPV Politburo adopted Resolution no. 13 which emphasized normalizing relations with China as one of the top foreign policy tasks of the country. On 27 August 1988, the Vietnamese National Assembly also voted to remove the reference to China as a "direct and dangerous threat" from the preamble of country's 1982 Constitution.

The CPV's persistent wish to normalize relations with China as expressed in Resolution no. 13 is noteworthy as the Resolution was adopted just two months after a brief naval clash on 14 March 1988 between the two countries in the Spratlys which destroyed three Vietnamese naval vessels and resulted in the death of sixty-four Vietnamese sailors. Although the naval clash did raise concerns among the Vietnamese leadership about Chinese hegemonism and expansionism, it did not diminish Vietnam's determination to pursue normalization with China. Apart from Vietnam's wish to break out of international diplomatic isolation and secure a peaceful and stable regional environment conducive to its domestic economic reform, there were at least two external factors that made Vietnam's resolve to normalize relations with China remain steadfast.

First, by the late 1980s, Vietnam had come under great pressure from the Soviet Union to repair ties with China (Thayer 1994a, p. 515). In the first round of Sino-Soviet negotiation on normalization in October 1982, China highlighted "three obstacles" to the process, namely, the Soviet military build-up along the Chinese border, Vietnam's occupation of Cambodia, and the Soviet occupation of Afghanistan (Goldstein and Freeman 1990, p. 125). After coming to power in 1985, Mikhail Gorbachev decided to accelerate efforts to restore relations with China. In his famous Vladivostok speech in July 1986, Gorbachev addressed these three obstacles with a view to moving the normalization process forward. On the Cambodian issue and Sino-Vietnamese relations, Gorbachev expressed hopes for improvements in the two countries' relations, adding that the settlement of the Cambodian issue as well as other problems of Southeast Asia depended on the normalization of their relations (Thakur and Thayer 1987, p. 223). Vietnam apparently felt great pressure from the Soviet Union, given the importance Gorbachev accorded to the process as well as the fact that the Soviet Union remained the country's most important political mentor and aid donor.

Second, and more importantly, in the light of China's crackdown on the Tiananmen pro-democracy demonstrations in June 1989, the Vietnamese leadership began to reassess the nature of the Chinese government. According to Co, the Tiananmen crackdown made a number of Vietnamese leaders believe that "no matter how expansionist it is, China remains a socialist country". In the same year, the collapse of communist governments in Eastern Europe also deepened the fear of a domino effect among Vietnamese leaders, causing a segment of them to believe that Vietnam should "join hands with China at any cost to protect socialism, repulse the United States and other imperialist forces". Such belief instigated a "rather sudden turnaround" in Vietnam's attitude towards China (Co 2003, pp. 31–32). Co's argument proved to be well founded if we look at developments in bilateral relations in 1990–91, especially Vietnam's concessions to China regarding the Cambodian issue.

In the first half of 1989, Vietnam and China conducted two rounds of negotiation on the Cambodian issue and normalizing bilateral relations, both in Beijing. The negotiation marked significant progress in bilateral relations given the fact that China had refused to resume talks since 1980. In the first round from 16 to 19 January, China proposed four main conditions for normalization: Vietnam's respect for China's claims to the Paracels and Spratlys Islands; an apology for mistreatment against ethnic Chinese in Vietnam; Soviet abandonment of Cam Ranh Bay; and Vietnam's removal of troops out of Cambodia and Laos (Duiker 1989, p. 5).

Meanwhile, according to Co's account, another major difference between the two sides was on how to solve two essential internal problems of Cambodia, namely power sharing arrangements and how to deal with the then existing armed forces of various Cambodian factions as a measure to facilitate the UN-sponsored peace building process in the country. While China insisted that solutions to these problems were critical to the resolution of the Cambodian issue, Vietnam refused to discuss these problems, maintaining that Cambodia's internal problems should be solved by the Cambodians themselves. In the second round from 8 to 10 May, China continued to emphasize that normalization would come only after the Cambodian issue was resolved, adding that it was Vietnam's responsibility to not only withdraw completely out of Cambodia but also to remove the aftermaths of its intervention, i.e. the Phnom Penh government and its armed forces (Co 2003, pp. 47–48).

Before the second round took place, the CPV Politburo announced in March that Vietnam would pull out of Cambodia completely in September 1989, earlier than its previously proposed deadline of 1990. The decision removed the most important obstacle to the normalization process that China had long been highlighting. However, Vietnam's position remained at odds with China's other conditions regarding the Cambodian issue for most of 1989. For example, in his speech at the Paris International Conference on Cambodia in July–August 1989, Foreign Minister Nguyen Co Thach described the Pol Pot regime as "genocidal" and "the most barbarous regime ever known in human history". In addressing the intra-Cambodian issues, Thach maintained that these issues must be solved by the Cambodian parties themselves, not foreign countries. He also repudiated the idea that the Khmer Rouge should be treated as an equal and legitimate party in any power-sharing arrangement for Cambodia, for which China had long been pressing Vietnam (Thach 1991, pp. 46–47).

From the beginning of 1990, however, Vietnam began to adopt a more flexible approach towards the Cambodian issue. On 8 March 1990, Advisor to the CPV Central Committee Le Duc Tho met with Deputy Foreign Ministers Dinh Nho Liem and Tran Quang Co, suggesting that Vietnam should make a strategic shift in its Cambodia policy. According to Tho, Vietnam should work with China to reach agreement on intra-Cambodian issues, abandon the idea of marginalizing the Khmer Rouge, and stop criticizing the Khmer Rouge for its genocidal record. Tho also stressed that there should be breakthroughs in the Cambodian issue prior to the CPV's seventh congress to pave the way for the solution of other issues (Co 2003, p. 59).

On 10 April, the CPV Politburo met to discuss the Cambodian issue and decided, among other things, that the Khmer Rouge should be allowed to participate in the coalition government, and Vietnam would try to get the United Nations to denounce the Khmer Rouge's genocidal atrocities on its behalf. A number of Politburo members also emphasized the need for Vietnam and China to work together to safeguard socialism against the U.S. "scheme" following the fall of socialism in Eastern Europe. They therefore advocated cooperation between Vietnam and China to help craft a socialist-oriented Cambodian state that would be friendly to both Vietnam and China. Right after the meeting, Foreign Minister Nguyen Co Thach was dispatched to Cambodia to persuade the Hun Sen government to accept the Khmer Rouge into power-sharing arrangements and play down its genocidal past. Hun Sen, however, turned down Thach's request, arguing that denouncing the Khmer Rouge's genocidal past was critical to the defence of the legality of Vietnam's military intervention into Cambodia as well as the legitimacy of the Phnom Penh government (Co 2003, pp. 61–62).

On 2 May 1990, Vietnam and China had another round of negotiation in Beijing between Deputy Foreign Minister Dinh Nho Liem and Assistant Foreign Minister Xu Dunxin. The negotiation focused on intra-Cambodian issues, particularly the scope of the Supreme National Council's (SNC) power, the disarmament of Cambodian parties' armies, and the transitional authority prior to general election. Xu Dunxin revealed China's intention to have the People's Republic of Kampuchea (PRK)/State of Cambodia (SOC)[4] and its army dismantled, while proposing that the transitional authority should be a quadripartite coalition government including the Khmer Rouge as a legitimate party.

He also demanded that Vietnam stop criticizing the Khmer Rouge's genocidal past. Liem, with prior direction from Ha Noi, conceded to Xu's demand regarding the Khmer Rouge's genocidal past, but avoided discussing the other Chinese proposals.

Following the negotiation, Beijing agreed to dispatch Xu Dunxin to Ha Noi for further discussion. As this was the first time in ten years that China had agreed to hold bilateral negotiations in Ha Noi rather than Beijing, the Vietnamese leadership saw it as a move of goodwill by China. In response, before Xu arrived in Ha Noi, General Secretary Nguyen Van Linh requested a courtesy call by Chinese ambassador Zhang Dewei on 5 June. It was also the first time in ten years that a Chinese ambassador had been received by a CPV General Secretary. At the reception, Linh acknowledged that Vietnam had committed certain "errors" in bilateral relations over the previous decade, adding that some — such as the 1982 Constitution's preamble — had been fixed. He also proposed to meet with Chinese leaders to discuss measures for safeguarding socialism against the scheme of "peaceful evolution". Despite the consensus reached at a prior Politburo meeting that the "red solution"[5] should not be mentioned during the reception, he suggested that the two countries adopt the "red solution" over the Cambodian question, arguing that "there's no reason why communists cannot talk to each other". The next day Defence Minister Le Duc Anh also met with Zhang Dewei to further explain Linh's points, especially the "red solution" (Co 2003, pp. 65–66).

In the subsequent negotiation between Xu Dunxin and Deputy Foreign Minister Tran Quang Co which started on 11 June, the two sides again focused on intra-Cambodian issues. When it came to the composition of the SNC, while Co maintained that it should be composed of two parties only,[6] Xu insisted that it should be composed of four parties, which would give the Khmer Rouge a legitimate and equal status as the Phnom Penh government. Facing Co's intransigence, Xu accused Co and the Foreign Ministry of acting against the CPV leadership's position, implying that, as the "red solution" would suggest, the Khmer Rouge had been acknowledged as a legitimate and equal party by the CPV's top leadership. In a latter reception by Foreign Minister Nguyen Co Thach on 13 June, Xu raised this point once again, eliciting an angry response from Thach (Co 2003, pp. 69–73). Following the incident, China showed its open dissatisfaction with Thach and started to ignore his Foreign Ministry in dealings with Vietnam.

Nevertheless, China tended to make further conciliatory moves towards Vietnam. On 12 August 1990, while on a visit to Singapore, Chinese Prime Minister Li Peng made a statement expressing hope that relations with Vietnam would finally be normalized. On 29 August, Chinese ambassador Zhang Dewei extended China's invitation to General Secretary Nguyen Van Linh, Prime Minister Do Muoi and Advisor Pham Van Dong to a secret meeting with General Secretary Jiang Zemin and Prime Minister Li Peng in Chengdu on 3–4 September to discuss the Cambodian issue and restoring bilateral relations. The invitation came as a surprise to the Vietnamese leadership as China still insisted several days earlier that only after the Cambodian issue was settled would China agree to hold bilateral summits to discuss normalization. The invitation as well as Li Peng's statement therefore signified a shift in China's policy toward Vietnam. By August 1990, China seemed to have judged from changes in the international context that it was in the interest of China itself to accelerate the Sino-Vietnamese normalization process.

First, after the crackdown on Tiananmen pro-democracy demonstrations in June 1989, China faced heavy criticism and even economic embargo from Japan and Western countries. Improving relations with neighbouring countries like Vietnam would ease China's isolation and relieve the effects of the economic embargo. Second, after Vietnam completed its troop withdrawal from Cambodia, Japan, ASEAN and Western countries began to repair their ties with Vietnam. For example, in July 1990, the United States declared that it would reopen negotiations with Vietnam. China's hostility towards Vietnam was therefore no longer relevant as it might cause China to be late in securing its interests in Vietnam. Third, regarding the Cambodian question, U.S. Secretary of State James Baker announced on 18 July 1990 that the United States would no longer recognize the Coalition Government of the Democratic Kampuchea (CGDK).[7] The U.S. goal was to prevent the possibility of the Khmer Rouge regaining power in Cambodia (Clymer 2004, p. 155). The sudden turnaround in the U.S. policy shocked China while giving Vietnam better leverage as the Khmer Rouge had been openly discredited by the United States. Meanwhile, at the United Nations, the five permanent members of the Security Council adopted on 28 August 1990 a framework document for a comprehensive political settlement of the Cambodian conflict which was accepted shortly afterwards almost in its entirety by the Cambodian parties (Findlay 1995, pp. 7–8). As a solution for Cambodia under the UN auspices became just a matter of time and with the above-mentioned factors taken into consideration, China found it was about time to push the Sino-Vietnamese normalization process forward.

In Chengdu, however, playing on Vietnam's greater anxiety to restore bilateral relations, China maintained its hope to pressure Vietnam into a Cambodian solution on China's terms. The bilateral discussion concentrated on eight points, in which seven points were related to the Cambodian issue, while the remaining one was on normalization. The most outstanding question was the composition of the SNC. In this regard, Vietnam conceded to China's formula, which was 6 + 2 + 2 + 2 + 1. Accordingly, the SOC would have six representatives; the three factions of the CGDK would have two representatives each, plus Prince Sihanouk himself. The concession, however, turned out to be a miscalculation for Vietnam. As the formula put the PRK/SOC in a disadvantaged position vis-à-vis the CGDK, it was later strongly rebuffed by the Hun Sen government and contributed to the further erosion of Phnom Penh's trust in Ha Noi.[8] At the Chengdu summit, China also openly dismissed the "red solution" as well as the idea of Vietnam and China working together to safeguard socialism (Co 2003, pp. 86–87). Nevertheless, the Chengdu summit was still a significant event for Vietnam as it marked the end of China's policy of "bleeding Vietnam white" and the official start of the Sino-Vietnamese normalization process (Thayer 1994*a*, p. 517).

After the Chengdu summit, the process gained further momentum and entered its final stages. In his report to the Fourth Session of the Seventh National People's Congress on 25 March, 1991, Li Peng declared that Sino-Vietnamese relations had thawed. More than two months later, at the CPV's seventh congress in June, Nguyen Co Thach, who was well known for his anti-China stance, was removed from the Politburo and the Central Committee. He also lost the post of Foreign Minister soon afterwards. The move was widely seen as a conciliatory gesture of Ha Noi to please Beijing and to further accelerate the normalization process. In late July, Vietnam dispatched Defence Minister Le Duc Anh, now the second top man of the new Politburo, and Hong Ha, Chief of the Central Committee's Foreign Affairs Department, to China to brief Chinese leaders on the outcome of the seventh congress. While in Beijing, however, Anh also discussed the Cambodian issue as well as Sino-Vietnamese relations with Chinese leaders. Accordingly, Anh secured Beijing's agreement to proceed with the normalization process (Thayer 1994a, p. 521).

On 23 October 1991, the Paris Peace Agreements on Cambodia were signed, marking the end of the Cambodian conflict as well as the removal of the greatest sticking point in Sino-Vietnamese relations. On 5 November 1991, General Secretary Do Muoi and Prime Minister Vo Van Kiet paid an official visit to Beijing. At the summit between Muoi and Kiet with their Chinese counterparts Jiang Zemin and Li Peng, the two sides officially declared the normalization of bilateral relations at both state and party levels in an eleven-point joint communiqué. In addition, the two sides also signed a trade agreement and a provisional agreement on the settlement of border affairs. Sino-Vietnamese relations thus entered a new chapter after more than a decade of armed hostilities and direct political confrontation.

Conclusion

Foreign policies of democratic states are significantly shaped by five major domestic factors, namely, domestic political conditions, electoral cycles, the government's accountability to the legislature and domestic constituencies, public opinion, and economic interests. In authoritarian states like Vietnam, however, domestic factors generally have a less significant impact on the making of their foreign policy. An examination of the domestic–foreign policy nexus in Vietnam's political context shows that economic interests are the most important domestic determinant of its foreign policy, while the CPV's wish to use foreign policies as a tool to maintain and consolidate its power is yet another factor that may also influence the country's foreign policy making.

In the late 1980s, Vietnam underwent an overhaul of its foreign policy, which ultimately resulted in the country's policy of diversifying and multilateralizing foreign relations, as adopted at the CPV's seventh congress. A combination of factors contributed to this process. As demonstrated by various official documents of the CPV, economic interests in terms of economic development under the banner of *Doi Moi* served as the most important basis for the reform, while changes in international conditions and renovation in the CPV's foreign policy thinking also played their part.

In implementing foreign policy reform, the Party consistently viewed diplomatic normalization with China as one of its top priorities.

However, Vietnam had a difficult time solving the Cambodian issue, a condition China had attached to the normalization process. Even as it tried to best protect its national interests, Vietnam also made a number of concessions to China along the way, which it considered a reasonable price for normalized relations with the northern neighbour. These various concessions ranged from adjustments in Vietnam's policy regarding the Cambodian issue to changes in its domestic politics to best accommodate China's conditions.

Vietnam's domestic conditions played an important role in bringing about the eventual bilateral normalization in November 1991. Vietnam's quest for normalized relations was necessitated by the CPV's adoption of economic renovation under *Doi Moi*. By 1989, however, the CPV's wish to maintain its regime security had become yet another domestic factor that helped accelerate the normalization process. As the CPV leadership wished to work with their Chinese counterparts to "safeguard socialism", they pushed for a quicker rapprochement between the two countries. As such, the bilateral normalization process is a relevant case for studying the domestic–foreign policy nexus in Vietnam's context in general, and for understanding the making of Vietnam's contemporary China policy in particular.

NOTES

1. All major resolutions of the CPV Politburo regarding the country's foreign policy during the 1986–91 period, including Resolution no. 32 (1986), Resolution no. 2 (1987), and Resolution no. 13 (1988), are still classified and not included in the publicly available *Van kien Dang toan tap* [Complete Collection of Party Documents]. The author therefore has to rely on a number of articles published in the *Tap chi Cong san* [Communist Review] by Vietnamese researchers associated with government-sponsored think-tanks for excerpts of Resolution no. 32 and Resolution no. 13. Meanwhile, Thayer (1994*b*) is used as the main source of reference for details on Resolution no. 2.
2. During the period of 1988–90, there were only 211 FDI projects licensed in Vietnam with the total registered capital of US$1.6 billion (GSO 2011, p. 161).
3. Based on scattered references to the resolution in the Vietnamese press, Thayer (1994*b*) argues that the resolution was probably entitled "On Strengthening National Defence in the New Revolutionary Stage" and was adopted between April and June 1987.

4. The PRK was established in 1979 following the removal of the Khmer Rouge regime. In late April 1989, the National Assembly of the PRK officially changed the name of the country into the SOC.

5. The idea of the "red solution" had been floated since early 1987. It suggests that the two communist rivals, namely the Phnom Penh government and the Khmer Rouge, should cease hostility and cooperate to form a united communist government, which would exclude non-communist factions of Sihanouk and Son San.

6. Which means the Phnom Penh government on one side and the Coalition Government of the Democratic Kampuchea as a single party on the other side.

7. The CGDK is composed of three factions: The Party of Democratic Kampuchea (the Khmer Rouge), the Khmer People's National Liberation Front (led by Son San), and the FUNCINPEC (led by Prince Sihanouk). The CGDK was formed on 22 June 1982 as a resistance force against the PRK/SOC government. The CGDK selected Sihanouk as its president.

8. It should be noted that in a meeting in Tokyo on 4–5 June 1990, Hun Sen and Sihanouk had agreed to the formula of 6 + 2 + 2 + 2 for the SNC. Accordingly, the Phnom Penh government and the CGDK would each have 6 representatives on the Council.

4

Overview of Vietnam's Economic Development and Relations with China under *Doi Moi*

Introduction

After a few years of unstable growth following the adoption of *Doi Moi* in 1986, Vietnam's economic reform began to stabilize and gather speed since 1989. Starting from a low base, Vietnam's economy has been growing rather quickly, at an average annual growth rate of 6.8 per cent for the period from 1990 to 2014. Over the past twenty-five years, Vietnam's economy has also become more open with external exchanges now playing an essential role in the nation's economic well-being. In 2014, for example, Vietnam's export and import turnovers amounted to 81 and 80 per cent of its GDP, respectively (World Bank 2015*b*).

The economy's current level of openness is impressive given the fact that it was only in the early 1990s, when the Soviet bloc collapsed, that the country effectively began to open up itself to economic interactions with countries outside the socialist bloc. The same observation is also true for Vietnam's economic relations with China. For example, when the two countries normalized their relations in 1991, official bilateral trade turnover stood modestly at US$30 million (Vinh 2001, p. 73). In 2013, however, two-way trade turnover reached US$50.2 billion, accounting for 19 per cent of Vietnam's total trade turnover of the same year and confirming China's status as Vietnam's biggest trade partner (General Department of Customs 2014). At the same time, Chinese investment into Vietnam, although still modest, has also increased considerably, especially in the recent years. In 2013, for example, China was the fourth largest foreign investor in Vietnam, with US$2.3 billion registered in 110 projects (GSO 2014*b*, p. 111).

Vietnam's deepened economic ties with China are just one of the three key features of Vietnam's relations with China since normalization in 1991. Over the last two decades, despite recurrent waves of tensions due to the territorial disputes in the South China Sea, Vietnam's overall relations with China have improved considerably. Apart from deepened economic exchanges, bilateral relations have generally benefited from the partial removal of territorial disputes and the continual promotion of political relations between the two states and the two communist parties, with the most visible landmark being the establishment of a "comprehensive strategic cooperative partnership" between the two countries in 2008. All these three features constitute the big picture of Vietnam–China relations since their normalization in 1991.

The current chapter aims to provide an overview of Vietnam's economic development under *Doi Moi* and its relations with China since bilateral normalization in 1991. Understanding Vietnam's economic development under *Doi Moi*, especially the role of foreign economic exchanges in this process, is essential as it helps locate the domestic dynamics of Vietnam's foreign policy in general and its China policy in particular. Meanwhile, understanding the big picture of bilateral relations is also important for one to fathom Vietnam's China policy, especially the way Vietnam has been handling new tensions emerging from deepened economic exchanges with China as well as those related to the South China Sea disputes. The chapter's purpose is therefore twofold: contributing to the book's objective of providing a comprehensive canvass of Vietnam's relations with China since normalization, and laying the background for the examination of the two case studies in subsequent chapters, namely the impact of economic exchanges on bilateral relations, and the political economy of the South China Sea disputes between the two countries.

Vietnam's Economic Performance under *Doi Moi*

Doi Moi was adopted in 1986, but it was not until the early 1990s that the macroeconomic conditions of the country started to stabilize and positive effects of the economic reform became visible. As shown in Figure 4.1, Vietnam achieved an annual GDP growth rate of roughly 6.8 per cent for the period 1990–2014, but the rate was not consistent for the whole period. During these twenty-five years, Vietnam's economy experienced two major waves of growth interrupted by the 1997–98 Asian Financial Crisis and the 2007–08 Global Financial Crisis and economic recession. The first wave of growth lasted from 1992 to 1997 with a record average annual growth rate of 8.75 per cent. After slowing down in 1998 and 1999, the economy recovered and experienced the second wave of growth from 2000 until 2007, registering an average growth rate of 7.63 per cent. Since 2011, Vietnam's economy began struggling again with slow growth, high inflation, amassing bad debt under an unhealthy banking system, and inefficient SOEs.

FIGURE 4.1
Vietnam's GDP and GDP Growth Rate (1990–2014)

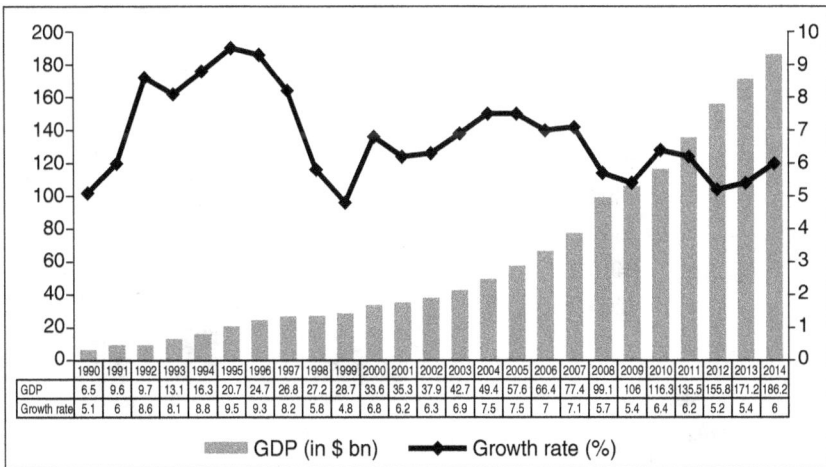

	1990	1991	1992	1993	1994	1995	1996	1997	1998	1999	2000	2001	2002	2003	2004	2005	2006	2007	2008	2009	2010	2011	2012	2013	2014
GDP	6.5	9.6	9.7	13.1	16.3	20.7	24.7	26.8	27.2	28.7	33.6	35.3	37.9	42.7	49.4	57.6	66.4	77.4	99.1	106	116.3	135.5	155.8	171.2	186.2
Growth rate	5.1	6	8.6	8.1	8.8	9.5	9.3	8.2	5.8	4.8	6.8	6.2	6.3	6.9	7.5	7.5	7	7.1	5.7	5.4	6.4	6.2	5.2	5.4	6

GDP (in $ bn)   Growth rate (%)

Note: The GDP is in current U.S. dollar.
Source: World Bank (2015*b*) and Vietnam Academy of Social Sciences (2011).

In 2009, however, by achieving the GNI per capita of US$1,030, Vietnam elevated itself into the low middle-income group of economies according to the World Bank's classification.[1] Economic growth over the last two decades has also lifted some 28 million people out of poverty and improved the economic well-being of almost the entire population. As shown in Figure 4.2, Vietnam's poverty rate decreased consistently from 58.1 per cent in 1993 to 11.1 per cent in 2012 (GSO 2015, p. 247; Vietnam Academy of Social Sciences 2011, p. 2). These economic successes have earned Vietnam wide international acclaim and served as a firm basis of the CPV's domestic political legitimacy.

The economic success of Vietnam so far would have been impossible without the implementation of *Doi Moi*. For example, Nghiep and Quy (2000, p. 331) estimate that *Doi Moi*'s impact on Vietnam's economy was as high as 42 per cent of the GDP in 1998. In other words, if Vietnam had not adopted *Doi Moi* in 1986, its GDP in 1998 would have been 42 per cent lower than the actual size. In their article, Nghiep and Quy specifically identify the improvement of productivity and the increase in investment as two major positive impacts that *Doi Moi* has

FIGURE 4.2
Vietnam's GNI per capita and Poverty Rate (1993–2012)

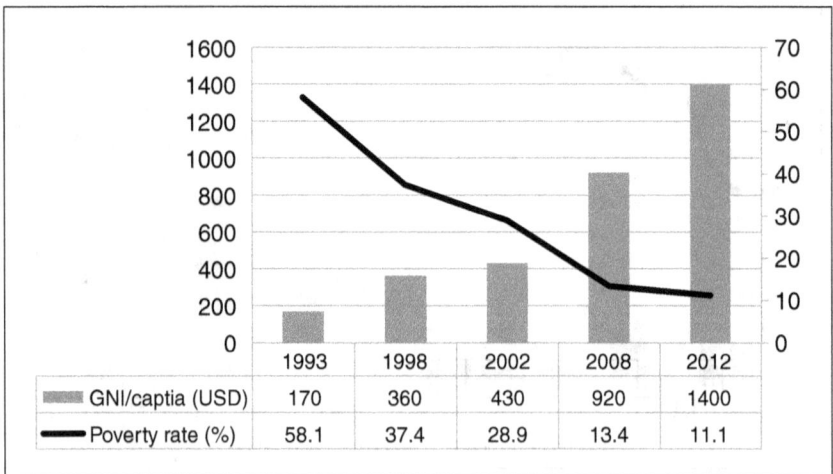

	1993	1998	2002	2008	2012
GNI/captia (USD)	170	360	430	920	1400
Poverty rate (%)	58.1	37.4	28.9	13.4	11.1

Source: World Bank (2015*b*); GSO (2015), p. 247; Vietnam Academy of Social Sciences (2011), p. 2.

generated on Vietnam's economic performance. While Vietnam's improved productivity has been mainly due to the diffusion of new technologies, its upward shift in investment has been made possible largely by the expansion of the non-state[2] and foreign-invested sectors since the late 1980s. For example, between 2000 and 2010, total investment of the whole economy increased by 5.5 times. While investment from the state sector increased by only 3.5 times, investment from non-state and foreign-invested sectors increased by 8.7 times and 7.9 times, respectively (GSO 2011, p. 151). As a result, the state sector's share in Vietnam's GDP has decreased from 38.4 per cent in 2005 down to 31.9 per cent in 2014, while those of non-state and foreign invested sectors have increased over the same period from 45.6 per cent to 48 per cent, and from 16 per cent to 20.1 per cent, respectively (GSO 2015, p. 62).

In addition, the improvement of Vietnam's economic conditions under *Doi Moi* would not have materialized without Vietnam's increasing integration into the global economy. Especially, Vietnam has benefited enormously from the inflows of FDI and the expansion of its exports.

Since the introduction of the first law on foreign investment in 1988, foreign capital has been playing an increasing role in Vietnam's economic development. By the end of 2014, the total registered FDI stock in Vietnam reached US$290.6 billion, of which US$124.2 billion had been implemented (GSO (2015), pp. 109, 113). FDI projects have generally contributed to Vietnam's economic growth, although the actual benefits vary across regions and industrial sectors (see, for example, Anwar and Nguyen 2010; Mai 2002, 2003; T.B. Vu, Gangnes and Noy, 2008). The productivity of the foreign invested sector is markedly higher than the other two sectors. In 2009, for instance, while the foreign-invested sector employed only 3.2 per cent of the workforce, it generated 18.3 per cent of the GDP and 11.5 per cent of government revenue (GSO 2011, pp. 99, 134, 144). As suggested by the literature on FDI into developing and transitional countries (see, for example, Aitken and Harrison, 1999; Blomström, Kokko and Zejan, 2000; Blomström and Sjöholm 1999; Borensztein, De Gregorio and Lee 1998; Haddad and Harrison 1993), foreign-invested projects also tend to help Vietnam improve the workforce's skills, absorb new technologies, and enhance the general performance of other economic sectors due to the spillover effect.

In addition, the inflows of FDI have also contributed considerably to the expansion of Vietnam's exports (Anwar and Nguyen 2011*a*, 2011*b*; Xuan and Xing 2008).[3] In 2009, for example, foreign invested enterprises accounted for up to 53.2 per cent of Vietnam's export turnover of goods (GSO 2011, p. 521). FDI enterprises have especially helped promote Vietnam's export to FDI source countries, with one research finding that a 1 per cent increase in FDI inflows could generate an increase of 0.13 per cent in Vietnam's exports to these countries (Xuan and Xing 2008). After Vietnam gained WTO membership in 2007, the country's export performance continued to improve although the 2007–08 global financial crisis and economic recession caused its export turnover to shrink in 2009.[4] In 2011, Vietnam's export of goods and services reached US$100 billion, which was greater than its combined export turnover during the first fourteen years of *Doi Moi* (World Bank 2015*b*). Exports have become an important source of economic growth for Vietnam, as the expansion of exports stimulates demand, encourages savings and capital accumulation, and increases the supply potential and the capacity to import of the economy (Thirlwall 1994). The impressive increase of export turnover during the last two decades, however, has also turned Vietnam into a trade-dependent economy, causing the country to become increasingly vulnerable to changes in global economic conditions.[5]

Nevertheless, recognizing the importance of exports performance and foreign capital to its economic well-being, Vietnam has consistently tried to expand its overseas markets and to attract more FDI into the country.

Since the adoption of *Doi Moi*, there have been three landmarks in Vietnam's efforts to expand its access to foreign markets. In 1995, Vietnam joined ASEAN, which paved the way for the country to become a party to the ASEAN Free Trade Area (AFTA) and five other ASEAN Plus FTAs.[6] In 2001, the Vietnam–US Bilateral Trade Agreement (BTA) came into effect, providing yet another important driving force for Vietnam's export performance. Under the BTA, Vietnam's export to the United States increased more than twelve times within just ten years to reach US$21.8 billion in 2011, and US$28.7 billion in 2014. The United States is now Vietnam's biggest export market, accounting for about one-fifth of Vietnam's annual exports by value. The third landmark was Vietnam's accession to the WTO in early 2007 after almost thirteen years of negotiation. Vietnam's entry into the WTO, while presenting the country with considerable challenges, also helped further improve the country's export performance and signified its full integration into the global trade regime.

Since 2008, Vietnam has also been pursuing a series of new Free Trade Agreements (FTAs), both bilateral and multilateral (see Table 4.1). Among these FTAs, the Trans-Pacific Partnership (TPP) is another landmark in Vietnam's international economic integration process and will likely further promote its economic growth and export performance.

In terms of FDI attraction, Vietnam issued in 1987 the first law on foreign investment which was considered as "arguably the most liberal" foreign investment law in Asia at the time (Business Monitor International Ltd 1993). The law was then revised in 1992, 1996 and 2000 before being superseded by the 2006 Unified Investment Law that treats domestic and foreign investors equally. The introduction of the 2006 Unified Investment Law resulted from both Vietnamese government's own initiative to improve the investment climate and external pressures to bring domestic law in line with international legal commitments, especially on the eve of Vietnam's accession to the WTO (N. N. Anh and Thang 2007, p. 13). Apart from developing a domestic FDI regulation framework, Vietnam has also entered into various bilateral and multilateral agreements to facilitate investment into the country. In addition to investment-related agreements under the umbrella of WTO and ASEAN, by March 2009, Vietnam had concluded bilateral agreements on investment encouragement and protection with fifty-five countries (OECD 2010, p. 25). Some bilateral trade agreements, such as the Vietnam–U.S. BTA and the Vietnam–Japan Economic Partnership Agreement, also contain sections on developing bilateral investment relations.

Vietnam's global economic integration under *Doi Moi* has first and foremost resulted from the CPV's determination to take advantage of the process to facilitate its economic reform agenda. Such determination can be tracked through various official documents of the Party. Apart from Party congresses' political reports, platforms or resolutions that provide the general guidelines, the Party has also issued a multitude of official documents outlining specific policy measures to promote the country's international economic integration. For example, the CPV Central Committee adopted a resolution dated 23 March 1989 in which the foreign ministry was directed as a matter of priority to shift its focus from political to politico-economic diplomacy (CPV 2006*b*, p. 527). At the third plenum of the Central Committee (seventh tenure)

TABLE 4.1
Vietnam's FTAs and Their Status by 2016

	Name	Status
1	ASEAN Free Trade Agreement (AFTA)	Effective
2	ASEAN-China Free Trade Agreement (ACFTA)	Effective
3	ASEAN-Korea Free Trade Agreement (AKFTA)	Effective
4	ASEAN-Japan Comprehensive Economic Partnership (AJCEP)	Effective
5	ASEAN – Australia – New Zealand Free Trade Agreement (AANZFTA)	Effective
6	ASEAN-India Free Trade Agreement (AIFTA)	Effective
7	Vietnam – Japan Economic Partnership Agreement	Effective
8	Vietnam – Chile FTA	Effective
9	Vietnam – Laos Trade Agreement	Effective 30 October 2015
10	Vietnam – Korea FTA	Effective 20 December 2015
11	Vietnam – Eurasian Economic Union FTA	Effective 5 October 2016
12	Vietnam – EU FTA	Negotiation concluded 1 December 2015, pending signing
13	Trans-Pacific Strategic Economic Partnership (TPP)	Signed 4 February 2016, pending ratification
14	Regional Comprehensive Economic Partnership (RCEP)	Negotiating

Source: Author's own compilation.

in June 1992, the CPV Politburo presented a report on developing external economic relations, in which the policy of multilateralizing and diversifying the country's foreign economic relations was again stressed as a key measure to support *Doi Moi* (CPV 2007*b*). Almost ten years later, the CPV Politburo adopted Resolution no. 7 dated 27 November 2001 on Vietnam's international economic integration, outlining specific measures to deepen the country's integration into the world economy. The adoption of the Resolution as well as the establishment of the National Committee on International Economic Cooperation in 1998 helped further accelerate Vietnam's integration process into the global economy, culminating in the country's accession to the WTO in 2007. More recently, in April 2013, the CPV Central Committee passed Resolution No. 22-NQ/TW on international integration, confirming that "proactive and active international integration is a major strategic orientation of the Party aimed to successfully implement the task of building and protecting the socialist Fatherland of Vietnam" (CPV 2013).

The trajectory of Vietnam's economic development and its international integration under *Doi Moi* shows that the decision of the CPV in the 1980s to change its foreign policy in order to help the country break out of international isolation and to expand its foreign relations has paid off. Despite the criticism by a number of Vietnamese intellectuals, the price that the CPV has paid for Vietnam's normalization with China have proven reasonable.[7] It is clear that without successfully solving the Cambodian issue and normalizing relations with China to secure a peaceful regional environment, it would have been impossible for Vietnam to promote its economic development and international integration. This background is therefore important for one to fully appreciate Vietnam's China policy in the post normalization period.

Evolution of Vietnam–China relations, 1991–2015

After the normalization of bilateral relations in 1991, despite sporadic waves of tension due to their disputes in the South China Sea, Vietnam and China have made numerous efforts to promote a peaceful, stable and cooperative relationship between the two countries. The improved bilateral relations have brought them significant benefits, especially in terms of trade, and contributed to a more stable and peaceful regional order in the post-Cold War era. The evolution of Vietnam–China relations since 1991 can be summarized by three key highlights: the partial solution of territorial disputes; the strengthening of political relations; and the promotion of bilateral economic ties.

Solving Territorial Disputes

A major sticking point that threatened to destabilize bilateral relations after normalization was the enduring territorial disputes between the two countries. By 1991, the two countries had territorial disputes regarding both land border and the South China Sea, including maritime boundaries in the Tonkin Gulf and ownership over the Paracel and Spratly Islands.

In order to help resolve the land border dispute, the two countries signed a provisional agreement on the settlement of border affairs on 7 November 1991, three days before the normalization summit. The purpose of the agreement was to maintain the status quo of the border line and facilitate cross-border transactions pending official negotiation and delimitation. Soon after that, the two sides conducted two rounds of negotiation in October 1992 and February 1993 which resulted in the 19 October 1993 agreement on fundamental principles governing the solution of border and territorial issues between the two countries.[8] Based on these principles, the two sides conducted nearly twenty more rounds of negotiations at different levels from 1994 to 1999 (Thao 2000, pp. 88–89). To accelerate the negotiation process, during CPV General Secretary Do Muoi's official visit to China in July 1997, leaders of the two countries agreed "to try to conclude the treaty on land border and another on the maritime delineation in the Gulf of Tonkin before the end of 2000". This political will was also reasserted in other high-level visits of the two countries' party and state leaders in 1998 and 1999 (Thao 2000, pp. 88–89). These efforts finally resulted in the Vietnam–China land border delimitation treaty which was signed in Hanoi on 30 December 1999 by Vietnamese Foreign Minister Nguyen Manh Cam and his Chinese counterpart Tang Jiaxuan. After the treaty was ratified by both sides in 2000, Vietnam and China established the Joint Committee for Land Boundary Demarcation to do field surveys and erect markers along the 1,450 kilometres of borderline. This effort took another eight years before the whole demarcation process was finalized on 31 December 2008.[9]

Along with negotiations on the land border, Vietnam and China also resumed talks on the delimitation of the Tonkin Gulf in 1994.[10] They accordingly held seven rounds of negotiation at the governmental level and eighteen rounds at joint working group level, plus nearly twenty other non-official meetings during seven years before the negotiation process concluded in 2000 (Thao 2005, p. 28). On 25 December 2000, the agreement on the delimitation of the Tonkin Gulf was finally signed in Beijing. Another agreement on fishery cooperation in the Gulf was also signed at the same time after only eight months of negotiation. The two agreements were then ratified by both parties and came into force in 2004.

The settlement of the land border disputes as well as the successful delimitation of the Tonkin Gulf have been significant landmarks in the evolution of Vietnam–China relations as they help narrow the scope of their territorial disputes, thereby lessening the potential of armed conflict and facilitating bilateral economic exchanges. There still remain, however, four unresolved maritime disputes between the two countries in the South China Sea.

The first dispute is related to the sea area beyond the mouth of the Tonkin Gulf. Although the two countries began talks on the delimitation of this sea area in January 2006 (BBC 2006), little progress has been made so far due to the discrepancy in the two countries' positions.[11] The second is related to the Paracels, which both Vietnam and China claim in full. Before 1974, the archipelago was administered by both China and the Republic of Vietnam (South Vietnam), with China occupying the northeastern (Amphitrite) group of the islands and South Vietnam the southwestern (Crescent) group. However, taking advantage of Vietnam's internal situation, China used force to seize the southwestern group of the islands from South Vietnam in January 1974. Since then, it has maintained control of the whole archipelago and consistently turned down Vietnam's request for negotiation on the dispute. The first two disputes are inter-related as the ownership of the Paracels will affect how the sea area beyond the mouth of the Tonkin Gulf should be delimited.

The third maritime dispute between the two countries is over the ownership of the Spratlys. Unlike the Paracels, the Spratlys is a multilateral rather than bilateral dispute, involving claims by Vietnam, China, the Philippines, Malaysia, Brunei and Taiwan. As such, the dispute is currently managed through both bilateral and multilateral mechanisms, such as the bilateral expert-level discussions on maritime issues which commenced in November 1995 (Thayer 2008) and the 2002 ASEAN-China Declaration on the Conducts of Parties in the South China Sea. Meanwhile, the fourth dispute is related to the maritime boundaries in the South China Sea caused by China's U-shaped line which overlaps a large part of Vietnam's EEZ and continental shelf.[12] Vietnam has denounced China's U-shaped line as illegal and baseless, and confirmed that its EEZ and continental shelf are not subject to bilateral dispute. Nevertheless, China's recent growing assertiveness in the South China Sea, which is in part to vindicate the validity of its U-shaped line, has generated unceasing tensions in bilateral relations.[13]

Improving Political Relations

At present, territorial disputes in the South China Sea are presenting themselves as the most serious source of threat to peace and stability in bilateral relations. However, since the normalization of Sino-Vietnamese relations in 1991, these disputes have never escalated into armed conflict, mainly thanks to the two countries' improved political relations. A major channel for the two countries to improve political relations has been the regular exchange of visits by high-ranking state and party officials. Table 4.2 shows that between 1991 and 2015, Vietnam and China exchanged thirty-eight visits by top party and state leaders.[14] On average, there were two high-level visits exchanged per year. The markedly high frequency of these visits testifies to the importance that the two countries accord to each other as well as the improved political ties between them. Most importantly, they play an important role in defining the political and legal framework for bilateral cooperation.

For example, the visit by CPV General Secretary Le Kha Phieu to China in February 1999 resulted in the adoption of the so-called "Sixteen Golden Words" of "long-term stability, good neighbourliness, mutual trust and all-round cooperation" as the guideline for the development of bilateral relations in the new century.[15] The adoption of the guideline not only marked the transition of bilateral relations from "normalization" into "normalcy" (Womack, 2006, p. 224), but also helped elevate bilateral relations to a higher level. During President

TABLE 4.2
Exchange of High-level Visits between Vietnam and China, 1991–2015

Visits by Vietnamese Leaders to China	Time	Visits by Chinese Leaders to Vietnam
General Secretary Do Muoi and Prime Minister Vo Van Kiet	Oct 1991	
	Dec 1992	Premier Li Peng
President Le Duc Anh	Nov 1993	
	Nov 1994	President Jiang Zemin
General Secretary Do Muoi	Nov, 1995	
	Jun 1996	Premier Li Peng
General Secretary Do Muoi	Jul 1997	
Prime Minister Phan Van Khai	Oct 1998	
	Dec 1998	Vice President Hu Jintao
General Secretary Le Kha Phieu	Feb 1999	
	Dec 1999	Premier Zhu Rongji
Prime Minister Phan Van Khai	Sep 2000	
President Tran Duc Luong	Dec 2000	
	Apr 2001	Vice-President Hu Jintao
General Secretary Nong Duc Manh	Nov 2001	
	Feb 2002	President Jiang Zemin
General Secretary Nong Duc Manh	Apr 2003	
Prime Minister Phan Van Khai	May 2004	
	Oct 2004	Premier Wen Jiabao
Prime Minister Phan Van Khai[1]	Jul 2005	
President Tran Duc Luong	Jul 2005	
	Oct 2005	President Hu Jintao
General Secretary Nong Duc Manh	Aug 2006	
	Nov 2006	President Hu Jintao
President Nguyen Minh Triet	May 2007	
General Secretary Nong Duc Manh	May 2008	
President Nguyen Minh Triet[2]	Aug 2008	
Prime Minister Nguyen Tan Dung	Oct 2008	
Prime Minister Nguyen Tan Dung[3]	Apr 2009	
Prime Minister Nguyen Tan Dung[4]	Oct 2009	
Prime Minister Nguyen Tan Dung[5]	May 2010	
	Oct 2010	Premier Wen Jiabao[6]

(*... continued on next page*)

TABLE 4.2 (*continued*)

Visits by Vietnamese Leaders to China	Time	Visits by Chinese Leaders to Vietnam
General Secretary Nguyen Phu Trong	Oct 2011	
	Dec 2011	Vice President Xi Jinping
President Truong Tan Sang	Jun 2013	
	Oct 2013	Premier Li Keqiang
General Secretary Nguyen Phu Trong	Apr 2015	
	Nov 2015	President Xi Jinping

Notes:
1. to attend the Greater Mekong Subregion Summit, Kunming; meets with Premier Wen Jiabao.
2. to attend the opening ceremony of the 2008 Olympic Games in Beijing.
3. to attend Boao Forum, Hainan Island; meets with Premier Wen Jiabao.
4. to attend the 10th Western China International Fair, Chengdu, meets with Premier Wen Jiabao.
5. to attend the opening ceremony of the Shanghai World Expo; meets with President Hu Jintao.
6. to attend the East Asia Summit, Ha Noi; meets with General Secretary Nong Duc Manh and Prime Minister Nguyen Tan Dung.
Source: Author's own compilation.

Tran Duc Luong's visit to China in December 2000, the two countries adopted a Joint Statement on Comprehensive Cooperation in the New Century that translated the sixteen-word guideline into specific measures to expand and deepen bilateral ties in all fields.[16] Five years later, during another visit by President Luong to China, the two countries agreed to further develop their relations in the spirit of the "four goods motto": "good neighbours, good friends, good comrades, and good partners".

After that, political ties between the two countries continued to further strengthen. During a visit by CPV General Secretary Nong Duc Manh to Beijing in May 2008, Vietnam and China issued a joint statement declaring the establishment of a "comprehensive strategic partnership" between the two countries (Vietnam News Agency 2008). As Thayer (2012b) argues, Vietnam uses the concept of "strategic partnership" to describe "a bilateral relationship that has breadth and depth" rather than a formal alliance.[17] In other words, Vietnam would not wish to return to the "lips and teeth" relationship with China in the 1950s and

1960s, yet the term "comprehensive strategic partnership" signifies the highest level of its relations with China since those "good old days". According to the statement, the two countries pledged to develop their "comprehensive strategic partnership" in accordance with the sixteen-word guideline and the spirit of the "four goods motto" to "ensure that bilateral relations would grow permanently, steadily and vigorously". The two sides also

> confirm that they will continue to support each other in all aspects, comprehensively strengthen mutual trust, deepen cooperation for mutual benefits, together promote [economic] development, and advance the socialist cause in each country toward success. Based on the principles of always taking the big picture into consideration [coi trong dai cuc], friendly consultation, equality, and fairness in search of mutual benefits and win-win solutions, the two sides will strictly implement the positions agreed upon by the two countries' leaders, and promote cooperation to effectively address the remaining issues in bilateral relations (Vietnam News Agency 2008).

It should be noted that "always taking the big picture into consideration" ("*coi trong dai cuc*", or "*gu quan da ju*" in Chinese) is considered as the most important principle governing the management of bilateral relations. By "taking the big picture into consideration", leaders of Vietnam and China imply that they attach importance to the maintenance of good general relations between the two countries and the two parties, and any dispute or problem between the two countries should be solved in a manner that overall bilateral relations will not be harmed. The principle also originates from the two Parties' concern that "hostile forces" may take advantage of strained relations between the two countries to split the two parties and weaken their rule. As such, the principle has served as a basis for the two countries to refrain from actions that may significantly damage bilateral relations, especially when tensions related to territorial disputes become intensified.

The 2008 statement also emphasized that the two countries would maintain the tradition of exchanging visits by high-ranking party and state leaders. In addition to consolidating the political foundation of bilateral relations, the frequent exchange of high-level visits also helped set up the legal framework for cooperation. Between 1991 and 2013, Vietnam and China entered into more than 130 bilateral agreements in different fields, most of which were signed on the occasion of high-level visits by the two countries' state or party leaders.[18] It is noteworthy that eighty (or 62 per cent) of these agreements directly or indirectly dealt with economic issues, showing that economic cooperation has become a matter of high priority in bilateral relations.

Along with the improvement of the legal framework also came the strengthening of the institutional structure for bilateral cooperation. In 1994, the two countries signed an agreement to establish the Committee on Economic and Trade Cooperation. Since then, the Committee has met annually to recommend measures for deepening bilateral economic ties, promote the implementation of bilateral agreements, and explore new avenues for economic cooperation. On 11 November 2006, Vietnam and China signed a Memorandum of Understanding that established the Steering Committee on Vietnam–China Bilateral Cooperation (Voice of Vietnam 2006). The inaugural meeting of the Committee took place on the same day. Composed of representatives from the two countries' key ministries, the mission of the Committee is to direct and coordinate bilateral cooperation at national level towards greater depth and efficiency. Under the Committee are different sub-committees to address various aspects of bilateral cooperation. As such, the Committee is now the most important mechanism at governmental level for the two countries to promote their comprehensive strategic partnership.

In addition, there also exist mechanisms for cooperation between the two countries' various ministries, agencies, and local authorities. For example, there have been cooperation mechanisms between the two countries' Ministries of Foreign Affairs, Ministries of Defence, Ministries of Public Security, and intelligence agencies (Vietnam News Agency 2013b). Especially, the two communist parties have also taken steps to strengthen their ties. In December 2008, the two parties signed agreements to establish the cooperation mechanisms between their departments of propaganda and departments of external affairs. Joint workshops have been held annually for the departments to exchange views and experiences on various themes and issues, such as socialist ideology, dealing with the "peaceful evolution" threat, party building, governance, economic reform and international integration. At local level, border province authorities on both sides have also taken steps to strengthen their ties. For example, Joint Working Committees between Vietnam's seven border provinces with China's two provinces of Guangxi and Yunnan were established in 2007 and have met annually since 2008 to discuss measures to promote cross-border cooperation, especially in the field of economics.

Strengthening Economic Ties

The third outstanding feature of Vietnam–China relations since their normalization is the unprecedented growth of bilateral economic ties. However, it should be noted that economic ties between Vietnam and China have always been heavily influenced by each country's domestic conditions as well as their political relations.

As mentioned in Chapter 2, during the colonial period, economic relations between Vietnam and China were distorted by the encroachment and exploitation of both countries by colonial powers. After Vietnam and China gained their independence in the 1940s, bilateral economic relationship returned to normalcy. After the two communist countries established their diplomatic relations in 1950, they signed the first trade agreement in 1952, which was renewed every year before becoming valid for triennial periods since 1959. In 1962, the two countries signed an agreement on trade and maritime transport, in which they granted each other the Most Favoured Nation treatment (Phong 2001, p. 50). By 1975, however, Vietnam's economic exchanges with China were still very modest due to two main reasons. First, both economies were still underdeveloped and remained relatively close. Second, Vietnam's two wars against France and the United States further limited the country's ability to expand its foreign economic relations in general and its economic ties with China in particular. As Phong (2001, p. 50) observes, Vietnam's economic relations with China during this period were restricted to the implementation of bilateral agreements and protocols through which China provided Vietnam with aid and loans. As such, bilateral economic relations were largely a one-way avenue in which Vietnam had very little to offer.

After Vietnam was unified in 1975, political conditions continue to shape the economic relations between the two countries. As political relations between Vietnam and China deteriorated quickly in the latter half of the 1970s, China cancelled all of its aid to Vietnam in 1978. After the 1979 Sino-Vietnamese border war broke out, economic exchanges between Vietnam and China were virtually non-existent until bilateral relations began to thaw in the late 1980s and early 1990s.

When the two countries finally normalized their relations in 1991, bilateral trade turnover was only US$37.7 million (GSO 2006*b*, pp. 56, 62). In order to boost economic exchanges, the two countries concluded a number of essential agreements soon after that. The most important ones include those on trade (1991), economic cooperation (1992), investment encouragement and protection (1993), payment (1993), avoidance of double taxation (1996), and a number of others on transportation. Apart from bilateral agreements, the two countries' economic exchanges have also been promoted by multilateral treaties. For example, the Framework Agreement on Comprehensive Economic Co-operation between ASEAN and China, which was signed on 5 November 2002 and entered into force on 1 July 2003, laid the foundation for the creation in 2010 of the ASEAN-China Free Trade Area, of which both Vietnam and China are members.

The desire to promote economic cooperation between the two countries as well as between China and ASEAN as a whole also led to the adoption of an initiative during Prime Minister Phan Van Khai's visit to China in 2004 to build the so-called "two corridors, one economic belt" connecting southern China and northern Vietnam. The two "economic corridors", namely the Kunming–Lao Cai–Ha Noi–Hai Phong–Quang Ninh corridor and the Nanning–Lang Son–Ha Noi–Hai Phong–Quang Ninh corridor, will improve connectivity and economic cooperation between Yunnan and Guangxi with twelve cities and provinces in northern Vietnam. Meanwhile, the Tonkin Gulf "economic belt" is designed to enhance economic cooperation between provinces of the two countries that are located around the Tonkin Gulf. By 2012, although the two countries had implemented many major transportation infrastructure projects to materialize the initiative, most of the progress had taken place on the Kunming–Quang Ninh corridor only. Nevertheless, once completed, the initiative will play an essential role in the promotion of connectivity and economic cooperation between Vietnam and China as well as between China and ASEAN countries, especially in terms of trade, investment and tourism.

Above efforts by both countries have helped bilateral economic exchanges expand rapidly ever since their normalization. Compared with 1991, two-way trade turnover between Vietnam and China increased more than 80 times to reach US$2.5 billion in 2000, and more than 1,355 times to reach US$50.2 billion in 2013. Political will played a certain role in this spectacular growth. For example, by 2011, leaders of the two countries had set targets for two-way trade turnover three times: US$2 billion in 2000, US$5 billion in 2005, and US$20 billion in 2010. All these targets have been achieved either earlier or with greater results than expected (Bien 2009). Since 2004, China has also been Vietnam's biggest trade partner. While trade is the main channel for the two countries to conduct economic exchanges, investment is also playing an increasingly important role. By the end of 2013, China had become the ninth largest foreign investor in Vietnam, with 992 projects and US$7.55 billion of registered capital. If investments from Hong Kong were included, China would be ranked as the fourth largest investor with the total registered capital reaching more than US$20 billion (GSO 2014*a*).

Apparently, the deepened economic ties between Vietnam and China are an unprecedented feature of the bilateral relations. Never before have the economies of the two countries been so well connected. The increasing level of economic interdependence tends to prevent the two countries from taking moves that may destabilize their relations and disrupt their economic exchanges. Therefore, while economic exchanges between Vietnam and China, as previously mentioned, have traditionally been conditioned by their political relations, a trend is emerging that economic considerations are now playing an increasingly important role in shaping the trajectory of the two countries' political relations. One should be reminded, however, that beneficial and conducive to peace as they might be, increased economic exchanges also present themselves as an emerging source of tension to bilateral relations. An in-depth analysis of the deepened economic ties between Vietnam and China since normalization and their dual effects on the bilateral relations will be presented in the next chapter.

Conclusion

Vietnam's economic performance under *Doi Moi* has been boosted significantly by the country's integration into the global economy. Exports and inflows of FDI, in particular, have played an essential role in boosting Vietnam's economic performance. This shows that the CPV's decision in the late 1980s to change its foreign policy to help the country get out of diplomatic isolation and facilitate its international integration was sensible. Similarly, Vietnam's quest for normalization with China even at certain costs more than twenty years ago has also proven to be a rational move. Without a peaceful relationship with the northern giant neighbour and a stable regional environment,

Vietnam would have been unable to successfully pursue its domestic development and international integration so far.

It is against this backdrop that since the normalization of bilateral relations in 1991, Vietnam has attached great importance to the development of its relations with China. After more than two decades, despite sporadic surge of tensions due to the South China Sea disputes, Vietnam's overall relations with China have improved considerably, with the most notable landmark being the establishment of a "comprehensive strategic partnership" between the two countries in 2008. Three major features illustrate the considerable improvement of bilateral relations since their normalization: the successful solution of the land border dispute and the delimitation of the Tonkin Gulf, the continual strengthening of political relations, and the deepening of economic ties. Flourishing economic ties have particularly become the central conduit of bilateral cooperation. One should be reminded, however, that while deepened economic ties have generally been mutually beneficial and conducive to peace, they are also emerging as a new source of tension to bilateral relations. At the same time, enduring disputes in the South China Sea are also threatening to destabilize and disrupt the two countries' peaceful and cooperative pattern of relationship. These two outstanding issues in will be further examined in the next two chapters of the book.

NOTES

1. The WB classifies economies into different income groups based on their GNI per capita calculated by its Atlas method. The groups are: low income, US$1,025 or less; lower middle income, US$1,026–US$4,035; upper middle income, US$4,036–US$12,475; and high income, US$12,476 or more. For information about WB's Atlas method, see: <http://data.worldbank.org/about/country-classifications/world-bank-atlas-method>.
2. The non-state sector is composed of collective, private and household enterprises.
3. It should be noted that the foreign-invested sector's impact on the country's net export may not be very significant as many foreign-invested enterprises rely heavily on imported inputs, which contributed to the expansion of the country's imports and its trade deficit.
4. Following the entry into WTO, Vietnam's imports also increased rapidly, causing the country to suffer from severe trade deficit in the period from 2007 to 2011.

5. Vietnam's exports as a share of GDP grew from 6 per cent in 1987 to 78 per cent in 2010 (see Table 3.1), among the highest ratios in the world and the third highest in ASEAN (only after Singapore and Malaysia).

6. As of 31 December 2014, ASEAN has entered into FTAs with Korea, Japan, China, Australia and New Zealand (jointly), and India.

7. For example, Nguyen Trung, a veteran diplomat and former ambassador of Vietnam to Thailand, has made a forthright criticism of the CPV that its "almost-at-any-cost" pursuit of normalization with China as showcased by the 1990 Chengdu summit was "a humiliating failure" of Vietnam that has made the country increasingly dependent on China (Trung 2012). Nguyen Trung, however, seems not to have taken into full account the fact that in the early 1990s, Vietnam had few options in its foreign policy in general and its dealing with China in particular, especially given its domestic problems. Without its timely normalization with China in 1991, Vietnam's economic reform and international integration might have been greatly impeded, which should have put the country in a much weaker position to deal with China than it is the case today.

8. A key principle identified by the agreement was that the two sides would recognize and base their negotiations on the two Franco-China Conventions of 1887 and 1895 on border delimitation.

9. For accounts of the negotiation on the agreement and the demarcation process, see Thao (2000) and Tang (2011, pp. 279–326).

10. Vietnam and China conducted two rounds of negotiations on the delimitation of the Tonkin Gulf in 1974 and 1977–78 but failed to achieve any result due to the unfavorable conditions of bilateral relations as well as their significantly different positions. While Vietnam wished to use the 108° 03'13" East longitude line mentioned in the 1887 Franco-China Convention as the maritime boundary in the Gulf (which would entitle Vietnam to 63 per cent of the Gulf area), China considered the 1887 line merely as a dividing line for the allocation of islands and looked for a more equitable share of the Gulf (Thao 2005; Zou 2005).

11. The major difference is that Vietnam prefers delimitation before the two countries can undertake joint development, while China insists on the opposite. The unresolved dispute over the Paracels also complicates the negotiation process.

12. China's position regarding the U-shaped line is ambiguous and it has never clarified what it claims through the line. Therefore, scholars have offered different interpretations of the line's meaning. For an updated summary of these interpretations, see Thang and Thao (2012, p. 50).

13. The South China Sea disputes will be addressed in greater detail in Chapter 6.

14. Besides summit meetings, official visits at lower level also take place frequently. In 2000, for example, there were more than 300 official visits between the two countries, of which 100 were at the vice ministerial level or above (Womack 2006, p. 224).

15. The number 16 corresponds to the number of words in the original Vietnamese and Chinese text of the guideline. The guideline reads *"Lang gieng huu nghi, hop tac toan dien, on dinh lau dai, huong toi tuong lai"* in Vietnamese, and *"Chang qi wen ding, mian xiang wei lai, mu lin you hao, quan mian he zuo"* in Chinese.

16. It should be noted that by 2000, China had signed long-term cooperative framework agreements with all ten Southeast Asian states. See Thayer (2003).

17. By 2015, Vietnam had established "strategic partnerships" with Russia (2001), Japan (2006), India (2007), China (2008), South Korea (2009), Spain (2009), the United Kingdom (2010), Germany (2011), Italy, Singapore, Thailand, Indonesia, France (2013), Malaysia and the Philippines (2015); and "comprehensive partnerships" with Australia (2009) and the United States (2013).

18. Author's own database.

5

The Political Economy Dimensions of Vietnam–China Economic Relations

Introduction

By the time Vietnam and China normalized their relations in 1991, official bilateral economic exchanges were virtually non-existent.[1] After normalization, however, favourable domestic and international conditions encouraged bilateral economic exchanges to expand rapidly. In China, Deng Xiaoping's famous southern tour took place just a few months after bilateral normalization. Deng's tour reasserted China's economic reform and openness against the conservative backlash following the Tiananmen demonstrations, and encouraged China's further expansion of foreign economic exchanges. Meanwhile, in Vietnam, the country's increasing economic stability was also favourable for its promotion of international integration. Vietnam's weak production base, in particular, caused a scarcity of even the most basic consumer goods and led to high demand for imports from China (Beresford and Phong 2000, p. 132). Internationally, the demise of the Council for Mutual Economic Assistance (CMEA) necessitated Vietnam's expansion of economic exchanges with any country that could help compensate for its loss of trade with former CMEA member economies. As a result, China, along with other East Asian economies such as Japan and Taiwan, conveniently emerged as an important trade partner for Vietnam due to the geographical proximity between the two countries. At the same time, bilateral economic ties also benefited from the end of the Cold War which accelerated the process of globalization and facilitated the economic liberalization and international integration of most countries, including both Vietnam and China.

Deepened economic ties have therefore become an outstanding feature of Vietnam–China relations since their normalization. The deepening of economic relations has brought significant benefits to both countries. In 2013, for example, China was the largest source of imports for Vietnam, providing the country with 28 per cent of its total (General Department of Customs 2013c). Vietnam's exports to China have also increased steadily over the recent years, almost tripling from US$4.9 billion in 2009 to US$13.2 billion in 2013 (General Department of Customs 2013b). Vietnam is accordingly becoming an increasingly important export market for Chinese manufacturers, especially those from southern provinces. Meanwhile, imports of raw materials such as crude oil and coals from Vietnam also help fuel China's economic growth. Other aspects of bilateral economic ties, such as aid, project contracting, and investment, have also enjoyed different levels of development.

As such, for the first time in history, economic issues have become a significant factor shaping each country's policy towards the other as well as the evolution of bilateral relations as a whole. In order to fully understand the dynamics of post-normalization Vietnam–China relations, it is therefore essential to investigate the political origins and effects of their deepened economic exchanges. The current chapter will address this issue by seeking answers to the following three key questions: What is the trajectory of economic relations between Vietnam and China since normalization? How have economic and political factors contributed to this process? And what economic and political implications has the process had on overall bilateral relations?

It should be noted that as China's economy is about sixty times larger than that of Vietnam (World Bank 2015a), the economic and political effects of strengthened bilateral economic ties are much more significant for Vietnam. As a result, Vietnam's reactions to such effects tend to be stronger than those from China. The impacts, if any, such reactions generate on overall bilateral relations also tend to be more consequential on the part of Vietnam. The chapter will therefore seek answers to the above questions mainly from a Vietnamese perspective.

In order to dissect the political economy dimensions of bilateral economic relations, the chapter will specifically examine four key aspects, namely Chinese aid and preferential export buyer's credits for Vietnam, project contracting, trade, and investment relations.

Chinese Aid and Preferential Export Buyer's Credits for Vietnam

Chinese aid to Vietnam used to be the most important form of economic interaction between the two countries in the pre-1979 period. Although there are no official statistics, some Chinese sources estimate that China provided North Vietnam with approximately US$20 billion worth of both economic and military aid during the 1949–75 period (Du and Zhao 1988; as cited in Khoo 2011, p. 1). After Vietnam's reunification in 1975, China continued to provide the country with the much-needed economic aid before cutting it off in 1977 due to deteriorated bilateral relations.

During the pre-1979 period, apart from military aid, China also provided Vietnam with a substantial amount of economic aid.[2] China's economic aid, however, was driven by political motivations as much as by altruistic considerations. Chairman Mao Zedong, for example, considered the protection of Vietnam from Western imperialism as a national security matter of paramount significance due to its close proximity to China. In addition, Mao's vision of himself and China as champions of national liberation movements and anti-imperialist revolutions in Asia and elsewhere also played an important part in China's decision to provide the North Vietnam with substantial amounts of aid (Zhai 2000, pp. 20–21). After the split between China and the Soviet Union in the late 1960s, China also intended to use its aid as a tool to prevent Hanoi from tilting towards Moscow. Deng Xiaoping also promised Vietnam a billion yuan of aid if Vietnam agreed to decline aid from the Soviet Union (MOFA 1979, p. 42). After 1975, as Vietnam became increasingly independent of Beijing and China's goal of using aid politically to influence Vietnam became irrelevant, China started to reduce and then cancel all of its aid to the country in 1977 (K.C. Chen 1987, p. 24).

After normalization, China's aid to Vietnam has ceased to be the most important aspect of bilateral economic relations. In addition, the nature and structure of its aid for Vietnam also changed.

First, the level of Chinese aid to Vietnam decreased significantly compared with the pre-1979 period.[3] While China's aid to Vietnam during the 1949–75 period probably reached as much as US$20 billion, China provided Vietnam with only US$312 million of aid in the period from 1992 to 2004 (*Asia Times* 2005). Meanwhile, according to a report by the Ministry of Finance (2011, p. 15), by the end of 2010, Vietnam's outstanding government debt to China through official arrangements had been US$551.7 million, accounting for only 1.98 per cent of Vietnam's total outstanding foreign debt. Although the Ministry did not clarify what constituted the debt, it can be inferred from the way the debt was categorized that it probably derived from interest-free and concessional loans that Vietnam had acquired from China through bilateral agreements.[4] Therefore, even when we account for the grants and the debt that Vietnam serviced, there is no doubt that China's aid to Vietnam since normalization has been insignificant compared with the pre-1979 level despite the fact that China's budget for foreign aid has increased in recent years.[5]

To compensate for the limited level of aid, however, China has increased its preferential export buyer's credit for Vietnam.[6] The MOF report revealed that Vietnam's government-guaranteed debt to China through official arrangements had been US$1.12 billion by the end of 2010. This amount of debt largely corresponds to the preferential export buyer's credits that Vietnamese SOEs had acquired from China under repayment guarantees from the Vietnamese government. It should be noted that the total preferential export buyer's credits that Vietnam had received from China might be larger than the statistics disclosed by the MOF report because a number of credits provided might not need repayment guarantee from Vietnamese government (China Eximbank 2012). In fact, according to Chinese Assistant Minister of Commerce Wang Chao, Chinese preferential export buyer's credits for Vietnam had already reached US$1 billion by the end of 2008 (Xinhua News Agency 2008). By now, it should have gone much higher. For example, according to the 2010–11 annual report of Electricity of Vietnam (2011, p. 29), preferential loans and export buyer credits provided by China Eximbank for the two projects of Vinh Tan 2 and Duyen Hai 1 Thermal Power Plant alone reached nearly US$2.14 billion.

Second, in terms of aid structure, unlike the pre-1979 period, China's grants for Vietnam since normalization have been insignificant.[7] From 1992 to 2004, China provided Vietnam with only US$50 million worth of grants (*Asia Times* 2005; Tien 2005). These grants were used for different purposes, ranging from upgrading factories financed by Chinese aid in the 1950s–1960s and building a hostel for the Ho Chi Minh National Political Academy, to sending Vietnamese officials to China for study tours and organizing youth exchange programmes. In 2003, on the occasion of CPV General Secretary Nong Duc Manh's visit to Beijing, China pledged to provide Vietnam with a grant of RMB150 million to build the Vietnam–China Friendship Palace in Hanoi. On the same occasion, China also agreed to relieve Vietnam from a rouble-denominated debt worth of RMB420 million (approximately US$50 million) left from the past (Vietnam News Agency 2003). Although China does not consider debt relief as official foreign aid, the OECD does (Brautigam 2010, p. 18). Therefore, according to OECD standards, the total amount of Chinese grants to Vietnam since 1992 until 2005 were approximately US$100 million. Nevertheless, this amount of grant is still insignificant if compared with the pre-1979 period. Moreover, there has been virtually no report of new Chinese grants to Vietnam since 2006 until November 2015, when China pledged to provide Vietnam with a grant of RMB1 billion during President Xi Jinping's visit to Hanoi.

While China's grants to Vietnam have decreased in comparison with the pre-1979 period, its preferential loans to the country have increased. According to incomplete statistics of the MPI (2009), by the end of 2009, China had provided preferential loans of at least RMB2.147 billion (approximately US$300 million) for sixteen projects of Vietnam (see Table 5.1). These projects were mainly in the fields of heavy industry, mining, railway transportation, power, textile, chemical industry, and infrastructure development. As the MPI's statistics were incomplete, the total amount of preferential loans that China provided Vietnam might have been larger. According to a more recent account by Vietnam News Agency, by June 2013, China had actually provided Vietnam with US$1.6 billion in concessional loans (Diep 2013), which is much larger than the amount of Chinese grants to Vietnam in the same period.

TABLE 5.1

Some Projects of Vietnam Using Chinese Interest-free and Concessional Loans

Project	Loan Value
Upgrading 8/3 Textile Factory	RMB17.5 million
Upgrading Sao Vang Rubber Factory	RMB12.5 million
Upgrading Hai Phong Enamelware Factory	RMB11.2 million
Providing small hydropower generator for five Northern provinces	RMB15 million
Upgrading Hai Duong Porcelain Factory	RMB11.2 million
Building Thai Nguyen Chipboard Factory	RMB40 million
Upgrading Vinh Phu Textile Factory	RMB41.5 million
Upgrading and Expanding Nam Dinh Textile Factory	RMB23.3 million
Upgrading 19/5 Textile Factory	RMB6 million
Procuring construction equipment for Cienco 6 Corporation	RMB52 million
Upgrading Thai Nguyen Iron and Steel Factory and Ha Bac Fertilizer and Chemical Factory	RMB36.8 million
Building Cao Ngan Thermal Power Plant	RMB710 million
Building Sin Quyen Copper Plant	US$40.5 million
Modernizing railway signal system	RMB1,08 billion
Building Plastic Mould Factory	RMB50 million

Note: Some of the projects used mixed credits. In addition to interest-free and concessional loans, their funding may also include grants and preferential export buyer's credits from China.
Source: MPI (2009).

The changing size and structure of Chinese aid to Vietnam since normalization can be explained in a number of ways. First, as China's White Paper on foreign aid put it, China's foreign aid policy has been designed to suit both "China's actual conditions and the needs of the recipient countries" (Information Office of the State Council 2011). Therefore, despite China's recent growing budget for foreign aid, Vietnam's relatively successful economic development under *Doi Moi* may have made China consider providing substantial aid for Vietnam, especially grants, unnecessary. Second, although the two countries have now normalized relations, bitter historical experiences of the 1970s and 1980s, in which China considered Vietnam "ungrateful" for its previous assistance, may also have played a role in China's aid policy for Vietnam since normalization. Third, despite improvements in bilateral relations, the increasing rivalry between the two countries in the South China Sea territorial disputes made any attempt by the Chinese government to maintain a high level of aid for Vietnam unjustifiable in the eyes of the Chinese public. Finally, unlike the pre-1979 period, China now tends to view its aid primarily as a tool to expand its economic rather than political interests in Vietnam. As a consequence, China finds it irrational to maintain a favourable aid policy for Vietnam in the post-normalization period.

That said, however, one should be reminded that China's political interests, especially regarding the Taiwan issue, now still carry some weight in its aid policy for Vietnam in the post-normalization period. China has long been known for using aid as a tool to win formal diplomatic recognition from recipient countries, especially in Africa, Latin America and South Pacific, at the expense of Taiwan (see, for example, Alden 2005; Erickson and Chen 2007; I. Taylor 1998; Van Fossen 2007). In the joint communiqué issued following the normalization summit in 1991, Vietnam had to reaffirm its recognition of the PRC as the only legal government representing the whole China and that Taiwan was an inalienable part of the PRC. Since then, the Taiwan issue has once again emerged as a major problem in Vietnam's relations with China. As China consistently sought to isolate Taiwan from multilateral international organizations and forums, it pressured Vietnam to exclude Taiwan from the 2006 APEC summit that Vietnam was hosting. However, Hanoi chose to adhere to previous hosts' convention of inviting Taiwan to APEC events, and refused to submit to Beijing's pressure. In response, Beijing decided to "punish" Vietnam by temporarily halting aid to the country (Mitton 2006; Thayer 2007). The decision, however, was rescinded soon after that. For example, in 2009, China agreed to increase the grant for building the Vietnam–China Friendship Palace, which was pledged in 2003, from the initial amount of RMB150 million to RMB200 million (Vietnam News Agency 2009).

The 2006 incident, to some extent, shows that although political motivations still matter in China's aid policy toward Vietnam, they tend to become less significant than the pre-1979 period. In the pre-1979 period, China used aid to politically influence Vietnam mainly for strategic purposes, such as maintaining Vietnam as a close ally, countering Soviet influence on the country, or preventing the U.S. military presence off China's southern border. In order to achieve these purposes, China both provided Vietnam with massive aid and designed its aid packages to comprise mainly grants. Since normalization, the decreased significance of aid as a tool for China to politically influence Vietnam is reflected not only by the size and composition of its aid, but also the attached conditions. For example, in the pre-1979 period, China's political conditions for Vietnam to receive its aid were highly demanding, such as staying politically loyal to China and distancing itself from the Soviet Union. Since normalization, however, China's main political condition has been Vietnam's observation of the one-China policy, a condition that any country maintaining diplomatic relations with China has to comply with no matter whether it receives aid from China or not. Furthermore, while economic conditions attached to Chinese aid for Vietnam were not significant in the pre-1979 period, they have now become far more consequential.

The increasing importance of economic conditions mainly originates from the changed structure of China's aid for Vietnam since normalization. As preferential loans rather than grants in the form of materials now account for most of China's aid to Vietnam, it becomes necessary for China to dictate how these loans should be used to promote its economic interests, especially given China's wish to support its businesses to go global. Accordingly, China requires Vietnam to use Chinese contractors, technology, equipment, and services for projects using Chinese preferential loans.[8] The same conditions apply to preferential export buyer's credits that Vietnam acquires from China (China Eximbank 2012). These conditions have generated some ramifications for Vietnam's relations with China, in which the most important is that these conditions have contributed to the rise of Chinese engineering contractors in Vietnam and Vietnam's persistent trade deficit with China over the last decade. These two issues will be further examined in the following sections.

Project Contracting

According to China's Ministry of Commerce (2010), Chinese engineering companies by the end of 2009 were involved in projects worth US$15.42 billion in Vietnam, turning the Vietnamese market into their largest in Southeast Asia. Various Vietnamese sources also confirm that these contractors have strongly outcompeted contractors from Japan, South Korea, and Western countries. On occasion, Chinese contractors have accounted for up to 90 per cent of EPC (Engineering/Procurement/Construction) contracts for thermal power plants in Vietnam (Nhat Minh 2012). This interesting phenomenon begs several questions. First, given their relative lack of international experience, how did Chinese engineering contractors manage to achieve their extraordinary success in Vietnam, and is it sustainable? Second, does this condition present special problems for the Vietnamese? And finally, what implications does this hold for Vietnam's economic and political relations with China?

As mentioned above, the conditions attached to China's concessional loans and preferential export buyer's credits partly account for the success of Chinese contractors. Projects funded by these financial sources are open to Chinese contractors only. For example, the construction of Cao Ngan Power Plant, which was funded by Chinese concessional loans, was open to four Chinese bidders and Harbin Electric Corporation was selected as the EPC contractor of the project. Similarly, Electricity of Vietnam had to choose Shanghai Electric Group Company Ltd. as the EPC contractor for the aforementioned Vinh Tan II Thermal Power Plant, which had 85 per cent of its investment coming from Chinese preferential export buyer's credits and ODA (Tuoitrenews 2010). In other words, the conditions attached to China's concessional loans and preferential export buyer's credits have undoubtedly contributed to the dominance of Chinese engineering companies in Vietnam.

In projects funded by other financial sources and open to international bidders, Chinese contractors normally play on loopholes in Vietnam's Law on Tendering which favours low prices over other technical factors.

Accordingly, Chinese contractors normally offer a markedly lower price than other competing bidders. A number of factors enabled Chinese contractors to pursue this low-price strategy. According to Dr Nguyen Thanh Son, who used to work for power plant projects of the state-owned Vietnam National Coal - Mineral Industries Corporation (Vinacomin) and had first-hand experience dealing with Chinese contractors, Chinese companies were able to offer low prices thanks to subsidies from the Chinese government given on presentation of contracts they had won. In addition, unlike Western contractors who normally offered a higher price but, once awarded the contract, would strictly implement its terms and conditions, Chinese contractors normally adopted a different strategy. They were willing to offer low prices, but after being awarded the contract, they would try to persuade project owners to change the contract's original terms and conditions, or just ignore them, in order to save costs. Consequently, components that did not meet project owners' technical requirements were still used and installed by Chinese contractors in a number of power plant projects, such as Quang Ninh, Hai Phong, Cao Ngan, and Na Duong (Thanh Phong 2010).

In addition, in some power plant projects which require swift implementation due to Vietnam's electricity shortage, project owners were allowed by Vietnamese government to appoint contractors without going through the bidding process. In such cases, Chinese contractors also got appointed because of the competitive prices they offer. Moreover, Chinese contractors are also interested in bidding for small-scaled projects which are normally ignored by engineering contractors from Vietnam and other countries (Pham Huyen 2010).

Such strategies seem to have worked. Chinese contractors have won contracts for many upstream projects of national importance in essential sectors such as energy and mining. Especially, as much as 90 per cent of Vietnam's thermal power plants have been built by Chinese contractors (Nhat Minh 2012). The increasingly dominant position of Chinese contractors, however, has produced a number of serious problems for Vietnam.

First, there have been numerous reports in the Vietnamese media about Chinese contractors' poor performance in projects in various fields (see, for example, Doan Cuong 2012; Linh Chi 2012; Pham Huyen 2010; Quoc Dung 2011; Thanh Phong 2010; Thanh Tung 2012; Ve Dinh 2011). The affected projects include both those funded by

Chinese concessional loans, such as Cao Ngan Power Plant and Sin Quyen Copper Plant, as well as commercially funded ones. The most common problems come from the contractors' failure to ensure quality; the inability to keep deadlines, or the violation of contractual terms and conditions. These problems have caused additional costs for Vietnamese project owners and hindered the sustainable development of Vietnam's infrastructure system.

For example, Vinacomin complained that some equipment Chinese contractors provided for its power plants were of inferior quality than equipment of Japanese or Western origin. The poor quality of equipment caused repeated incidents in such projects as Hai Phong Thermal Power Plant No. 1 (Le Thu and Van Thinh 2010). The Vietnam Energy Association (VEA) also reported in 2011 that many power plants constructed by Chinese contractors had faced protracted delay. Meanwhile, the Dinh Vu DAP Fertilizer Factory, which was built by China National Chemical Engineering Group Corporation as the EPC contractor, could not produce fertilizer of pledged quality. The problem caused the Ministry of Industry and Trade (MOIT) to lower the Vietnamese Standards on diammonium phosphate chemical fertilizer so that the factory's products could be sold on the market (Chi Hieu 2011). In this particular case, the Chinese contractor was fined US$6 million for failing to meet requirements set in the contract (Quoc Dung 2011). In projects which are funded by Chinese preferential loans and export buyer's credits, however, it would be hard to financially sanction Chinese contractors as the funding is transferred directly to Chinese contractors from China Eximbank (Thanh Phong 2010).

Second, the condition that projects funded by Chinese preferential loans and export buyer's credits must import technology, equipment and services from China has also contributed to Vietnam's perennial trade deficit with China. Although China provides Vietnam with preferential loans and export buyer's credits, the money actually never leaves China. In any project funded by Chinese concessional loans and preferential export buyer's credits, the Chinese contractor selected by Vietnam will receive money directly from China Eximbank for the equipment and technology they import into the country as well as the services they provide to implement the project. In projects funded by other financial sources, Chinese companies who act as the EPC contractors also normally import most of the machinery and equipment from China, including basics such as washers (Hoang Lan 2010). This practice helps Chinese contractors save costs, which is almost a must given the low prices that they have offered to project owners. However, it has also caused Vietnam's imports from China to surge and its trade deficit with the latter to remain high. Vietnam's trade deficit with China, for example, increased from US$4.1 billion in 2006 to US$23.7 billion in 2013 (see Table 5.2 for more details). Vietnam also imported US$6.6 billion worth of machinery and equipment for its industrial projects in 2011, accounting for almost 18 per cent of its total import turnover from China the same year (General Department of Customs 2014). The next section will analyse Vietnam's trade deficit with China in more detail.

Finally, Chinese contractors' use of Chinese labourers is yet another important issue that has added friction to Vietnam's relations with China. According to the Ministry of Labour, War Invalids and Social Affairs (MOLISA), by September 2011, there were 78,440 foreign workers in Vietnam, of which 31,330 were illegal (Phong Cam 2012). Various reports suggested that most of the illegal workers were brought into the country by Chinese contractors. For example, among about 1,700 Chinese workers working at Ca Mau Gas–Electricity–Fertilizer complex in August 2011, more than 1,000 did not have a working permit (Thien Phuoc 2011). Similarly, many of the 1,300 Chinese labourers working at the construction site of Hai Phong Thermal Power Plant No. 2 in June 2012 were also illegal. Chinese contractors explained their preference for Chinese workers by referring to the language barrier, their lack of trust in Vietnamese labourers, and Chinese workers' more advanced skills (Giang Linh 2012).

The problems presented by Chinese contractors have also brought about significant implications for Vietnam's economic and political relations with China.

First, Vietnam's dependence on Chinese contractors has conjured up concerns about Vietnam's national security, especially energy security. For example, such concerns have been officially voiced by Ms Pham Thi Loan, member of the National Assembly's Finance and Budget Committee, at a conference in 2010 (Hoang Lan 2010). The concerns about the country's energy security, in particular, have originated from the delay and poor quality of power plants constructed by Chinese contractors. Officials from VEA have pointed out that some power plants constructed by Chinese contractors could not start operation at expected deadlines, while others repeatedly had to halt operation for maintenance. These problems further exacerbated the country's power shortage (Pham Tuyen 2011). Such concerns may ultimately contribute to the rise of policies aimed at restricting China's unwarranted economic influence on Vietnam, which, in turn, would negatively impact Vietnam's overall relations with its northern neighbour.

Second, the presence of Chinese workers, whether legal or illegal, has caused public resentment in Vietnam. Chinese workers have been criticized for taking away jobs from local labourers, especially when many jobs performed by Chinese workers, in contradiction to claims made by Chinese contractors, are simple manual ones that require no advanced skills. Chinese contractors' discrimination between Chinese and local labourers in terms of wage and working conditions has also caused grievances among locals. For example, for the same job, Chinese workers are normally paid a significantly higher wage than wages paid to Vietnamese (Giang Linh 2012; Nam Cuong and Nguyen Thanh 2011).

Especially, the presence of Chinese workers has also caused security concerns. There have been reports of Chinese workers violating laws, causing social disorder, or even engaging in violent confrontation with local communities (*Vietnamnet* 2009). The presence of hundreds of Chinese labourers working for EPC contractor China Aluminium Engineering Corporation (Chalieco) at Nhan Co and Tan Rai Aluminium Plants in the Central Highlands also elicited objection from a segment of Vietnamese high-profile figures, including the late General Vo Nguyen Giap (U.S. Embassy in Hanoi 2009c). In addition to environmental concerns, General Giap argued that the large numbers of Chinese working in the Central Highlands would give China a foothold in this strategically important area of the country (Marston 2012, p. 183). His argument was one of the rationales behind the strong protests mounted by Vietnamese civil society against bauxite mining in the Central Highlands.[9]

Third, the poor quality of a number of their projects has created a negative perception of Chinese contractors among a large segment of Vietnamese population. They further deepened Vietnamese distrust in China in general and Chinese products and services in particular. More importantly, they have also triggered certain official responses from Vietnamese organizations and policymakers. In September 2011, for example, the VEA sent a petition to Party and State leaders calling for, among other things, a restriction on Chinese contractors' participation in Vietnam's power plants projects (Bao Anh 2011). The VEA cited the above-mentioned problems, especially the prolonged delay and poor quality of power plants projects undertaken by Chinese contractors, to support their recommendation.

At the same time, there were also calls for revising the Law on Tendering to fix the loopholes that had facilitated the rise of Chinese contractors. In response, the MPI submitted a revised Law on Tendering to the National Assembly in 2013. Although the revised law aimed at multiple purposes, it seemed to have the problems presented by the dominance of Chinese contractors as a hidden target. Accordingly, it introduced the quality-price trade-off tender evaluation method.[10] Under this method, project owners would be able to disqualify bidders who offered low prices but seemed unlikely to provide the expected quality. In addition, the revised Law also put restrictions on the use of foreign workers and the importation of locally available goods and equipment. The revised law was passed in November 2013 and will undoubtedly undermine Chinese contractors' competitiveness in Vietnam.

The case of Chinese contractors is reminiscent of the dominance of Chinese consumer goods in Vietnam in the 1990s. After Vietnam normalized its relations with China in 1991, Chinese consumer goods quickly flooded the Vietnamese market. As the massive influx of Chinese goods was detrimental to its domestic production, Vietnam introduced a protectionist policy in September 1992 to ban seventeen varieties of imports from China. The ban, however, proved to be ineffective (Womack 1994, p. 506). It was only when Vietnamese consumers became disappointed with the poor quality of "made-in-China" products several years later that the market share of Chinese consumer goods in Vietnam began to contract. In the case of Chinese engineering contractors, however, their poor performance and tainted reputation, at least until recently, have not affected their dominant position. Instead, it is changes in Vietnam's legal and policy framework that will probably play a more decisive role in bringing that about.

Bilateral Trade

Since normalization, trade has remained the most important aspect of bilateral economic relations that showcases the growing interdependence between the two economies. Table 5.2 shows statistics on Vietnam's

TABLE 5.2
Vietnam's Official Trade in Goods with China, 1991–2013

Year	Vietnam's Export to China (US$ million)	Vietnam's Total Export (US$ million)	Share of Vietnam's Total Export (%)	Vietnam's Import from China (US$ million)	Vietnam's Total Import (US$ million)	Share of Vietnam's Total Import (%)	Total Bilateral Trade (US$ million)	Annual Growth Rate (%)	Trade Balance (US$ million)
1991	19	2,087	0.9	18	2,338	0.8	37	—	1
1992	96	2,581	3.7	32	2,541	1.3	128	246	64
1993	136	2,985	4.6	86	3,924	2.2	222	73	50
1994	296	4,054	7.3	144	5,826	2.5	440	98	152
1995	362	5,449	6.6	330	8,155	4.0	692	57	32
1996	340	7,256	4.7	329	11,144	3.0	669	-3	11
1997	474	9,185	5.2	404	11,592	3.5	878	31	70
1998	440	9,360	4.7	515	11,500	4.5	955	9	-75
1999	746	11,541	6.5	673	11,742	5.7	1,419	49	73
2000	1,536	14,483	10.6	1,401	15,637	9.0	2,937	107	135
2001	1,417	15,029	9.4	1,606	16,218	9.9	3,023	3	-189
2002	1,518	16,706	9.1	2,159	19,745	10.9	3,677	22	-641
2003	1,883	20,149	9.3	3,139	25,256	12.4	5,022	37	-1,256
2004	2,899	26,485	10.9	4,595	31,969	14.4	7,494	49	-1,696
2005	3,228	32,447	9.9	5,900	36,761	16.0	9,128	22	-2,672
2006	3,243	39,826	8.1	7,391	44,891	16.5	10,634	16	-4,148
2007	3,646	48,561	7.5	12,710	62,765	20.3	16,356	54	-9,064
2008	4,850	62,685	7.7	15,974	80,713	19.8	20,824	27	-11,124
2009	5,403	57,096	9.5	15,411	69,949	22.0	20,814	0	-10,008
2010	7,743	72,237	10.7	20,204	84,839	23.8	27,947	34	-12,461
2011	11,125	96,906	10	24,594	106,750	23	35,719	28	-13,469
2012	12,388	114,573	10.8	28,786	113,792	25.3	41,174	15	-16,398
2013	13,233	132,134	10	36,938	132,033	28	50,171	22	-23,705

Source: GSO (2006b, 2008, 2012); General Department of Customs (2014).

official trade in goods with China from 1991 to 2013. Bilateral trade has increased exponentially over this period, reaching US$50.17 billion in 2013, which was 1,356 times greater than in 1991. In 2013, Vietnam's exports to and imports from China accounted for 10 per cent and 28 per cent of its respective totals. Taken together, China accounted for 19 per cent of Vietnam's total foreign trade turnover in 2013, further confirming its status as Vietnam's biggest trade partner since 2004 (see Table 5.3 for more details).

The impressive growth of bilateral trade is undoubtedly both a source and a consequence of sustained economic development in the two countries. On the part of Vietnam, China is an important market for some Vietnamese agricultural products and raw materials. For example, China accounted for 86 per cent of cassava and cassava products, 64 per cent of coal, 45 per cent of rubber, and 31 per cent of rice that Vietnam exported in 2013 (General Department of Customs 2014). The increased exports to China therefore helps promote Vietnam's total exports as well as its overall economic performance. Meanwhile, imports from China also play an important role in the development of Vietnam's economy. China has been a major provider of many input materials, parts and components for Vietnam's key export industries, such as mobile phone and electronics, garment and textile, or footwear (see Table 5.4 for more details). Especially, China has also emerged as an important source of technology for Vietnam. For example, in 2013, China provided Vietnam with 35 per cent of its imports of machine, equipment, tools and instruments (General Department of Customs 2014). China has also been an important source of electricity import for Vietnam. In 2010, for example, electricity import, mostly from China, accounted for 5.8 per cent of Vietnam's total electricity generation output (Vietnam Electricity 2011, p. 16). Anticipating the continued power shortage of Vietnam, Vietnam Electricity also struck a deal in 2011 with China Southern Power Grid for electricity import until 2015 (Vietnam Electricity 2011, p. 27).

Apart from the conditions of geographical proximity, improved political relations, and growing import demands thanks to robust economic development in both countries, three major factors have accounted for the significant growth of bilateral trade over the last two decades.

First, the export structures of the two countries tend to be highly complementary to each other. Table 5.5 shows the list of top product

TABLE 5.3
Share of Trade with Biggest Trade Partners in Vietnam's GDP (2013)

Country	Exports to Vietnam (US$ billion)	Imports from Vietnam (US$ billion)	Total Trade Turnover (US$ billion)	Share of Vietnam's Total Trade (%)	Share of Total Trade in Vietnam's GDP (%)
China	36.94	13.23	50.17	19	29.3
ASEAN	21.33	18.42	39.75	15	23.2
EU	9.46	24.32	33.78	12.8	19.7
United States	5.23	23.84	29.04	11	17
South Korea	20.71	6.62	27.33	10.4	16
Japan	11.61	13.63	25.24	9.6	14.7

Source: GSO (2014*a*), pp. 531–41.

TABLE 5.4
The Importance of China as a Source of Imports for Vietnam in 2011 and 2013

Product	2011			2013		
	Import from China (US$ million)	Total Import (US$ million)	Share of Total Import (%)	Import from China (US$ million)	Total Import (US$ million)	Share of Total Import (%)
Telephones, mobile phones & parts thereof	1,768	2,721	65	5,698	8,048	71
Pharmaceutical materials	79	174	45	160	308	52
Fabrics	2,799	6,731	42	3,870	8,340	46
Machine, equipment, tools & instruments	5,262	15,533	34	6,561	18,685	35
Computers, electrical products, spare parts and components thereof	2,282	7,851	29	4,501	17,713	25
Textile, leather & footwear materials & auxiliaries	814	2,949	28	1,210	3,779	32
Chemical	694	2,717	26	834	3,032	28
Iron & steel	1,489	6,431	23	2,393	6,657	36
Yarn	339	1,537	22	464	1,517	31
Electric consumer products & parts thereof	124	688	18	206	903	23

Source: General Department of Customs (2014).

TABLE 5.5
Top Product Categories Traded between Vietnam and China (in US$ million)

Year/ Rank	Vietnam Imports from China		Vietnam Exports to China	
	Product	Value	Product	Value
1994				
1	Insecticides	7.8	Rubber	83.8
2	Wheat flour	7.7	Motor cars	56.3
3	Chemicals	5.5	Cashew nut	33
4	Disodium carbonate	3.4	Rice	19.3
5	Silk & fibres	2.1	Coal	9.1
6	Motor vehicles	1.9	Crude oil	8.5
2002				
1	Petroleum products	474	Crude oil	689
2	Fabrics	183	Fishery products	174
3	Motorcycles	96	Rubber	90
4	Chemicals	96	Vegetables & fruits	60
5	Footwear materials	78	Coal	44
6	Iron & Steel	70	Cashew nut	38
2011				
1	Machine, equipment, tools & instruments	5,262	Rubber	1,937
2	Fabrics	2,799	Crude oil	1,076
3	Computers, electrical products, spare-parts & components thereof	2,282	Computers, electrical products, spare-parts & components thereof	1,051
4	Telephones, mobile phones & parts thereof	1,768	Coal	1,023
5	Iron & steel	1,489	Cassava & cassava products	860
6	Petroleum products	1,300	Petroleum products	754

TABLE 5.5 (continued)

Year/Rank	Vietnam Imports from China		Vietnam Exports to China	
	Product	Value	Product	Value
2013				
1	Machine, equipment, tools & instruments	6,561	Computers, electrical products, spare-parts and components thereof	2,090
2	Telephones, mobile phones & parts thereof	5,698	Rubber	1,129
3	Computers, electrical products, spare-parts and components thereof	4,501	Wood and wooden products	1,051
4	Fabrics	3,870	Cassava & cassava products	942
5	Iron & steel	2,393	Rice	900
6	Petroleum products	1,268	Yarn	900

Note: The list of 1994 seems to provide an inaccurate description of top product categories traded between the two countries during the year. According to GSO, Vietnam imported US$144.2 million worth of products from China in 1994, but the combined value of all the imported products it had statistics on was only US$34.3 million (GSO 2006b, pp. 124–25). Apparently missing from the list are some major Chinese products that were very popular in Vietnam during that time, such as bicycles, beer, clothing, and consumer products. The data collection method that GSO used back then largely accounts for this incompleteness of the data. Before 1996, GSO compiled the national trade data based on reports of companies engaging in foreign trade activities. It was not until 1996 that the GSO started using customs declaration submitted to the General Department of Customs as the main source of trade statistics (GSO 2006b, p. 369).
Source: GSO (2006b); General Department of Customs (2014).

categories that the two countries exported to each other in 1994, 2002, 2011, and 2013. While the largest components of Vietnamese exports to China are dominated by agricultural products and raw materials, the main exports from China are mainly composed of industrial input materials, components and parts. A significant portion of Chinese exports to Vietnam are also products of medium-high and high technologies according to the OECD classification. For example, the top three product categories that China exported to Vietnam in 2013 were machine, equipment, tools and instruments; telephones, mobile phones and parts thereof; and computers, electrical products, spare parts and components thereof. The structure of bilateral trade generally reflects the difference in development level of the two economies and is an important factor accounting for the continuous increase of bilateral trade since normalization.

Second, the deeper integration of both China and Vietnam into free trade regimes has also facilitated the expansion of bilateral trade. China joined the WTO in 2001, and Vietnam did the same six years later. WTO membership has led to further market opening by both countries to each other's products. A more relevant free trade regime that has helped promote bilateral trade is the China–ASEAN Free Trade Agreement (CAFTA).[11] Although the Agreement came into effect on 1 January 2010, an Early Harvest Programme (EHP) has been implemented since 1 January 2004 to reduce tariff on some identified products. Research conducted by the EU-Vietnam Multilateral Trade Assistance Project (MUTRAP) in 2010 revealed that the CAFTA had a generally positive impact on bilateral trade. For example, the research found that under the Agreement, Vietnam's trade in manufactures with China grew faster than corresponding trade flows with third countries (Vergano et al. 2010, p. 1).

Finally, the expansion of bilateral trade has also benefited from growth of FDI into both countries. Investments from multinational corporations have turned China into a central hub of the global production network, providing the international market with varieties of not only finished products but also parts and components. The increasing importance of China as a major provider of information and communication technology (ICT) parts and components is a primary example for this observation (see, for example, Amighini 2005). As multinational corporations establish their production facilities in Vietnam, China naturally became a convenient source of input materials, parts, and components for them. For example, Samsung Electronics Vietnam, which contributed US$23.9 billion to Vietnam's export turnover in 2013, imported a large part of components for its smartphone assembly facility in Bac Ninh province from China (Pham Huyen 2012). A portion of the final products then would be exported back to its northern neighbour. The operation of multinational corporations like Samsung thus partly accounted for the surge in Vietnam's import of mobile phone parts from China in recent years.

Growing bilateral trade ties, however, has brought Vietnam not only benefits but also problems. First, Vietnam has been running a perennial trade deficit with China since 2002. Figure 5.1 shows the level of Vietnam's trade deficit with China from 2002 to 2013.

As shown by Figure 5.1, Vietnam's trade deficit with China swelled from US$641 million in 2002 to US$23.7 billion in 2013. This is in stark contrast with Vietnam's trade relations with the United States, its second largest trade partner after China. Since 1997, Vietnam's trade balance with the United States has always been in surplus. In 2013, for example, Vietnam's trade surplus with the Unites States stood at US$18.6 billion (General Department of Customs 2014).

The enduring and burgeoning trade deficit with China has been a major concern for policymakers as well as the public in Vietnam. The deficit implies that Vietnam is more trade-dependent on China than China is on Vietnam, which causes Vietnam to be more sensitive and

FIGURE 5.1
Vietnam's Trade Deficit with China, 2002–13

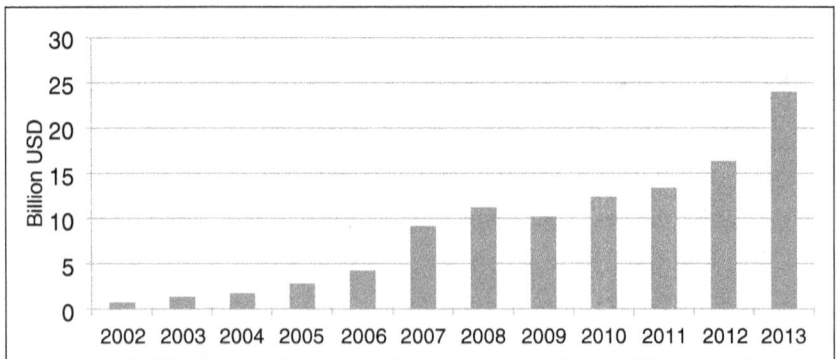

Source: GSO (2006b, 2012), General Department of Customs (2014).

vulnerable to the disruption of bilateral trade. The problem has become even more significant as a matter of national economic security when China has shown that in certain cases it is willing to use economic interests as a coercive diplomatic tool. Following a stand-off over the Scarborough Shoal in the South China Sea in early 2012, for example, China decided to disrupt tourist exchange and halt its importation of bananas from the Philippines to mount pressure on the latter. In the case of Vietnam, a senior official from the General Statistics Office estimated in June 2014 that in case China decided to disrupt bilateral trade, Vietnam's GDP would contract 10 per cent as a consequence (Phuong Linh 2014). Therefore, given the rising tensions over the South China Sea disputes in recent years, the potential disruption of bilateral trade by China as a coercive tactic has become a legitimate concern for Vietnamese policymakers.

In order to mitigate the consequences of this prospect, Vietnam has to seek ways to improve the bilateral trade balance. However, Vietnam has few options for achieving this goal. As the two countries are now bound together in regional and global free trade regimes, Vietnam cannot adopt protectionist measures to effectively restrict imports from China except for rare cases in which it can resort to safeguard mechanisms to protect certain domestic industries from excessive harm caused by imports from China.[12] As a result, there are only two feasible ways for Vietnam to narrow its trade deficit with China. First, it needs to improve the bilateral trade structure so that Vietnam can export more high value-added products to China, while becoming less reliant on China for expensive imported items, such as machinery and equipment. Second, Vietnam needs to increase its total exports to China. This measure was adopted by Vietnam's Ministry of Trade (now MOIT) in a blueprint for developing trade ties with China for the period of 2007–15 (MOIT 2007). In addition, Vietnamese leadership also showed strong political will in reducing the trade deficit.[13] However, at least by 2014, it remained an unattainable goal as the country's trade deficit with China still kept rising.

The next major problem that growing trade ties with China have presented Vietnam is the rampant smuggling along its northern border that stretches for 1,450 kilometres. In the early 1990s when bilateral trade resumed, smuggling was informally estimated by some experts to exceed regular trade in volume (Xiaosong and Womack 2000, p. 1048). Twenty years later, the problem still persists although the scale of smuggling has been dwarfed by regular trade in both volume and value. Smuggling is particularly widespread along border areas where road systems on both sides have been well established. In the provinces of Lang Son and Quang Ninh, which host major border gates and border crossings such as Dong Dang, Huu Nghi and Mong Cai, smuggling from China is a serious problem that Vietnamese authorities have to deal with, especially during the months leading to the Lunar New Year (Tet). From January to mid-December 2012, for example, customs authorities of Quang Ninh and Lang Son uncovered 639 and 570 cases of smuggling from China, respectively. Nevertheless, detecting the true scale of smuggling from China is almost impossible as smugglers also take advantage of the lawful duty-free, small-scaled trade activities by border residents to smuggle goods into the country.[14] Therefore, as acknowledged by anti-smuggling forces of the two above-mentioned provinces, the smuggling cases exposed are just the tip of an iceberg (*Sai Gon Giai Phong* 2012).

It should also be noted that many categories of smuggled goods are illegal and banned by Vietnamese government. These include drugs, counterfeit money, small weapons, fire crackers and fireworks, and fake goods. Preventing the infiltration of these harmful goods through the border is undoubtedly the focus of Vietnamese anti-smuggling forces, especially when some of these goods can cause potential threats to the country's security, social order, and the people's safety. As shown by historical precedents, for example, counterfeit money may well be used by China to disrupt Vietnam's economy when bilateral relations turn sour.[15]

Another issue arising from Vietnam's trade relations with China is the exposure of Vietnamese consumers to sub-standard Chinese products. Health problems caused by sub-standard Chinese products are not unique to Vietnam, and even Chinese consumers themselves fall victim to such products. In the case of Vietnam, the booming of bilateral trade and the condition of geographical proximity facilitate the infiltration of sub-standard Chinese products into the country, mainly by means of border trade and smuggling. Although both the value and volume of sub-standard Chinese products may be small in comparison with the total value of Vietnam's imports from China, they are still capable of instilling a widespread negative perception among Vietnamese people as most of the sub-standard Chinese products are consumer goods that Vietnamese people use every day.

For example, a study in 2011 which surveyed 1,000 students at Vietnam National University – Ho Chi Minh City (VNU-HCM) shows that up to 70 per cent of respondents said they either "extremely disliked" or "disliked" Chinese products (see Figure 5.2). Due to widespread negative perception of Chinese products, some traders even sought to deceive consumers by changing the label or origin statement of products imported from China,[16] which further undermined the confidence of Vietnamese consumers in Chinese products.

Vietnamese consumers' negative perception of Chinese products has been made possible in a large part by the extensive coverage of the topic by the Vietnamese media. There have been numerous reports in the media about health and safety problems caused by sub-standard Chinese products, ranging from cars, motorbikes, to toys, food and clothes. While media reports on the topic are intended to inform consumers of problems associated with Chinese products, they also generate unintended consequences. The poor quality of Chinese products as reported in the media tends to undermine China's image in Vietnam and, to a certain extent, generate a negative impact on bilateral relations. In 2009, for example, in response to an expert roundtable on the topic of sub-standard Chinese products published

FIGURE 5.2
Perception of VNU-HCM Students of Chinese Products

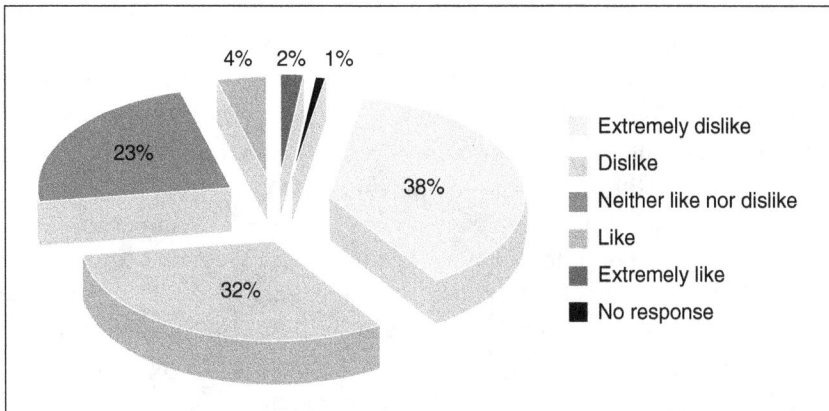

Source: Sang et al. (2011), p. 53.

on the popular news site *Vietnamnet*, Commercial and Economic Counsellor at the Chinese Embassy in Hanoi Hu Suojin reportedly registered a complaint with the Ministry of Information and Communications and asked the Ministry to reprimand *Vietnamnet* for publishing what he considered "unfriendly remarks" on China. He also added sarcastically that sub-standard Chinese products were available on the Vietnamese market due to local demands, which elicited angry responses from Vietnamese bloggers (Radio Free Asia 2009). Following the contact, however, *Vietnamnet* neither withdrew nor changed the content of its articles.

After China became increasingly assertive in the South China Sea in 2011–12, calls for boycotting Chinese products also began to appear on the Internet. As a reporter of Radio Free Asia pointed out, while the poor quality of Chinese products was sound enough a reason for consumers in Vietnam to boycott Chinese products, it was China's growing assertiveness in the South China Sea that gave them an extra reason to do so (Radio Free Asia 2012). Nevertheless, such calls have met with little response from the public. While Chinese products are so ubiquitous that boycotting them is almost impossible, Vietnamese authorities also seem unwilling to let the problem become another strain on bilateral relations.[17]

Bilateral Investment Relations

While trade is the key pillar of bilateral economic relations, direct investment is also becoming an increasingly significant channel of economic cooperation between Vietnam and China. In 2013, for example, China was the fourth largest foreign investor in Vietnam with US$2.39 billion registered for 110 projects (GSO 2014b, p. 111).[18] However, despite vigorous growth in recent years, bilateral investment relations have still been facing major setbacks.

First, just like trade ties, bilateral investment is asymmetric. While China's investment into Vietnam keeps rising, Vietnam's investment into China has remained modest. By the end of 2013, Vietnamese enterprises had invested only US$16 million in thirteen projects in China, and US$14 million in fifteen projects in Hong Kong (GSO 2014b, p. 123). Meanwhile, as shown by Figure 5.3, by the end of 2013, there were 992 Chinese FDI projects registered in Vietnam with

FIGURE 5.3
China's FDI in Vietnam
(as of 31 December 2013)

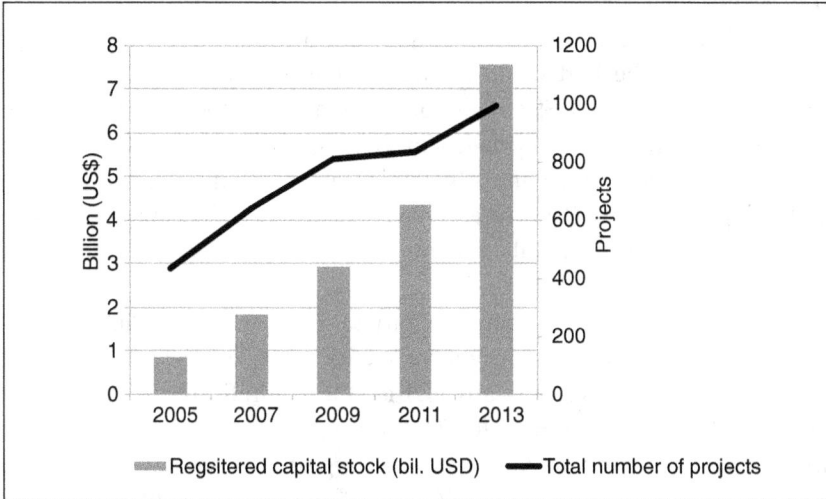

Source: Sang et al. (2011), p. 53.

capital stock reaching over US$7.55 billion. The value of Vietnam's investment in China was merely a fraction of Chinese investment in Vietnam. The situation reflects to some extent the difference in the level of economic development between the two countries. It was not until the latter half of the 2000s that Vietnamese companies began to pursue significant outward FDI projects, while Chinese counterparts had done so long before that.[19]

Second, Chinese investment into Vietnam has increased significantly, but only since the mid-2000s. During the fourteen years from 1991 to 2005, Chinese companies invested only US$841 million into 431 projects in Vietnam. Meanwhile, by the end of 2013, Chinese investors had committed US$7.55 billion to a total of 992 projects. In other words, the eight years from 2005 to 2013 witnessed Chinese investment into Vietnam increase almost eight times than the fourteen previous years combined. However, the increase of Chinese FDI is not unique to Vietnam. During the period from 2005 to 2012, for example, Chinese outward FDI stock increased 9.3 times, from US$57.2 billion to US$ 531.94 billion (*Beijing Review* 2013; Ministry of Commerce

2011, p. 81). The increase of Chinese investment into Vietnam over the past decade therefore reflects both the general pattern of Chinese outward FDI and Vietnam's increased attractiveness to Chinese investors.

Third, Chinese FDI projects in Vietnam are relatively small in size. Specifically, at the end of 2013, each Chinese project had an average registered capital of US$7.6 million compared to the average size of US$15.4 million of all FDI projects in Vietnam. As a result, most Chinese FDI projects tend to be more labour-intensive rather than capital or technology-intensive (Kubny and Voss 2010, p. 9). The spillover effect that these projects generate on the Vietnamese economy is therefore rather limited.

At the same time, although Chinese investment in Vietnam has increased considerably in recent years, its share of Vietnam's inward FDI as well as China's outward FDI is still insignificant. By the end of 2013, while China accounted for 3.23 per cent of the total FDI registered in Vietnam and was ranked its ninth largest FDI source in terms of registered capital stock (see Table 5.6), China's investment in Vietnam represented only 1.18 per cent of its outward FDI stock (UNCTAD, 2015).

The flow of Chinese FDI into Vietnam is therefore not significant enough to offset Vietnam's trade deficit with China. It also fails to meet the expectations of both Vietnamese and Chinese policymakers. While Chinese central and local governments reportedly showed their strong support for Chinese companies to invest in Vietnam (Yi 2006, p. 44), Vietnamese policymakers also expected that the conditions of geographical proximity, Vietnam's improved investment environment as well as China's state-sponsored "going-outside" strategy would boost Chinese investment in the country. The current modest level of Chinese FDI into Vietnam is also in stark contrast with the booming of bilateral trade. What then can explain the difference in trade and investment patterns between the two countries?

The mainstream theory of FDI suggests that there are three primary motivations for firms to decide on their foreign investment locations: seeking foreign markets; seeking efficiency; and seeking resources (Buckley et al. 2007, p. 501). In the case of Chinese firms, when it comes to deciding whether or not to invest in Vietnam, it is rational for them to base their decision on Vietnam's economic conditions and FDI policy framework that may affect the achievement of these goals.

TABLE 5.6
Top 20 FDI Sources of Vietnam by Registered Capital Stock (as of 31 December 2013)

Country	Projects	Capital (US$ million)	Country	Projects	Capital (US$ million)
1. Japan	2,186	35,180	11. Netherlands	198	6,311
2. Singapore	1,243	29,942	12. Cayman Islands	55	5,863
3. South Korea	3,611	29,653	13. Brunei	114	4,882
4. Taiwan	2,290	28,020	14. Canada	130	4,698
5. British Virgin Islands	523	17,152	15. Samoa	103	3,967
6. Hong Kong	772	12,524	16. France	401	3,273
7. United States	682	10,696	17. United Kingdom	177	2,813
8. Malaysia	453	10,376	18. Russia	97	1,946
9. China	992	7,551	19. Switzerland	95	1,827
10. Thailand	339	6,401	20. Luxembourg	27	1,518

Source: GSO (2014*b*), pp. 103–104.

However, as suggested by a number of researchers (see, for example, Buckley et al. 2007; Kolstad and Wiig 2012; Q. Li and Liang 2012), Vietnam's political relations with China may also play a role in their decision. Therefore, both economic and political factors should be taken into consideration when explaining the rather limited flow of Chinese FDI into Vietnam so far.

First, although Vietnam with a population of 93.4 million people (as of 2015) is a significant market that Chinese firms may be interested in, the condition of geographical proximity and the emergence of free trade regimes like ACFTA have to some extent discouraged Chinese firms from investing in Vietnam as a measure to penetrate its market. Instead of establishing their manufacturing facilities in the country, some firms, especially those based in southern China, have chosen to ship their products from China for sale in Vietnam. This may also partly account for the strong growth of Vietnam's imports from China. In addition, as the number of Vietnam's FTAs is rather limited,[20] there is little incentive for Chinese firms to manufacture and export their products from Vietnam in order to take advantage of preferential treatment Vietnam enjoys under these arrangements. However, this may change if the TPP comes into effect. As China is not a TPP member, China's investment into Vietnam may surge as its investors seek to take advantage of the trade deal by setting up production facilities in Vietnam.

Second, as labour cost is an essential input affecting a firm's efficiency, Vietnam's low labour cost is undoubtedly an incentive for Chinese firms to invest in the country. However, while some firms decide to set up their manufacturing facilities in Vietnam, some prefer other destinations, such as Cambodia, which has an even lower labour cost than Vietnam.[21] By the end of July 2012, Chinese investments in Cambodia, which concentrate heavily on the labour-intensive industries of garment, textile, agriculture and mining, had reached US$9.1 billion (Kunmakara 2013), more than double China's investments in Vietnam by the end of 2011. Cambodia's lower labour cost undoubtedly plays a significant role in this process. It also helps turn Cambodia into a major competitor of Vietnam in terms of attracting Chinese FDI, especially in labour-intensive industries.[22] As a result, the rather limited flow of Chinese FDI into Vietnam is also attributable to the efficiency-seeking behaviours of Chinese firms.

Third, although resource-seeking is a dominant motivation of Chinese FDI, Chinese investment in Vietnam in the field of mining and resource extraction is limited, in which political reasons seem to play an important role. On the one hand, maritime disputes between Vietnam and China in the South China Sea have prevented Chinese oil companies from investing in Vietnamese oil fields, although oil companies from Russia and Western countries have long been present in Vietnam. Meanwhile, the widespread anti-China sentiment in Vietnam is also a major obstacle to Chinese mining companies seeking to invest in the country. The bauxite mining project in the Central Highlands is a relevant example for this observation. Although Vietnam's state-owned Vinacomin is the project owner, the involvement of Chinese company Chalieco as the EPC contractor of the project as well as the political agreements between Vietnam and China to cooperate on developing the mines has also rekindled anti-Chinese sentiment (*The Economist* 2009; U.S. Embassy in Hanoi 2009*b*). Along with environmental concerns, these were important rationales behind the strong public protests against the project in Vietnam.[23]

Furthermore, as most mining deposits are located in remote or border areas, where activities of foreign companies and its workers are hard to monitor and thus pose a potential threat to the country's national defence and security, there was some reservation on the part of Vietnamese authorities regarding foreign investments into these areas.[24] Such circumstances further discouraged Chinese investment in the country's mining industry. Instead of running the risk, some Chinese companies chose to import ores and minerals from Vietnam, which is economically viable due to the geographical proximity between the two countries. In 2012, Vietnam exported US$1 billion of crude oil, US$809 million of coal, and US$90 million of ores and other minerals to China through official channels (General Department of Customs 2013*a*). However, the flow of Vietnamese ores and minerals to China may be significantly higher due to smuggling. A report in *Sai Gon Tiep thi* (Ky 2011), for example, estimates that about 2,000 tons of iron ore are smuggled from Cao Bang province into China every day. Meanwhile, in the first six months of 2013, 2 million tons of coals also were reportedly smuggled from Quang Ninh province into China (Le Viet 2013).

In sum, contrary to the booming of bilateral trade, post-normalization investment relations between Vietnam and China, despite recent surges, have stayed rather limited. Although the situation is largely attributable to firm-level FDI motivations, political relations between Vietnam and China also play a part. On the bright side of the issue, plenty of room is still available for bilateral investment ties to grow in the future. However, the negative side is that economic ties between Vietnam and China are not evenly developed. In other words, investment ties have failed to match bilateral trade in promoting the economic interdependence between the two countries.

Conclusion

Vietnam's economic relations with China have undergone significant developments since bilateral normalization in 1991. The above analysis of four key aspects of bilateral economic cooperation shows that an intertwined matrix of economic and political factors has helped shape the trajectory of bilateral economic ties. For example, while various economic factors and improved political relations have contributed to the booming of bilateral trade, the South China Sea disputes between the two countries and pervasive anti-China sentiment in Vietnam tend to discourage Chinese investment into the country. At the same time, increased economic interactions have also generated complex implications for overall relations between the two countries. Although increased economic interactions tend to promote economic interdependence[25] and discourage the two countries from engaging in actions that may harm their mutually beneficial economic ties, they also create certain negative side effects, especially from Vietnam's perspective. Vietnam's perennial trade deficit with China and the dominance of Chinese engineering contractors in Vietnam, for example, have given rise to concerns about Vietnamese vulnerability to China's economic preponderance as well as its unwarranted economic influence on the country.

The post-normalization period has also witnessed the unprecedented emergence of economic factors as an essential determinant of bilateral relations. Unlike previous historical periods when economic interactions were limited or shallow, all-round and intense economic interactions now entangle the two countries in a network of economic interdependence. In such a network, economic calculations now play a no less important role than political considerations in the making of each country's policy toward the other. Nevertheless, on the dyadic level, how much significance the current status of economic interdependence between the two countries, given its asymmetrical nature, will hold for the prospect of a more peaceful, cooperative and stable relationship between them is still unclear and merits further assessment.

NOTES

1. The two governments, however, agreed to resume unofficial "small volume trade" across their border in 1988.
2. China's development aid to North Vietnam was particularly popular during the period from 1955 when North Vietnam started its national reconstruction following the First Indochina War until 1965 when the United States started bombing the DRV. For example, in an article on the *Nhan Dan (People's Daily)*, Nguyen Van Tran, Assistant Director of the DRV's State Planning Committee revealed that by 1959 China had provided North Vietnam with grants totalling 900 million yuan, which was equal to North Vietnam's total domestic income of 1955, 1956, 1957 budgets combined. Tran also mentioned that Chinese aid played a significant role in North Vietnam's development of such sectors as industry and mining, communications and postal services, and agriculture and water management (Tran 1959).
3. The lack of coherent and transparent statistics from both Vietnam and China makes it difficult to determine the amount of aid that China has provided Vietnam so far. Although the author attempts to rely on statistics provided by official sources, such as Vietnam's MOIT and MPI, aid statistics presented in this section should still be treated with reservation.
4. China was categorized as an official bilateral creditor together with other bilateral donors. The table also listed multilateral donors to Vietnam such as ADB, IBRD, IDA, and IMF.
5. According to China's 2011 White Paper on foreign aid, by the end of 2009, China had provided foreign countries with a total of RMB256.29 billion in aid, including RMB106.2 billion in grants, RMB76.54 billion in interest-free loans and RMB73.55 billion in concessional loans. The White Paper also confirmed that since 2004, China's rapid economic growth has enabled its foreign aid to increase rapidly, averaging 29.4 per cent from 2004 to 2009 (Information Office of the State Council 2011).
6. According to China's definition, its foreign aid is composed of three major categories, namely grants (aid gratis), interest-free loans, and concessional loans (Information Office of the State Council 2011). These three types of funding are primarily aimed at promoting development and welfare in

recipient states. Meanwhile, China's preferential export buyer's credits, although offered at a better-than-market interest rate, do not qualify as aid as their primary purpose is to promote Chinese exports rather than recipient countries' development and welfare.

7. At the normalization summit in November 1991, China insisted on Vietnam's acknowledgement of all Chinese aid since 1950 as debt. However, Hanoi only agreed to debt repayments for aid received since 1973 (Gainsborough 1992, p. 205), which implied that all aid Vietnam received from China in the 1950–72 period was considered grants.

8. Therefore, China's statement that no strings are attached to its foreign aid is only partially true. China does not demand recipient countries to adhere to certain governance and transparency standards or adopt changes to economic policy, but other economic conditions still apply (Mattlin and Nojonen 2011).

9. For more information on protests against bauxite mining in the Central Highlands, see Marston (2012), Thayer (2009a), and Vuving (2010).

10. In the final text of the law, the method is called *"phuong phap ket hop giua ky thuat va gia"* (method of combining technical and price factors).

11. A background of the CAFTA and Vietnam's participation can be found in Vergano et al. (2010, pp. 14–20).

12. Even in such cases, Vietnam's exports to China may be affected due to China's retaliatory measures.

13. For example, the joint communiqué released after CPV General Secretary Nguyen Phu Trong's visit to China in October 2011 stated that the two sides would work together to improve bilateral trade balance.

14. There are two major types of trade between the two countries, namely official trade (*thuong mai chinh ngach*) and border trade (*thuong mai bien gioi/bien mau*). Official trade is conducted by large trading companies in accordance with regular international trade practices (i.e. through contracts, payments made through banks, etc.). Meanwhile, border trade is composed of three types: non-official trade (*thuong mai tieu ngach*) not conducted in accordance with regular international trade practices (e.g. without contracts and cash payments are possible); trade by border residents; and trade at border markets, border gate markets, and markets in border economic zones. Goods traded by border residents are duty-free if the value of the traded goods does not exceed VND2 million/person/day. Smuggling is therefore legally possible in cases where a trader splits the goods into small packages valued under VND2 million and hires border residents to carry them across the border.

15. Vietnam used to condemn China for using counterfeit money to sabotage its economy (MOFA 1979, p. 96).

16. For example, there have been reports of Chinese garment items' labels being replaced by those of Vietnamese producers, and traders falsely declaring Chinese fruits as produce of Vietnam.

17. For example, a shop-owner in Ho Chi Minh City was harassed by local authorities and forced to close her shop in December 2012 after displaying a signboard pledging not to sell any Chinese products. See Radio Free Asia (2012).

18. Implemented capital is more important as an indicator of FDI than registered capital. However, due to the unavailability or incompleteness of Vietnam's data on implemented capital, the section will rely mainly on Chinese investors' registered capital as provided by GSO, unless otherwise stated.

19. By 2013, Vietnamese companies had invested only US$19.5 billion in outward FDI projects.

20. See Chapter 4 for further information on Vietnam's multilateral and bilateral FTAs.

21. For a comparison of labour costs in Vietnam and Cambodia, see Ishida (2010).

22. Other factors that may also play to Cambodia's advantage include its good relations with China and its early accession to the WTO. Cambodia joined the WTO in October 2004, more than two years before Vietnam.

23. In December 2001, on the occasion of CPV General Secretary Nong Duc Manh's visit to China, the two countries released a communiqué announcing that they would encourage their enterprises to cooperate on the bauxite mining project in Dak Nong province. Another joint communiqué released during Hu Jintao's visit to Vietnam in November 2006 again stressed that the two parties would "promptly discuss and implement big projects such as the bauxite mining project in Dak Nong". Vietnamese government's determination to push the project ahead and the involvement of Chinese companies therefore gave rise to criticisms that Vietnamese government had been subject to Chinese pressure, adding further momentum to public protests against the project.

24. A primary example is the strong backlash against foreign-invested projects (such as those by Taiwanese company Innovgreen) for leasing land along Vietnam's remote border areas to grow trees. Widespread concerns about security implications of these projects prompted the National Assembly's Committee on National Defence and Security to undertake investigations. The government also ordered local authorities to stop granting new land leasing contracts to foreign investors in these areas pending the review of the projects. By mid-2014, the government had also cancelled the lease of 53,000 hectares of land in these areas (Bich Ngoc 2014).

25. Due to the asymmetrical nature of Vietnam-China economic relations, especially in terms of trade, some observers suggest that "dependency" rather "interdependence" is a more proper term to describe the relationship. However, "dependency" is the not the right concept in this regard because dependency is a one way relationship, which means Vietnam is dependent on China, while China is not dependent on Vietnam. However, in fact, although Vietnam is more dependent on China, China is also dependent to some extent on Vietnam for its exports and imports. Therefore, interdependence, albeit asymmetrical, is still the right concept to describe bilateral economic relations. This is what political scientists call "complex interdependence" (see, for example, Keohane and Nye 2001).

6

The Economic Determinants of Vietnam's South China Sea Disputes with China

Introduction

Despite significant developments in bilateral relations since normalization, a number of problems still threaten to unsettle Vietnam's relations with China in the long term. The South China Sea[1] disputes stand out as the single most challenging issue. Resurfacing since the 1970s, the disputes not only remain the most serious sticking point in bilateral relations but have even pitted the two countries against each other in deadly armed confrontation on a number of occasions as well. The management and resolution (if ever) of the disputes therefore bear significant implications for the future evolution of bilateral relations.

Since 1991, South China Sea disputes between Vietnam and China have witnessed both positive and negative developments. While the two countries successfully signed a treaty on the maritime delimitation of the Gulf of Tonkin in 2000,[2] thereby removing part of the disputes, other disputes over the sovereignty of the Paracels and the Spratlys as well as maritime boundaries in the sea remain intractable. In recent years, as both countries step up their military modernization and China pursues more assertive measures in pressing its claims, the disputes tend to become even more intense and threaten to undo hitherto positive developments in other fields of the bilateral relations.

Contributing to the dynamics of the disputes is a wide range of drivers, in which geo-strategic and economic ones are the most important. While both geo-strategic and economic factors driving China's moves in the South China Sea have been extensively studied (see, for example, Buszynski 2012; Buszynski and Sazlan 2007; Fravel 2011; Garrison 2009; Leifer, 1995; Lo 1989; N.A. Owen and Schofield 2012; Storey 1999; Zhao 2008), they have not been equally examined on the part of Vietnam. So far, most of the studies on the dynamics of Vietnam's South China Sea disputes with China have focused on the geo-strategic aspect (see, for example, Butterfield 1996; Storey and Thayer 2001; Thayer 2011b; Tonnesson 2000), leaving the economic aspect largely under-examined. Specifically, there has been no major study that exclusively and comprehensively examines the role of economic factors in Vietnam's disputes with China. This gap in the literature makes it difficult to fully appreciate the dynamics of the disputes at a time when economic factors, following Vietnam's launch of economic reforms under *Doi Moi*, have been playing an increasingly important role in shaping the country's foreign policy in general and South China Sea strategy in particular.

This chapter will address this literature gap by providing an examination of economic factors' influence on the dynamics of Vietnam's South China Sea disputes with China as well as the shaping of its related strategy. As such, although several aspects of the South China Sea disputes are multilateral in nature, the chapter will strictly focus on the disputes between Vietnam and China, the two claimants that have the most overlapping claims. At the same time, as its title suggests, this chapter will mainly focus on the implications for the disputes of economic factors originated or as seen from the Vietnamese perspective. However, the role of economic factors in China's South China Sea policy will also be discussed whenever relevant to provide a more comprehensive and balanced analysis of the issue.

This chapter argues that economic factors have contributed considerably to the evolving dynamics of Vietnam's South China Sea disputes with China over the past few decades, especially since Vietnam launched its economic reform under *Doi Moi*. Vietnam's effective exploitation of the sea's resources for economic development and China's moves to counter such an effort have generated constant tensions in their relations. At the same time, Vietnam's perception of the South China Sea in terms of economic interests has also strengthened. It is therefore adopting measures to protect and advance its interests in the sea against China's expansive claims. These measures include various policies and strategies to develop a marine economy, and considerable investments in naval modernization and maritime enforcement capacity building. Meanwhile, the growing economic interdependence between Vietnam and China under *Doi Moi* is not likely to provide pacifying effects on the disputes due to the asymmetrical nature of the relationship.

The South China Sea Disputes as a Constant Irritant in Vietnam–China Relations

Vietnam's South China Sea disputes with China can be divided into two separate but related categories. The first is related to their respective sovereignty claims over the Paracels and the Spratlys. While the Paracels dispute is just between the two of them, the Spratlys row is multilateral, involving also the Philippines, Malaysia, Brunei and Taiwan. At the same time, the two also have another dispute over maritime boundaries in the sea. What makes the disputes highly relevant for future bilateral relations is that they have proved intractable, leaving the possibility of their eventual solution a matter of almost infinite uncertainty.

The intractability of the disputes is rooted in their complicated nature as well as setbacks suffered by possible settlement arrangements.

First, both countries' claims, especially those regarding the sovereignty of the two archipelagos, are mainly grounded in historical evidence that both sides present. The assessment of such evidence is undoubtedly a very complicated and painstaking enterprise. That said, it should be stressed that such an enterprise is not impossible if both sides submit themselves to a jointly agreed competent arbitration authority. While an evaluation of each country's claims as well as their basis is beyond the scope of this chapter, it is important to point out that China has always refused to seek international arbitration regarding its claims in the area.[3] Such an attitude generates an impression that China may feel the historical as well as legal bases of its claims to be weaker than those of other claimants.[4] However, given the complicated nature of the disputes that make a mutually acceptable solution through bilateral negotiation almost impossible, the use of international arbitration remains the most important, if not the only feasible measure, for reaching a permanent peaceful solution to the dispute.

Second, while international legal rules governing territorial sovereignty disputes, especially those on territorial acquisition, have been well defined and caused little controversy, those governing the arbitration of maritime claims in the case of the South China Sea disputes are less so. This is due to the different views on the status of features forming the two archipelagos and their maritime entitlements. According to Article 121 of the UN Convention on the Law of the Sea (UNCLOS) on the regime of islands, any feature in the South China Sea will be considered an island and entitled to its own exclusive economic zone (EEZ) and continental shelf only if it is "a naturally formed area of land, surrounded by water, which is above water at high tide", and can "sustain human habitation or economic life of their own". In its two submissions to the Commission on the Limits of the Continental Shelf (one jointly with Malaysia, one on its own) in early May 2009, Vietnam implicitly held the position that features in the two archipelagos do not meet criteria set out under Article 121, and thus they possess no EEZ or continental shelf of their own.

However, in its *Note Verbale* to the UN Secretary General protesting the joint submission of Malaysia and Vietnam, China stated that it "has indisputable sovereignty over the islands in the South China Sea and the adjacent waters, and enjoys sovereign rights and jurisdiction over the relevant waters as well as the seabed and subsoil thereof" (PRC Permanent Mission to the UN, 2009). In can be inferred from China's statement that China views at least a number of features in the South China Sea to be qualified islands and thus entitled to their own territorial sea, EEZ and continental shelf (Beckman 2010). Such different views derive from divergent interests of the two countries: While China wants to maximize the disputed areas to include the EEZ and continental shelf of other claimants, Vietnam seeks to minimize them, especially to protect its economic interests in its lawful EEZ and continental shelf. Obviously, such differing views can also be settled through an arbitrational process. However, as the judgments offered by such a process are likely to be based on the interpretation of

Article 121 rather than concrete evidence that can be verified on factual basis, not only China but also Vietnam may feel discouraged from taking that path for fear of being disadvantaged.

Third, the dispute is made ever more intractable by the infamous nine-dotted line that China has been using to assert its claims. As China has never clarified the meaning as well as the legal basis of the line, scholars have tried to interpret what it is that China actually wants to claim in at least four different ways:

1. it defines Chinese sovereignty over only the islands enclosed by the line (e.g., Gao 1994);
2. it claims China's sovereignty of all islands and its rights to their adjacent waters (e.g., Zou 1999);
3. it represents China's traditional maritime boundary in the South China Sea (e.g., J. Li and Li 2003); and
4. it delimits China's historic waters (e.g., Yu 2003) or the scope of China's historic rights (e.g., Zou 2001).

The *Note Verbale* mentioned above did add some light to China's claims and the meaning of the nine-dotted line, but failed to completely remove the obscurity shrouding it (Thang and Thao 2012). It asserted that China not only had "sovereignty over the islands in the South China Sea and the adjacent waters", but also enjoyed "sovereign rights and jurisdiction over the relevant waters". The terms "adjacent waters" and "relevant waters" are rather ambiguous, leaving one to wonder whether these waters correspond to those defined under the UNCLOS, or whether they refer to the entire water column enclosed by the nine-dotted line. As the nine-dotted line cuts deep into Vietnam's EEZ and continental shelf, the ambiguity around its meaning makes it difficult even to define clearly the disputed areas, thereby further straining efforts to manage and settle the dispute.[5]

The unresolved claims have undergone different phases of actual development over the last four decades, ranging from joint efforts of peaceful dispute management to lethal armed confrontations. The worst episode of the disputes took place before bilateral normalization in 1991, when two brief armed clashes actually took place. The first was in February 1974 when China invaded the southwestern (Crescent) group of the Paracels then held by South Vietnamese forces.[6] Since then, Vietnam has continuously confirmed its undisputable sovereignty of the Paracels and requested China to open negotiation to peacefully resolve the dispute, to which China has persistently turned a deaf ear. The second incident took place in the Spratlys fourteen years later. On 14 March 1988, Chinese warships opened fire on three Vietnamese naval ships and a group of mostly unarmed combat engineers who were trying to build new structures on the Johnson South Reef. The clash claimed sixty-four Vietnamese lives and resulted in the sinking of two Vietnamese ships and serious damage to the third.[7] The clash was also the most violent episode in a campaign that China started in late 1987 to establish for the first time a physical presence in the Spratlys. The timing of both incidents shows that China intentionally exploited Vietnam's weaknesses of internal division in 1974 and international isolation in 1988 to advance its strategic interests in the South China Sea.

Since bilateral normalization in 1991, tensions between the two countries over the South China Sea have been fluctuating and efforts to better manage the disputes have produced mixed results. In October 1992 and February 1993, the two sides conducted two rounds of negotiation that resulted in the 19 October 1993 agreement on fundamental principles governing the solution of border and territorial issues between the two countries. Following the agreement, the two sides started negotiations on the delimitation of the Tonkin Gulf and, separately, on the demarcation of their land border. After seven rounds of negotiation at the governmental level and eighteen rounds of negotiations at joint working group level, plus nearly twenty other non-official meetings over seven years, the agreement on the delimitation of the Tonkin Gulf was signed in Beijing on 25 December 2000 (Thao 2005, p. 28). Another agreement on fishery cooperation in the Gulf was also signed at the same time after only eight months of negotiation. Both agreements came into force in 2004 and have permanently settled one of the disputes between the two countries.

Other disputes, however, remain intractable, and efforts for resolving them have witnessed little progress. The bilateral expert-level meetings on "maritime issues" launched in November 1995 were cancelled in 2006 after eleven rounds due to lack of progress.[8] One of the main reasons was the two countries' disagreement on the meeting agenda. Vietnam had insisted on the inclusion of the Paracels, which China had consistently refused to do (Thao and Amer 2007, p. 313). Before the meetings were cancelled, the two sides launched another round of negotiations in January 2006 on the delimitation of the sea area beyond the mouth of the Tonkin Gulf (BBC 2006). However, they quickly ran into stalemate again. While Vietnam preferred delimitation of the sea area before the two countries could undertake joint development, China insisted on the opposite.

In August 2009, in an effort to break the stalemate, the two sides agreed to start negotiating on basic principles guiding the settlement of sea issues. This followed a meeting between Vietnamese Deputy Foreign Minister Ho Xuan Son and his Chinese counterpart Wu Dawei in Hanoi. The negotiation officially started in early 2010. After seven rounds of negotiation at expert level and a few other rounds at deputy foreign minister level, an agreement finally took shape and was signed on 11 October 2011 on the occasion of CPV General Secretary Nguyen Phu Trong's official visit to Beijing.[9] Under the agreement, the bilateral expert-level meetings on "maritime issues" have been revived in a new format which consists of two simultaneous series of meetings, one on the delimitation and joint development of the sea area beyond the mouth of the Tonkin Gulf,[10] and the other on bilateral cooperation in "less sensitive" fields in the South China Sea.[11]

This agreement is reminiscent of the 19 October 1993 agreement on fundamental principles governing the solution of border and territorial issues, which ultimately resulted in the conclusion of two bilateral treaties on land border demarcation and Tonkin Gulf delimitation in 1999 and 2000, respectively. The agreement therefore raised hopes that similar positive results would ultimately be achieved regarding remaining maritime disputes. However, given the much more complex nature of these, especially due to the actual occupation of the two archipelagos, the possibility of a permanent solution is highly unlikely in the near to mid-term future.

While bilateral efforts have witnessed slow progress, multilateral efforts have not produced any significant result either. The most significant multilateral tool for the two sides to manage their disputes has been the 2002 ASEAN–China Declaration on the Conduct of Parties in the South China Sea (DOC). The DOC, as a non-binding political document, has shown many weaknesses in maintaining stability and reducing tension between claimant parties.[12] The overdue Code of Conduct of Parties in the South China Sea (COC), which is expected to be more legally binding than the DOC, has failed to take shape so far despite the enormous effort invested by ASEAN states, especially Vietnam and the Philippines.[13] This failure is mainly due to China's reluctance to be constrained by such an instrument. What should also be noted is that even when a COC is eventually established, it is in essence just a tool to manage the disputes, not to settle them. As long as the disputes persist, relations between claimant states in general and between Vietnam and China in particular, will continue to be tense.

Since normalization in 1991, the South China Sea disputes have in fact made bilateral relations "warm outside but cold inside". Various incidents have happened due to the two sides' conflicting claims in the sea. The most recent notable incidents include the cutting of a Vietnamese seismic survey ship's cable by Chinese maritime surveillance vessels within Vietnam's EEZ in May 2011, China's offering of nine blocks within Vietnam's EEZ to international bidders in June 2012, China's placement of the giant oil rig *Haiyang Shiyou 981* in Vietnam's EEZ in May 2014, and China's construction of artificial islands in the Spratlys since 2014. Such incidents have generated incessant tensions between the two countries.

For example, following the cable cutting incident, anti-China demonstrations broke out in Hanoi on Sundays over eleven consecutive weeks in the summer of 2011. Vietnamese leaders also spoke strongly against China's aggressive actions. While President Nguyen Minh Triet stated that "we are ready to dedicate all to defend our native villages and defend sea and island sovereignty", Prime Minister Nguyen Tan Dung, in an address to the National Assembly, also openly denounced China's use of force to seize the Paracels from South Vietnam in 1974, the first time a Vietnamese high-ranking leader had ever done so (Associated Press 2011). Meanwhile, incidents with Vietnam in the South China Sea have also generated hostile responses from China. For example, in March 2013, the *Global Times* ran an op-ed stating that "the Philippines and Vietnam would face more troubles if they choose to seek fierce confrontation with China" (*Global Times* 2013).

One useful way to see how constant the South China Sea disputes present themselves as an irritant to bilateral relations is to look at statements issued by the Vietnamese MOFA spokesperson. For example, although 2012 was a relatively calm year for the South China Sea, the bilateral disputes still featured prominently in twenty out of forty-nine press releases and statements of the MOFA spokesperson throughout the year.[14] These statements addressed a multitude of incidents and problems related to the disputes, ranging from protesting China's unilateral fishing moratorium and seizure of Vietnamese fishing boats, condemning Chinese offer of blocks within Vietnam's EEZ to international bidding, to denouncing various activities China conducted with regards to the two archipelagos. If the frequency of the South China Sea disputes being featured in the Vietnamese MOFA spokesperson is to be used as a barometer for Vietnam–China relations, there will be no doubt that the disputes are the most important factor shaping the mood for the relations, and that the mood, at least over the last five years, has been going from bad to worse.

Vietnam's South China Sea Disputes with China: Geo-strategic vs. Economic Drivers

Vietnam's South China Sea disputes with China have been driven by both geo-strategic and economic factors. As both interests are inextricably intertwined, it is difficult to determine which one is more important as a driver of Vietnam's strategy regarding the disputes. A careful examination of both factors, however, shows that while geo-strategic interests have long been fundamental in Vietnam's view of the South China Sea, it is only in recent decades that economic considerations have emerged as an increasingly important determinant of Vietnam's strategic thinking regarding the sea as well as its disputes with China.

Vietnam's traditional geo-strategic view of the South China Sea has been framed by its particular geographical features. With more than 3,200 kilometres of coastline stretching along the South China Sea and the Gulf of Thailand, Vietnam is highly vulnerable to seaborne invasions. In the past, Chinese dynasties invaded Vietnam from the sea on several occasions, such as in the years 938, 1285 and 1287. A more recent historical example that shows the importance of the sea to Vietnam's defence was the invasion by France, which started with a seaborne attack on Da Nang in 1858. Moreover, in light of the traditional power asymmetry between the two countries, should Vietnam lose its control of the South China Sea to China, Vietnam's ability to resist a military invasion from its northern neighbour would be further undermined. In other words, securing a favourable foothold in the South China Sea will help Vietnam constrain China's superior military advantage, thereby mitigating the adverse effects of the power asymmetry between the two countries on its national security.

Meanwhile, the control of the Paracels and the Spratlys is also geo-strategically important for Vietnam. As the South China Sea is the only gateway for Vietnam to access international maritime trade routes in both the Pacific and Indian oceans, if Vietnam lost control of the two archipelagos, its vital sea lanes of communication would be subject to serious threats as its enemy might use forces on and around the two archipelagos to impose a naval blockade on the country. Moreover, the two archipelagos, especially the Spratlys, are strategically vital for Vietnam's essential military assets, such as Cam Ranh Port and the submarine base there. If Vietnam lost control over the Spratlys and the surrounding waters, for example, the safety and accessibility of Cam Ranh Port as well as the manoeuvrability of its submarine fleet would be significantly constrained.

In sum, the South China Sea's geo-strategic importance for Vietnam is shaped by its particular geographical conditions, and to a lesser extent, its historical experience. As geographical features are permanent, Vietnam's geo-strategic perception of the South China Sea has been long-established. Accordingly, the country's traditional perception of the sea has been mainly defined by the recognition of its importance for national defence. On the contrary, from a historical perspective, Vietnam's traditional perception of the sea in economic terms seems to have been much less pronounced. This argument is substantiated by a number of observations.

First, in the past, Vietnam's traditional economic activities were mainly restricted to the mainland with wet rice agriculture being the most important source of livelihood for the people. As argued in Chapter 2, although maritime foreign trade used to blossom in Vietnam during certain historical periods, Vietnamese feudal economy was mainly autarkic and the small scale of maritime foreign trade could hardly turn it into a significant source of wealth for the country. Second, as maritime disputes with China only emerged since the early twentieth century, Vietnam for a long time had taken its uncontested maritime economic benefits from the South China Sea for granted. Third, after maritime disputes over the sea became more visible, Vietnam, at least until the 1970s, was mired in its own domestic problems, such as seeking independence and fighting for national unification. Such historical conditions prevented Vietnam from pursuing economic development and diverted its attention away from the South China Sea's economic resources. The situation also caused its disputes with foreign countries over the sea to remain a matter of relatively low priority for an extended period of time.

Nevertheless, after Vietnam gradually rose out of domestic turmoil and started focusing on its economic reform in the 1980s, its perception of the South China Sea as well as the two archipelagos in economic terms began to heighten. The extraction of oil and gas from the South China Sea, for example, has contributed significantly to Vietnam's economic development and export performance ever since. Its demand for living resources from the sea has also grown. Other sea-related industries, such as shipbuilding, maritime transport and tourism, have also enjoyed fast expansion and become important to the economy. Vietnam's increased awareness of the sea's economic resources has therefore made the adoption of proper policies to exploit and protect them a matter of strategic importance.

Such tendency could be traced back to the early 1990s. On 6 May 1993, for example, the CPV Politburo adopted Resolution no. 03-NQ/TW entitled "On a number of tasks for developing the marine economy in the forthcoming years". The Resolution stated that "becoming a strong marine economy is a strategic goal derived from the objective demands and conditions of the cause of building and defending the Vietnamese Fatherland" (CPV 2007*b*, p. 576). The Resolution also set guidelines for the development of sea-related industries, especially oil and gas and fishery. Since then, a number of other official documents and policies on the issue have been released. The most important one has been the "Vietnam Maritime Strategy toward the Year 2020" adopted by the CPV Central Committee in February 2007. As the culmination of Vietnam's growing awareness of the South China Sea's importance to its economic well-being, the Strategy set the target that sea-related economic activities should account for 53–55 per cent of Vietnam's GDP and 55–60 per cent of its exports by 2020 (CPV 2007*a*).

In June 2012, Vietnam's National Assembly also passed the Sea Law of Vietnam. The law confirms Vietnam's sovereignty over its islands and archipelagos, including the Paracels and the Spratlys, as well as its sovereignty, sovereign rights and jurisdiction over its South China Sea waters in accordance with the UNCLOS. The law also has a section dedicated to marine economic development (Vietnam National Assembly 2012). All this testifies to the fact that Vietnam is actively consolidating its maritime policy and legal framework while pursuing ambitious plans to protect and advance its economic interests in the South China Sea.

The above comparative analysis of geo-strategic versus economic drivers of Vietnam's South China Sea disputes with China shows that while the former are long established, the latter have gained momentum only after Vietnam started its economic reform under *Doi Moi*. Nevertheless, economic drivers are now playing a no less significant role in shaping Vietnam's perception of and strategy towards the South China Sea. Therefore, in order to better understand the evolving dynamics of Vietnam's maritime disputes with China, it is important to investigate how economic drivers are contributing to Vietnam's South China Sea strategy and the resultant course of action it is undertaking, as well as evaluate their implications for future prospects of the disputes.

Vietnam's Economic Development and Implications for South China Sea Disputes

Since the late 1980s, Vietnam's reliance on the South China Sea for its economic development has been increasing. In particular, the sea plays a vital role in the development of Vietnam's oil and gas and fishery industries, which in turn help boost the country's economic growth under *Doi Moi* significantly. The current section therefore uses these two key industries as case studies to examine the importance of the sea to the country's economic well-being and explain why Vietnam is taking measures to protect its interests there. The section will also shed light on how Vietnam's economic considerations have added to growing bilateral rivalry over the sea during recent decades.

Oil and Gas Industry

Soon after the fall of Saigon, the CPV Politburo issued Resolution no. 244 NQ/TW dated 9 August 1975 guiding the promotion of oil and gas exploration in the whole country. The Resolution identified the continental shelf off the southern coast along with the Tonkin Gulf as the most important areas for exploration efforts (CPV 2004, p. 285). The southern continental shelf was particularly the top target as documents retrieved from the Saigon regime showed that there was a great potential for oil and gas there.[15] In April 1978, PetroVietnam signed its first Production Sharing Contracts with foreign partners and in 1979, the first exploration drills were conducted in the Nam Con Son basin on the southern continental shelf. However, it was not until 24 May 1984 that oil of commercial value was discovered at Bach Ho (White Tiger) field. Two years later, production began in the field in June 1986, providing Vietnam with its first barrels of crude oil from the South China Sea (PetroVietnam 2011a, pp. 281–86).

After this important event, Vietnam began to lay more emphasis on the oil and gas industry. In July 1988, the CPV Politburo passed Resolution no. 15-NQ/TW providing guidelines for the development of the industry. Based on the resolution, PetroVietnam adopted in 1989 a development strategy until 2000. Both the resolution and the strategy stated that Vietnam would strive to "step by step turn oil and gas into an important technical and economic industry in the [country's] economic development strategy for the coming decades" (PetroVietnam 2011a, p. 206). The "Strategy for socio-economic stabilization and development until 2000" adopted by the CPV's seventh congress in 1991 also emphasized the importance of the industry. According to the strategy, Vietnam would "actively promote cooperation with foreign countries to explore, exploit and process oil and gas" (CPV 2007c, p. 164). One year later, the 1993 Petroleum Law was adopted by the National Assembly, providing for the first time a comprehensive legal framework for the development of the industry.

Against this backdrop, Vietnam's oil and gas production developed quickly and soon became a major source of wealth for the country, contributing greatly to its socio-economic development. By the early 2010s, PetroVietnam had become Vietnam's biggest conglomerate, accounting for about 20 per cent of the country's GDP and generating up to 25–30 per cent of the government's annual revenue (PetroVietnam 2012, p. 3). By September 2009, PetroVietnam's accumulated production had reached 300 million tons of oil equivalent, most of which came from the South China Sea (PetroVietnam 2011b, p. 45).

In recent years, South China Sea oil and gas have become even more important to the country as continued economic development has caused its energy demand to soar. For example, from 2001 to 2011, Vietnam's oil consumption increased by 6.4 per cent annually, reaching 16.5 million tons in 2011 (BP 2012, p. 11). However, Vietnam's recent annual oil production has generally been in decline, falling from peak production of 20.1 million tons in 2004 down to 15.2 million tons in 2011 before rising again to 17.4 million tons in 2014 (GSO 2008, p. 415; 2012, p. 463; *Nguoi Lao Dong* 2015). As a consequence, Vietnam became a net oil importer in 2008 (GSO 2010, pp. 459, 466).[16] This has raised Vietnam's concern for energy security and led to PetroVietnam's both increased investment in foreign oil fields[17] and intensified exploration and exploitation activities within Vietnam's continental shelf. For example, by 2010, PetroVietnam had entered into twenty-seven contracts over foreign oil fields, nineteen of which were signed from 2007 to 2010 (PetroVietnam 2011b, pp. 363–70). At the same time, in addition to expanding its activities on the southern and northern continental shelf, PetroVietnam has also been engaging foreign partners since 2006 to explore for oil and gas in the Phu Khanh basin off the central part of the country.

As a consequent, China has shown its resentment against Vietnam's active exploitation of hydrocarbon resources in the South China Sea. In December 2012, for example, the *Global Times* ran an editorial accusing Vietnam of "stealing resources" by "constantly seeking to expand offshore oil and gas businesses within the nine-dash line" (*Global Times* 2012). As China's energy demand surged dramatically due to its fast economic development,[18] China persistently seeks to tap hydrocarbon resources of the South China Sea, for which it has very optimistic reserve estimates.[19] Accordingly, China has long proposed the formula of "shelving disputes for joint development" in contested areas. Vietnam, however, has consistently rejected such proposals.[20] The main reason is that China's proposals target Vietnam's lawful Exclusive Economic Zone (EEZ) and continental shelf, which Vietnam does not view as disputed areas (Thao 2001, p. 110).

Unable to persuade Vietnam into joint development projects in the South China Sea, China has resorted to a number of "low intensity actions to increase the risks of Vietnam's oil and gas exploration efforts within the nine-dash line," and to cause Vietnam to realize that "this exploration is only bringing itself trouble" (*Global Times* 2012). The most serious incident of this nature was the cable cutting of PetroVietnam's seismic survey ship *Binh Minh 02* by China's maritime surveillance vessels on 26 May 2011. The *Binh Minh 02* was then operating in Block 148 within Vietnam's EEZ. Another similar incident happened only two weeks later on 9 June 2011 when a Chinese fishing trawler supported by two Chinese fishery patrol vessels cut the cable of the *Viking II*, which was chartered by PetroVietnam to undertake seismic surveys in Block 136/03 further south. The two incidents, as mentioned in the first section, caused an angry response from Vietnam and sent bilateral relations to their lowest ebb in years.[21]

Facing China's rising aggressiveness, Vietnam chose to "name and shame" China publicly in international forums, while actively engaging partners from various countries in its oil exploration and exploitation efforts. From 1988 to the end of 2010, PetroVietnam signed ninety-nine contracts with various partners from different countries, including the United States, Russia, the United Kingdom, India, Canada, South Korea, Malaysia, and Australia.[22] Vietnam obviously sought to enlist support from these countries in protecting their legitimate interests in Vietnam, thereby countering against China's undue pressures. On its part, China has long used its economic clout to coerce a number of oil companies to abandon their businesses in Vietnam. Leaked cables from the U.S. embassy in Hanoi reported a campaign since 2006 in which China routinely pressured oil companies, such as Exxon Mobil, BP, Chevron and Petronas, to cancel oil exploration deals with Vietnam. In July 2008, for example, Chinese diplomats repeatedly threatened Exxon Mobil that if it did not cancel deals with Vietnam, it might face punishment against its businesses in China. Although Exxon did not back down, a number of other companies did. The cable confirmed that by July 2007 four U.S. and eight foreign companies faced similar threats from China, and about five deals were suspended or cancelled (U.S. Embassy in Hanoi 2009a). In response, Vietnam vowed that it would do its best to protect the operation of foreign oil companies in its waters.

Another source of bilateral tension arose from Vietnam's efforts to prevent China from exploring for oil and gas in its waters. For example, soon after bilateral normalization, the China National Offshore Oil Corporation (CNOOC) signed an agreement with Crestone Energy Corporation to conduct exploration in Vietnam's Tu Chinh (Wan'an Bei in Chinese) basin in May 1992 (Thayer 1994a, pp. 524–25). Vietnam fiercely protested the move and a prolonged exchange of claims and counterclaims between the two countries ensued. While China contended that the Tu Chinh area was part of the disputed Spratlys, Vietnam stated that the basin was not subject to disputes as it was situated completely within Vietnam's EEZ and continental shelf and in no way related to the Spratlys and adjacent waters (Amer 1997, pp. 91–93).[23] Tensions between the two over the Crestone contract lingered on at least until September 1998 when China reported that Crestone and China were continuing their survey of the Spratlys and Tu Chinh area (Zou 2006, pp. 88–89).

In addition, bilateral tensions have also built up around the CNOOC's offer of blocks that lie within Vietnam's EEZ in the South China Sea to international bidders. For example, China opened nine such blocks to international bidding in June 2012 (Ma and Hookway 2012). Due to Vietnam's firm protest as well as the vague legal basis of China's offer, oil companies have not shown interest in the offer. This is likely the reason why China decided to conduct its own exploration activities in Vietnam's waters several times in the past.

In March 1997, China dispatched the Kantan-3 floating oil platform to drill in Vietnam's Block 113 off Thua Thien-Hue province. The oil platform was also involved in a similar incident in the same area in late 2004. In both cases, China had to withdraw the platform after Vietnam issued diplomatic protests. However, in some other cases, Vietnam had to resort to more effective measures. For example, in December 1997, Vietnam had to dispatch its naval ships to escort away China's Exploration Ship No. 8 and two supply ships that intended to undertake exploration in the Tu Chinh area (Zou 2006, p. 88).

In a more serious incident that started in May 2014, China deployed the giant floating oil rig *Haiyang Shiyou 981* well within Vietnam's lawful EEZ, just 120 nautical miles from its maritime baseline, for an exploratory mission. At the same time, China acted aggressively by dispatching more than eighty vessels from different forces, including naval warships, to the scene to protect the rig and to intimidate the Vietnamese vessels. Chinese vessels reportedly rammed and fired water cannons at Vietnamese ships (see, for example, Linh and Martina 2014; Perlez and Gladstone 2014). The crisis also sparked anti-Chinese riots in Vietnam and sent bilateral relations to the lowest ebb since normalization.

Facing growing Chinese aggression in the South China Sea, Vietnam has been increasing investments in upgrading the capabilities of the Vietnam People's Navy (VPN) as well as the Vietnam Coast Guard (VCG).[24] As the involvement of naval ships may lead to a higher possibility of armed clash, the VCG is set to play a more important role in protecting Vietnam's resources in its EEZ and continental shelf.

Established in 1998 as a branch of the Navy, the VCG became an independent force under the Ministry of Defence in 2008 and by 2012 had received some significant investments, including two Damen offshore patrol vessels of 2,500-ton displacement and three CASA C-212 aircrafts. In an interview in 2011, VCG Commander Lieut. Gen. Pham Duc Linh confirmed that the VCG would work closely with the VPN and PetroVietnam to protect the country's oil and gas exploration activities and "resolutely" prevent "foreign countries" (read: China) from installing drilling rigs in the country's waters (Thanh Huy, 2011). As China steps up its effort to extract oil and gas in the South China Sea and Vietnam is getting geared up to protect its resources, it is very likely that tensions between the two over the South China Sea disputes will keep escalating in the foreseeable future.

Fisheries

Similar to the oil and gas industry, fisheries have played an important role in Vietnam's socio-economic development under *Doi Moi*. In 2011, the industry's production reached 5.2 million tons and accounted for 6.34 per cent of the country's GDP. The industry also provided 4.5 million jobs to the country's workforce and helped lift thousands of people out of poverty (Directorate of Fisheries 2012, pp. 12, 40). Fishery products are also a major export of Vietnam. In 2010, for example, the industry contributed US$5.1 billion to Vietnam's export turnover, turning the country into the world's fourth largest exporter of fishery commodities only after China, Norway, and Thailand (FAO 2012, p. 45).

Vietnam's fishery industry has benefited greatly from the South China Sea, which is a rich fishing ground with the highest species diversity in the world (Franckx 2012, p. 734). In 2013, Vietnam's capture fishery production reached 2.8 million tons, of which 2.6 million tons came from the South China Sea (GSO 2015, p. 161). At the same time, offshore fishing is becoming increasingly important for the country. For example, the share of offshore fishing in the country's marine capture production increased from 31.8 per cent in 2001 to reach 49.4 per cent in 2010 (Directorate of Fisheries 2012, p. 22). As such, there is little doubt that offshore fishing will soon replace near-shore fishing to become Vietnam's key source of marine capture production.

Two major reasons have accounted for this particular trend. First, Vietnam's near-shore fish stocks are being either fully exploited or overexploited, causing its production to increase very slowly at an average rate of 1.1 per cent per annum for the 2001–10 period. Meanwhile, offshore production increased 10.3 per cent annually during the same period, not only because Vietnam's offshore fishing grounds in the South China Sea had not been fully exploited but also due to the migratory pattern of fish stocks in the Tonkin Gulf (Directorate of Fisheries 2012, pp. 22–23).[25] Second, like China, Vietnam has always considered the active operation of its offshore fishing fleet, especially around the Paracels and the Spratlys, as a key measure to defend its sovereignty over the two archipelagos. This has been confirmed in various official documents regarding the country's fishery industry. One of the most recent examples is the "Master Plan for Developing Vietnam's Fishery Industry until 2020, with a Vision to 2030". Accordingly, the Plan stresses offshore fishing as a measure to "monitor activities at sea", "prevent foreign ships from intruding Vietnam's waters", and "implement tasks regarding sea and islands security and defence" (Directorate of Fisheries 2012, p. 103). Vietnam has therefore invested considerably in upgrading the capacity of its offshore fishing fleet.

In effect, Vietnam started promoting the development of offshore fishery in the early 1990s. The "Strategy for Socio-Economic Stabilization and Development until 2000" adopted by the CPV in 1991 was the party's first major official document to stress the importance of "developing fishing fleets to exploit offshore areas" (CPV 2007c, p. 162). Two years later, Politburo's Resolution no. 03-NQ/TW specifically set the target of increasing the share of offshore fishing in the country's total marine capture production (CPV 2007b, p. 580). Such policy guidelines were soon translated into concrete measures.

In April 1997, Vietnam launched the Program on Offshore Fishing (*Chuong trinh danh bat xa bo*) and established an inter-ministerial steering committee to monitor its implementation. The key mission of the Program was to provide financial assistance for fishermen to build high-capacity offshore fishing boats. Under the program, by 2004, the government had disbursed about 1,400 billion dongs in preferential credits for fishermen in twenty-nine selected provinces, with which about 1,300 high-capacity boats had been built or upgraded. Although the Program was later cancelled due to poor implementation, it did contribute to Vietnam's growing fleet of offshore fishing boats. From

2001 to 2010, for example, the number of fishing boats with the capacity of 90HP upwards suitable for offshore fishing quadrupled from 6,005 to 24,970 (Directorate of Fisheries 2012, p. 20). Vietnam set the target of increasing the number to 28,000 by 2020. Its offshore capture production by then is also planned to reach 1.4 million tons, accounting for about 64 per cent of its total marine capture production (Directorate of Fisheries 2012, p. 58).

The development of Vietnam's marine capture capacity, especially the growth of its offshore fishing fleet, has generated some important implications for Vietnam's South China Sea disputes with China.

First, competition between Vietnam and China over living resources in the sea, including contested areas, will intensify. While Vietnam's offshore fishing fleet grows, China has also invested heavily in promoting its offshore fishing capacity in the sea. For example, in May 2012, China launched and dispatched the *Hainan Baosha* 001, a 32,000-ton seafood-processing ship, along with three supporting vessels, to the South China Sea. The fleet was said to help China both better exploit fishery resources and enhance its "maritime enforcement capability" (Tianran 2012). Second, the intensified competition is likely to cause both sides to harden their respective positions regarding the disputes. China, in particular, will likely maintain its nine-dotted line claim at the most, or the view that certain disputed features in the South China Sea are qualified islands at the least, in order to maximize its possible access to the sea's living as well as non-living resources. Third, as the offshore fishing capacity of both sides increases, confrontations between each side's maritime enforcement agencies and fishermen of the other side are likely to become more frequent. This will undoubtedly generate further tensions between the two disputants in the future.

In fact, over the past decade, incidents involving fishing boats of both sides have already been a major source of friction between the two countries. The most violent incident happened on 8 January 2005 when Chinese coast guards killed nine Vietnamese fishermen while they were fishing in Vietnamese waters in the Tonkin Gulf.[26] Other incidents, in which China drove off or seized Vietnamese fishermen fishing around the Paracels, have occurred more often. For example, from 2005 to 2010, China seized 63 fishing boats and 725 fishermen from Quang Ngai province alone (BBC 2010*a*). Apart from Vietnam's greater offshore fishing capacity, the number of seizures also tends to rise due to the increasingly active operation of Chinese maritime enforcement agencies, especially around the Paracels, as well as China's unilateral imposition of annual fishing moratorium in the South China Sea since 1999, which Vietnam has consistently protested (Phan Le 2012).

For its part, Vietnam has taken measures to deal with the situation. For example, as mentioned above, Vietnam has invested in upgrading the VCG's capacity. One of the key responsibilities of the VCG is to protect Vietnamese fishermen and preventing foreign fishing boats from illegally intruding into Vietnamese waters. As the Paracels is where many Vietnamese fishing boats have been captured or harassed, there is a possibility that in the future, the VCG may send its vessels to the area to protect Vietnamese fishermen and to exercise Vietnam's sovereignty over the archipelago. In January 2013, Vietnam also established the Vietnam Fisheries Resources Surveillance (VFRS) under the Directorate of Fisheries. There have been plans for the VFRS to build four 3,000 HP patrol vessels and 18 other vessels of smaller capacity (The Dung 2012). Apart from maintaining the sustainability of Vietnam's marine living resources, the VFRS is also tasked with suppressing foreign boats illegally fishing in Vietnamese waters. A few years back, although hundreds of Chinese fishing boats were illegally operating in Vietnamese waters on a daily basis, Vietnam reacted merely by instructing them to leave its waters (BBC 2010b). However, the proliferation and enhanced capacity of Vietnam's maritime enforcement agencies will likely cause the number of Chinese fishing boats seized or fined to increase. Bilateral tensions over living resources in the South China Sea are therefore also due to intensify in the future.

The Pacifying Effects of Economic Interdependence?

The above section has found that Vietnam's economic development under *Doi Moi*, especially the growth of its oil and gas and fishery industries, has deepened Vietnam's economic interests in the South China Sea and tended to add tensions to its disputes with China. At the same time, there are other economic factors stemming from Vietnam's pursuit of *Doi Moi* that may work to balance against such a negative trend. At least on the surface, the most notable one is the growing economic interdependence between the two countries. An important question therefore merits further examination: How significant are the pacifying effects that the growing economic interdependence may generate on bilateral relations?

As examined in Chapter 5, the economic interdependence between Vietnam and China has been growing continuously over the past two decades. This particular trend, according to liberal peace theory, may hold significant implications for future bilateral relations. A thread in the theory's literature, for example, argues that economic interdependence tends to discourage countries from engaging in armed conflicts with each other for fear of losing the welfare gains associated with the economic relationship, especially in terms of trade and investment. In the same vein, liberal peace theorists believe that the convergent national interests through the interdependent relationship will help improve communication and foster cooperation between countries, through which peace rather than conflict will thrive (see, e.g., Domke 1988; Gartzke et al. 2001; Gasiorowski and Polachek 1982; Maoz, 2009; Oneal et al. 1996; Oneal and Ray 1997; Oneal and Russett 1997; Polachek 1980, 1992; Polachek and McDonald 1992). Accordingly, the theory suggests that the growing economic interdependence between Vietnam and China will prevent them from pushing their South China Sea disputes to the point of an armed conflict in the future.

However, critics of the liberal peace theory argue otherwise.[27] They contend that the pacifying effects (if any) of economic interdependence are also conditioned by other independent variables, such as the dyad's joint democracy score, their geographical proximity, the closeness of their political ties, the symmetry of their interdependence, or their relative capabilities, which are sometimes even more important than the interdependence itself.[28] Barbieri (1996, p. 44) also found that "it is not interdependence itself that determines the impact on interstate relations, but some characteristic of the type of interdependence present in the relationship".

Therefore, while some critics of the liberal peace theory believe that economic interdependence is not relevant to peace, some contend that it even increases the probability of conflict. In particular, they have pointed to the fact that interdependence tends to, among other things, cultivate asymmetric dependence between the countries in question. The less dependent one may take advantage of its position to elicit economic and/or political concessions from the more dependent, which tends to damage their overall relations (Gasiorowski 1986;

Keohane and Nye 1973). The situation is worse for the more dependent states if structural linkages make them unable to change their trade patterns, further subjecting themselves to manipulation. Therefore, although costs are unavoidable in all economic relationships, the negative consequences of interdependence are more pronounced in asymmetrical ones (Cooper 1968).

In the case of Vietnam and China, it is undeniable that mutual benefits brought about by deepened economic exchanges and growing interdependence have provided an important common ground for the two countries to promote cooperation. Tensions over South China Sea disputes notwithstanding, improvements in overall bilateral relations, as analysed in Chapter 4, have been remarkable. Economic cooperation, in particular, has been an essential pillar of overall bilateral ties since normalization. Nevertheless, whether the mutual benefits derived from the growing economic interdependence are significant enough to constrain both countries from pursuing aggressive actions against each other in the South China Sea remains uncertain. The uncertainty is mainly rooted in the heavily asymmetrical nature of the relationship.

First, in terms of direct investment, by 2013, Vietnamese companies had invested US$16 million in China, only a tiny fraction of Chinese investment in Vietnam, which reached US$7.5 billion of registered capital by the same time (GSO 2014b). One may argue that if another armed conflict were to break out between the two over the South China Sea, it would very likely be the much more powerful China rather than the weaker Vietnam that started the hostility. Therefore, China's greater investment in Vietnam may not necessarily be a bad thing, as it may constrain China from pursuing such an action for fear of putting its investments in Vietnam at risk. However, this logic may not apply for two major reasons. On the one hand, Vietnam is bound by domestic and international legal commitments to protect foreign investments. It will not be in the country's interest to expropriate Chinese investments in case of worsening bilateral relations as such a move will irrevocably damage its investment environment and, ultimately, its economic performance. On the other hand, and more importantly, although China's investments in Vietnam have grown at a considerable rate in recent years, they remain too modest to influence both countries' policymakers. By the end of 2013, while China accounted for 3.23 per cent of total registered FDI into Vietnam, Vietnam had absorbed only 1.18 per cent of China's accumulative outward FDI stock (UNCTAD 2015). For these reasons, bilateral investments are not likely to have a major impact on China's South China Sea calculations vis-à-vis Vietnam.

Second, in terms of trade, Vietnam is much more dependent on China than China is on Vietnam. As shown in Table 6.1, from 2001 to 2013, the share of trade with China increased from 9.7 to 19 per cent of Vietnam's total, while the share of trade with Vietnam only grew from 0.6 to 1.2 per cent of China's total. The asymmetry in the bilateral trade structure therefore tended to expand in China's favour, as the difference between the shares of the two-way trade in each country's total increased from 9.1 to 17.8 per cent. Given the fact that China's GDP is about fifty-five times larger than that of Vietnam,[29] the asymmetrical bilateral trade structure is not surprising. However, the asymmetry is aggravated by Vietnam's widening trade deficit with China, which increased from US$189 million in 2001 to US$23.7 billion in 2013 (see Figure 5.1 for more details). Such an unbalanced trade structure causes Vietnam to be even more trade-dependent on China, especially in terms of imports. In 2013, for example, Vietnam's imports from China accounted for 28 per cent of Vietnam's total imports but only 1.7 per cent of China's total exports. The situation therefore subjects Vietnam to further economic vulnerabilities and has become more of a national security issue for the country as any possible disruption of bilateral trade will cause far greater damage to Vietnam than China.

The above analysis shows that although growing economic interdependence as well as the associated mutual benefits has been an important driver of bilateral cooperation, its pacifying effects on Vietnam's relations with China are heavily constrained by the asymmetrical nature of the relationship. Therefore, economic interdependence is not going to help Vietnam constrain China from aggressive actions in the South China Sea. To the contrary, in extreme cases, there is a possibility that China might even take advantage of Vietnam's trade dependence on itself to elicit concessions regarding the South China Sea disputes. This is particularly worrisome for Vietnam as China has recently shown its willingness to use economic power as a tool of coercion in territorial disputes. Following a spat in the South China Sea in early 2012, for example, China disrupted tourist

TABLE 6.1
The Asymmetrical Vietnam–China Trade Structure (2001–11)

Year	Total Two-way Trade (US$ billion)	Vietnam's Total Trade (US$ billion)	Share of Vietnam's Total Trade (%)	China's Total Trade (US$ billion)	Share of China's Total Trade (%)
2001	3.0	31.2	9.7	509.8	0.6
2003	5.0	45.4	11.1	851.2	0.6
2005	9.1	69.2	13.2	1,422.1	0.6
2007	16.4	111.3	14.7	2,173.8	0.8
2009	20.8	127.0	16.4	2,205.9	0.9
2011	35.7	203.7	17.5	3,640.7	1.0
2013	50.2	264.1	19	4,160	1.2

Source: GSO (2006*b*, 2008, 2012, 2014*a*); Global Trade Atlas, cited in Morrison (2012, p. 18); Xinhua (2014).

exchanges and halted its importation of bananas from the Philippines to mount pressure on the latter (Associated Press 2012). In 2010, China also briefly stopped exports of rare earth elements to Japan following a collision between a Chinese trawler and two Japanese Coast Guard vessels near the Senkaku/Diaoyu islands (*The Telegraph* 2010). Such precedents have raised concerns among Vietnamese policymakers. For example, Deputy Foreign Minister Pham Quang Vinh stated in an interview that "economic force should not be applied in the case of settlement of territorial disputes" (*Bloomberg* 2012). Although the statement was made when he commented on the Senkaku/Diaoyu dispute between China and Japan, Vinh obviously had Vietnam's South China Sea disputes with China at the back of his mind.

Conclusion

The intractable South China Sea disputes have generated incessant tensions between Vietnam and China since their normalization in 1991. The peaceful management and resolution of the disputes therefore bear extremely important implications for the current and future trajectory of bilateral relations. Such endeavours, however, have been further complicated by the economic reform that Vietnam has been pursuing under *Doi Moi*. Since the late 1980s, economic factors have indeed emerged as an increasingly important determinant of Vietnam's disputes with its northern neighbour. In particular, Vietnam's effective exploitation of the sea's resources for economic development and China's moves to counter such an effort have intensified bilateral rivalry over the sea and put their relations under constant stress. Under *Doi Moi*, Vietnam's awareness of the South China Sea's economic benefits has also deepened, further strengthening its determination to protect its territorial and maritime interests against China's expansive claims. Vietnam is accordingly adopting measures to protect and advance its interests in the sea, including various policies and strategies to develop its marine economy, with the oil and gas and fishery industries being the key priorities. In addition, it has also invested considerably in modernizing its navy and building capacities for maritime enforcement agencies.

Under *Doi Moi*, the growing economic interdependence between Vietnam and China has been serving as an important common ground for the two countries to promote cooperation. However, its potential pacifying effects on bilateral relations in general and the South China Sea disputes in particular are largely dampened by the asymmetrical nature of the relationship. As Vietnam is much more economically dependent on China than China is on Vietnam, China's actions in the South China Sea are not likely to be constrained by potential costs associated with a possible disruption of economic exchanges. Meanwhile, Vietnam feels much more vulnerable, as China may take advantage of the asymmetrical interdependence to coerce Vietnam into tactical compromises, or even strategic concessions over the South China Sea disputes.

Nevertheless, a more balanced interdependent relationship in which China has more economic stakes at risk if it pursues aggressive actions may, to a certain extent, work in Vietnam's favour and help to maintain peace and stability in the South China Sea. Accordingly, Vietnam needs to promote a more balanced trade structure, through which increasing its exports to China while diversifying import sources to become less reliant on the latter are key objectives. At the same time, Vietnam also needs to attract more Chinese direct investment. A broader and more balanced structure of economic exchanges may make China think twice before taking aggressive actions against Vietnam in the South China Sea.

That said, it should be noted that it will take Vietnam a lot of time and effort to forge a more balanced economic relationship with China. Some measures, such as increasing exports to China and diversifying import sources, have actually been implemented but achieved limited results. Therefore, in order to deal with China in general and the South China Sea disputes in particular, Vietnam has resorted to a comprehensive, multi-dimensional strategy, in which promoting a more symmetrical economic interdependence is just one of the components. The overall objective of such a strategy is twofold: While continuously nurturing a cooperative and stable relationship with China, Vietnam also aims to narrow down the gap in power between the two countries, through both hard and soft balancing. This "hedging strategy" of Vietnam against China will be investigated in detail in the next chapter.

NOTES

1. The sea is called Bien Dong, or East Sea, in Vietnamese.
2. The Agreement came into force in 2004. Its full title is "Agreement between the Socialist Republic of Viet Nam and the People's Republic of China on the Delimitation of the Territorial Seas, Exclusive Economic Zones and Continental Shelves of the Two Countries in Bac Bo/Beibu Gulf". Full texts of the Agreement in Vietnamese and Chinese, and its English translation, are available in United Nations (2007, pp. 179–99).
3. In early 2013, for example, China rejected the Philippines' proposal to bring their territorial dispute to the UN's Permanent Court of Arbitration in The Hague, through which the Philippines was seeking to challenge the validity of China's claims based on the nine-dotted line.
4. For analyses of the weight of Vietnam's and China's claims, see Valencia, Van Dyke and Ludwig (1999, pp. 17–76), and especially Nguyen (2012). If official maps were to be used as the main evidence verifying historical bases of a disputant's claims and its government's exercise of sovereignty over the disputed territories, China's claims that the Paracels and Spratlys have belonged to China "since ancient times" would be seriously undermined. For example, the Chinese official map titled *Huang chao zhi sheng yu di quan tu* and published by the Qing imperial government in 1904 shows that the two archipelagos were not part of China's territory. Meanwhile, the two archipelagos have long been included in Vietnamese official maps, such as the *Dai Nam nhat thong toan do* published by the Nguyen Dynasty as early as 1838.
5. In July 2016, an international arbitral tribunal delivered its ruling on the *Philippines vs. China* case on the South China Sea disputes. The tribunal found that China's claims to historic rights in the South China Sea based on the nine-dotted line are invalid. The tribunal also ruled that none of the features in the Spratlys met the criteria of an island under Article 121(3) of the UNCLOS. As such, these features are only entitled to a territorial water of 12 nautical miles at most, not an EEZ that may stretch up to 200 nautical miles. However, due to China's non-acceptance and non-implementation of the ruling, it is likely that conflicting claims between China and Vietnam as well as other claimant states will persist.
6. An account of the naval clash can be found in Lo (1989, pp. 53–83).
7. Some authors have reported the death toll of seventy-three on the Vietnamese side. However, the actual death toll was sixty-four. Nine Vietnamese soldiers were captured alive and released in 1991. Six Chinese were also killed in the clash.

8. The author is grateful to Dr Nguyen Dang Thang for his kind help in verifying this information.
9. The Vietnamese text of the agreement is available in the *Official Gazette of the Socialist Republic of Vietnam*, No. 581+582 (11 November 2011), accessed 29 March 2013 at <http://congbao.chinhphu.vn/noi-dung-van-ban-so-58_2011_TB-LPQT-(2561)?cbid=2552>.
10. As such, the meetings would replace the negotiation on the same matter that the two countries launched in 2006. The first round of the meetings was held in Hanoi in May 2012 (Thanh Mai 2012).
11. The term "less sensitive" is used to refer to the fields that are not necessarily related to the sensitive question of sovereignty and may serve to nurture mutual trust and cooperation between the two parties. The agreement names a number of such fields as marine scientific research and environmental protection; search and rescue at sea; and prevention and mitigation of damages caused by natural disasters.
12. For an analysis of the DOC's flaws, see Thang and Ha (2011).
13. For a useful summary of the ongoing ASEAN-China consultations on the COC, see Thayer (2013).
14. An archive of statements by the MOFA spokesperson is available at <http://www.mofa.gov.vn/vi/tt_baochi/pbnfn>.
15. From 1973 until 1975, Saigon signed thirteen concession contracts with foreign oil companies. By 1975, oil and gas of commercial value had been discovered by Mobil at Bach Ho 1-X field (PetroVietnam 2011a, p. 169).
16. The US Energy Information Administration (EIA), however, estimated that Vietnam became a net oil importer in 2011. See EIA (2012).
17. PetroVietnam made its first foreign investment in 1999.
18. China became a net oil importer in 1993 and is currently the world's second-largest consumer of oil behind the United States.
19. The China National Offshore Oil Company (CNOOC), for example, estimates the area's undiscovered resources to be around 125 billion barrels of oil and 500 trillion cubic feet of natural gas. This estimate is considered overly optimistic. The EIA estimates there to be only about 11 billion barrels of oil reserves and 190 trillion cubic feet of natural gas reserves in the sea (EIA 2013).
20. The only exception so far is an agreement between PetroVietnam and CNOOC on joint development of a defined area in the Tonkin Gulf signed in November 2006. However, the Tonkin Gulf was delimitated in 2000 and no longer a subject of dispute between the two countries.
21. The two countries were supposed to celebrate the sixtieth anniversary of their diplomatic ties in 2011. However, no major activities were organized during the year due to rising tensions over the South China Sea.

22. For the full list of the contracts, see PetroVietnam (2011*b*, pp. 341–62).

23. For an analysis of the validity of each side's claims, see Claget (1995).

24. Originally known as Vietnam Marine Police (Canh sát bien Viet Nam in Vietnamese), the force's English name was officially changed into Vietnam Coast Guard in October 2013 to be consistent with international practice, although its Vietnamese name remains the same. For an account of Vietnam's military modernization, see Thayer (2009*c*).

25. Due to low temperature during winter, fish stocks in the Tonkin Gulf tend to migrate to warmer offshore areas.

26. China, however, claimed that these fishermen were in Chinese waters and committing armed robbery against Chinese fishing boats (*Bloomberg* 2012).

27. For summaries of different views on the relation between economic interdependence and conflict, see Barbieri (1996) and Copeland (1996).

28. For the list of coefficients, see, for example, Barbieri (1996) and Oneal and Ray (1997).

29. In 2013, China's GDP was US$9,490 billion, while Vietnam's was US$171 billion (in current U.S. dollars) (World Bank 2015*a*).

7

Vietnam's Hedging Strategy against China since Normalization

Introduction

Vietnam's relations with China reflect a typical pattern of interactions between asymmetrical powers, with the smaller and greater powers pursuing divergent, sometimes conflicting, interests. Each power employs different strategies to handle the relationship (see, for example, Thayer 2002; Womack 2006). As summarized in Chapter 2, Vietnam's long-standing objective vis-à-vis China has been to maintain its sovereignty, territorial integrity and political autonomy against the threat of Chinese expansionism, while taking advantage of cultural and trade opportunities for its own national development made possible by its geographical proximity to China. Since independence, Vietnam has pursued a two-pronged strategy to handle a preponderant China: on the one hand, Vietnam has shown its unwavering determination to stand up against any Chinese attempts to undermine its political autonomy or territorial integrity. On the other hand, Vietnam has also paid due deference to China as long as its own independence and autonomy were respected.

In short, Vietnam's approach towards China can be characterized as a calibrated mixture of deference and defiance. In recent decades, this approach has been reinforced by two contradictory tendencies that have shaped bilateral relations. While ideological affinity and growing economic interdependence have strengthened bilateral relations, Vietnam's entrenched awareness of the China threat — primarily due to China's increasing assertiveness in the South China Sea — has deepened its suspicion of Beijing's intentions and hence its efforts to counter any undue pressure from China.

Although living next to a powerful China is not a new experience for Vietnam, China's re-emergence as a proto-superpower in recent decades — especially in terms of its military strength and power projection capabilities — has necessarily renewed and intensified Vietnam's China challenge. Furthermore, unlike previous historical periods, bilateral relations after the Cold War have also been increasingly conditioned by the international and regional frameworks in which the bilateral relationship is situated. In particular, this is due to the unprecedented expansion of both countries' foreign relations, their deeper integration into regional and global institutions and arrangements, as well as their gradual embrace of prevalent norms and practices. Against this backdrop, although the dichotomy of deference and defiance still represents the general tendencies in contemporary Vietnam's China policy, Hanoi's attempts to manage bilateral relations and uncertainties with the rise of China have been much more sophisticated and nuanced than they may appear. For this reason, an examination of the origins, developments and implications of Vietnam's China policy since normalization — with special reference to how Vietnam's economic and political integration into global and regional systems under *Doi Moi* has influenced such a policy — is necessary in order to understand the dynamics and evolution of bilateral relations.

This chapter argues that since normalization Vietnam's China policy has been shaped by a delicate combination of various approaches best described as a multi-tiered omni-directional hedging strategy. The strategy is made up of four major components: economic pragmatism; direct engagement; hard balancing; and soft balancing. Accordingly, Vietnam has made efforts to promote economic cooperation with China and directly engage it in various bilateral arrangements to boost mutual trust and cooperation. At the same time, it has also pursued a balancing strategy against China, which is composed of a "hard" component, represented by its military modernization programme, and a "soft" one aimed at constraining China's freedom of action and shaping its behaviours through regional multilateral arrangements. The soft balancing component also involves Vietnam's efforts to deepen its ties with foreign powers to counter undue pressures from China. As such, Vietnam's hedging strategy against China is premised upon the economic and diplomatic successes that it has achieved under *Doi Moi*, without which all components of the strategy would be either irrelevant or unfeasible.

Hedging Strategy: The Theoretical Framework

How to manage relations with the Great Powers presents a fundamental and challenging problem for small and medium-sized states as far as their national survival and autonomy are concerned. Mainstream theories of international relations, especially Realism, suggest three principal approaches: balancing against the more powerful or threatening state; bandwagoning with it; or hedging against it.

In terms of balancing, the less powerful state can increase defence spending and modernize its armed forces (internal balancing) to deter the stronger power from pursuing aggressive behaviour. Alternatively, or simultaneously, it can forge an alliance with other countries to counter the stronger power (external balancing) (Walt 1985; Waltz 1979). Theorists also differentiate between "hard balancing" and "soft balancing". Hard balancing refers to strategies by smaller states "to build and update their military capabilities, as well as create and maintain formal [and informal] alliances and counter-alliances" to match the capabilities of the stronger power. Meanwhile, soft balancing involves "tacit balancing short of formal alliances", mainly in the form of "limited arms build-up, *ad hoc* cooperative exercises, or collaboration in regional or international institutions" (Paul 2004, p. 3).[1] In this connection, it should be noted that a number of scholars categorize smaller states' efforts to engage the Great Powers in international institutions in order to shape their behaviour and reduce security threats from them as a separate security strategy under the term of "engagement" (see, for example, Johnston and Ross 1999; Roy 2005; Shambaugh 1996), or "enmeshment" (see, for example, Goh 2005, 2008; Roy 1996). However, given the ultimate purpose of these approaches, rather than being classified as separate strategies, they should be grouped under the broader strategy of soft balancing as suggested by the above-mentioned definition.[2]

If a small state chooses to bandwagon with a stronger power, it opts not to challenge but to pay deference to the latter and accept an inferior status in the bilateral relationship with the hope of gaining security or economic benefits. Hence, bandwagoning is defined in terms of the smaller state's political and/or military alignment with the greater power to avoid being attacked (Walt 1987, p. 17), or its choice to be "on the winning side" to reap economic gains from its relationship with the stronger power (Schweller 1994). While the first definition of bandwagoning is straightforward, the second one is more contentious. For example, Denny Roy (2005, p. 307) contends that "the interpretation of bandwagoning as profit-seeking is broad and divorced from security considerations, allowing for bandwagoning to be equated with economic cooperation". However, as intentions of states could not be easily and clearly identified, and economic, political and security considerations are normally interrelated drivers of states' foreign policy, it could be argued that even when a smaller state seeks favourable relations with a more powerful one mainly for economic gains, the policy has security implications for the former as well. This is because the promotion of a favourable relationship with the greater power — no matter for what reasons the smaller state may have in mind — will encourage the greater power to view the smaller state as a friendly partner. The favourable bilateral relationship may also generate economic benefits for the stronger power as well, which, as argued by liberal peace theorists (see, for example, Domke, 1988; Gartzke et al. 2001; Gasiorowski and Polachek 1982; Maoz 2009; Oneal et al. 1996; Oneal and Ray 1997; Oneal and Russett 1997; Polachek 1980, 1992; Polachek and McDonald 1992), may deter it from taking aggressive actions against the smaller one, especially at the additional risk of pushing it into a strategic relationship with rival powers. In other words, as far as bandwagoning is concerned, the policy's intended purposes are not as important as its actual effects. For that reason, it could be argued that the promotion of a favourable relationship with the greater power, even allegedly for economic gains, is still an act of bandwagoning with security implications for the smaller state.

However, pure forms of balancing and bandwagoning are hardly desirable strategies for states, especially under the normal conditions of international relations short of imminent threats or crises. This is because these strategies tend to limit a state's scope of choices and freedom of action. Therefore, theorists have proposed another major strategy called "hedging", which has been defined in various ways by scholars of international relations.[3] In essence, hedging is a strategy to enable states to deal with uncertainties in their partners' future behaviour by relying on a basket of policy tools that, while helping to promote bilateral cooperation, also entails competitive elements aimed at preparing themselves against potential security threats posed by their partners. The policy tools available in this basket are virtually the same for every state and situated anywhere along a continuum extending from pure bandwagoning to pure balancing. According to Cheng-Chwee (2008, p. 166), for example, these tools include limited bandwagoning, binding engagement, economic pragmatism, dominance denial, and indirect balancing. However, the adoption of specific tools — as well as the significance of each selected tool — depends on a state's security perception of the partner to which the strategy is to be applied. The diversity and convertibility of the tools therefore enable states to easily move back and forth along the bandwagoning–balancing continuum, depending on developments in bilateral relations and changes in the international environment. In extreme cases, a state may even quickly switch to pure balancing or bandwagoning strategies without requiring a major overhaul of its foreign and security policy. As such, hedging strategy offers states the much-needed flexibility to best deal with their partners' uncertain future behaviour while enabling them to get the most out of the existing relationship.

With the rise of China over the last three decades, regional states have been faced with the question of how best to handle the uncertainties around China's ascension to global power status. Scholars have captured regional responses to the rise of China in different ways and advocated different policy prescriptions, which undoubtedly reflects the diversity of theoretical formulations discussed above. For example, Friedberg (1993) argues that the end of the Cold War ushered in an age of unstable multipolarity for Asia, in which power politics dominates and countries in the region are likely to rely on balancing as the primary measure to deal with emergent security threats, including those related to China's rise. Meanwhile, David Kang (2003, p. 58) finds that "Asian states do not appear to be balancing against ... China. Rather they seem to be bandwagoning." He goes on to contend that a hierarchical regional order centred upon an emergent and benign China as the core will help shape a peaceful and stable future for Asia, as it did in the past. These perspectives, however, have been criticized as too simplistic, as the balancing–bandwagoning dichotomy, in Amitav Acharya's words, "is too limited to capture the range of choices a state has in responding to a rising power" (2004, p. 152).

Therefore, hedging strategy in the above-mentioned broad sense has been identified by many scholars as the key approach that regional states are pursuing to manage the rise of China.[4] In Southeast Asia, the literature also suggests that hedging is the favoured strategic option. However, each country's position on the bandwagoning–balancing continuum, as well as the significance of specific tools used in the strategy, varies from country to country, mainly depending on their security concerns vis-à-vis China (see, for example, Cheng-Chwee 2008; Goh 2005). In the case of Vietnam, scholars such as Goh (2005), Roy (2005) and Thayer (2008, 2011b) have also directly or indirectly argued that the country has employed a hedging strategy to deal with China. The chapter will now examine the foundations of Vietnam's hedging strategy and detail how it has been operationalized since normalization.

Hedging as an Option in Vietnam's China Strategy

Vietnam's adoption of hedging as its key strategy vis-à-vis China after 1991 was a rational choice given its historical experience, domestic and bilateral conditions, and changes in Vietnam's external relations and international environment.

Historical Experience

Prior to normalization, Vietnam pursued pure forms of either bandwagoning or balancing as its key strategies towards China. Specifically, in the period from the early 1950s to the mid-1970s, Vietnam arguably adopted a bandwagoning strategy towards China in the form of an informal alliance that was described by both Chinese and Vietnamese leaders as close as "lips and teeth" (Thayer 2002, p. 272). As a result, the long-standing threat that China posed to the country was played down during this period.[5] Furthermore, Vietnam also enjoyed significant economic benefits from the relationship as Beijing provided it with considerable economic and military aid during this period.

However, from the mid-1970s, this strategy became irrelevant due to the deterioration of the bilateral relationship, which culminated in the 1979 border war following Vietnam's military intervention in Cambodia the previous year. After the war, China maintained military pressure on Vietnam along the northern border and used the Cambodian issue to drain Vietnam economically and isolate the country diplomatically. China's re-emergence as a major source of threat therefore prompted Vietnam to switch to balancing as its key China strategy. The strategy was conducted both internally and externally, and underlined by Vietnam's 1978 friendship and cooperation treaty with the Soviet Union. Accordingly, Moscow provided Vietnam with a limited form of security assurance and moral support, and, more importantly, the much-needed economic and military aid for the country to maintain its resistance against China's pressures. Unfortunately, the balancing strategy and the enduring hostilities against China, as examined in Chapter 3, became a major national security and economic liability for Vietnam until the two countries normalized their relations in late 1991. Therefore, although Cold War conditions constrained much of Vietnam's strategic choices, it is obvious that neither bandwagoning nor balancing could help Vietnam ensure its security in the face of a more powerful China. Moreover, such strategies also undermined Vietnam's autonomy as they required a significant level of dependence on external powers, be it China in the case of bandwagoning or the Soviet Union in the case of balancing. Vietnam's historical experience, therefore, encouraged its leaders to explore other strategic options vis-à-vis China following normalization in 1991.

Vietnam's traditional strategic culture is arguably another important factor that led Vietnam to adopt a hedging strategy towards China. Jack Snyder, who coined the term "strategic culture", described it as a "body of attitudes and beliefs that guides and circumscribes thought on strategic questions, influences the way strategic issues are formulated, and sets the vocabulary and the perceptual parameters of strategic debate" (Snyder 1977, p. 9). Accordingly, Vietnam's strategic culture, and Vietnamese leaders' "attitude and belief" in essence, have necessarily been conditioned by the country's historical experience in dealing with its northern neighbour. As Butterfield (1996, p. 18) rightly points out, "Vietnam's strategic culture is still marked by sometimes conflicting desires regarding China: to seek and receive help from China, but also to resist undue Chinese influence or domination." This dual perception persists, and can find its manifestation in Vietnam's hedging strategy vis-à-vis China. Mirroring the past, Vietnamese leaders today seek harmonious and cooperative ties with China to maintain peace and promote the country's domestic economic development, but at the same time look for measures to ensure its security against a rising China.

Domestic and Bilateral Conditions

When Vietnam normalized its relations with China, the country's socio-economic reform under the banner of *Doi Moi* were already well underway. Therefore, the question of how to maintain a favourable relationship with China that would enable the country to both minimize the potential threats posed by China and make the most of the bilateral relationship for its domestic agenda acquired great significance to Vietnamese strategists. The hedging strategy therefore emerged as a rational choice, as its balanced and flexible nature was an essential merit that could facilitate the country's attainment of both strategic objectives.

In addition, some dynamics of Vietnam's domestic politics have also shaped the country's hedging strategy. On the one hand, Vietnam's communist rule and its political affinity with China tend to push Vietnam further to the bandwagoning end of the bandwagoning–balancing continuum. This tendency is well reflected in the contemplation by a segment of Vietnamese leadership to form a *de facto* alliance with China to safeguard socialism in both countries following the collapse of communist regimes in Eastern Europe in the late 1980s and early 1990s. On the other hand, nationalist sentiments underlined by the historical experience of Chinese domination and accentuated by the ongoing bilateral disputes over the South China Sea tend to push the country towards the balancing option.

In particular, the ongoing disputes in the South China Sea against the backdrop of China's emergence as a global superpower is arguably the most important variable in the shaping of Vietnam's current perception of China and its contemporary China policy. The effects of the disputes are substantial, in at least three ways. First, they revive and reinforce Vietnam's traditional perception of China as an expansionist and aggressive power. Second, it highlights the power asymmetry between the two countries and Vietnam's vulnerabilities, causing the country to favour balancing measures, which may invite hostile responses from China and further destabilize the bilateral relationship. Third, the disputes are central to the rise of anti-China nationalism in the country and thus minimize any positive influence that the ideological and cultural affinity as well as the growing economic interdependence may generate in bilateral relations. As such, the disputes are complicating Vietnam's efforts to handle the rise of China, and work as a pendulum that swing its China strategy between the two extremes of balancing and bandwagoning. If the disputes intensify, Vietnam is likely to reinforce its balancing strategies. On the other hand, if the disputes are well managed, or eventually resolved, a less threatening China will encourage Vietnam to contemplate a more accommodating posture that tilts towards the bandwagoning end of the spectrum.

Changes in Vietnam's External Relations and International Strategic Environment

Taking into account the above two conditions, hedging becomes a rational — if not convenient — strategy for Vietnam to handle China. The question remains, however, as to why Vietnam adopted the strategy only after the normalization of bilateral relations, given the fact that most of those conditions had been in place long before that. The answer lies in the changes in Vietnam's foreign policy in the late 1980s and shifts in the regional strategic landscape following the end of the Cold War.

As hedging requires substantial linkages with foreign partners and international institutions, Vietnam's pursuit of the strategy would have been impossible if the country had not successfully "diversified and multilateralized" its foreign relations in the early 1990s. Therefore, changes in Vietnam's foreign policy, as analysed in Chapter 3, played a crucial part in the formulation and operationalization of its hedging strategy. At the same time, shifts in regional geopolitics over the last few decades have also facilitated Vietnam's hedging strategy. Specifically, post-Cold War trends, such as China's rise and regional wariness about its growing power, the emergence of ASEAN as the key broker of multilateral security arrangements, the renewed interest and involvement of external powers in the region, and the likely future intensification of strategic rivalry between the United States and China have all been favourable to Vietnam's efforts to deepen its linkages with other countries and strengthen the external foundations of its hedging strategy vis-à-vis China. Without these external conditions, the strategy would not have been a viable option for Vietnam.

In sum, Vietnam's adoption of hedging as its main China strategy since normalization is the result of a combination of various factors. While historical experience as well as domestic and bilateral characteristics of the bilateral relations serve as necessary conditions, changes in the country's external relations and shifts in the regional strategic environment have been sufficient ones that make the strategy viable.

Operationalizing the Hedging Strategy

Evolving Policy Foundations

As mentioned above, around the time of normalization, a segment of the Vietnamese leadership still contemplated the idea of forming an alliance with China to safeguard socialism and the CPV's rule. However, Vietnamese leaders soon woke up to the reality when China began to increase its pressure in the South China Sea shortly after normalization. For example, in February 1992, China occupied Da Ba Dau (Three-headed Rock), a feature in the Spratlys. Three months later, during a visit to Beijing by CPV Central Committee Senior Advisor Nguyen Van Linh, China signed an agreement with Crestone Energy Corporation to conduct exploration activities in the Tu Chinh basin located on Vietnam's continental shelf (Thayer 1994a, pp. 524–25). These events disabused Vietnamese leaders of the illusion that China would adopt a compromising posture towards Vietnam based on a shared ideology, and tended to further strengthen their preference for hedging as the key strategy to deal with China.

The foundation for such a strategy was basically laid out in official documents adopted by the CPV at its seventh Congress, which, among other things, provided guidelines for the country's foreign policy. Accordingly, Vietnam sought to diversify and multilateralize its foreign relations, "to be friends with all countries in the world community"

(CPV 2010, p. 403). Without a broad base of foreign relations, Vietnam would be subject to greater dependence on China, rendering any attempt to hedge against it impossible. Along with the emergence of this new foreign policy was a transformation in the Vietnamese leadership's strategic mindset. Specifically, Vietnam departed from the rigid ideology-based strategic approach to embrace a more flexible, pragmatic one, embodied in what CPV strategists label the cooperation-struggle strategy (Ninh 1998; Thayer 2011*b*). Hong Ha, then secretary of the CPV Central Committee and head of the Party's External Relations Department, explained this strategy as follows:

> [In international relations] depending on the opposite side, on the issue and at a different point in time, the cooperative side or the struggle side may be more prominent. One-way cooperation or one-way conflict both lead to a losing and unfavourable situation. We push for cooperation but we still have to struggle in a form and at a pace appropriate to each opponent in order to safeguard our people's interest, establish equal relations that are mutually beneficial and maintain peace. But we struggle in order to push forward cooperation, avoiding the weak spots that would push us into a corner and generate provocation (quoted in Ninh 1998, p. 458).

By 1993–94, the approach had been incorporated into the CPV's official documents as a guiding foreign policy principle. For example, in July 1994 the CPV Politburo concluded that with regard to Vietnam's accession to ASEAN, "The motto of 'cooperating while struggling' [*vua hop tac vua dau tranh*] should be fully grasped in order to take advantage of common points and minimize discrepancies [between Vietnam and other countries], while staying vigilant to guard against schemes of certain forces that seek to make use of ASEAN against our interests" (CPV 2007*d*, p. 410). Obviously, the struggle-cooperation approach resonates the essential logic of the hedging strategy and plays a central role in shaping transformations that followed in Vietnam's relations with major foreign partners, especially China and the United States.

The cooperation-struggle approach was further elaborated and supplemented by the introduction of two related strategic concepts, namely *doi tac* and *doi tuong*. Specifically, the "Strategy of Fatherland Defence in a New Situation" adopted by the CPV Central Committee in July 2003 used the two terms to refer to "objects of cooperation" and "objects of struggle", respectively (Thayer 2011*b*, p. 351; Vuving

2006, p. 818). However, the introduction of the terms did not necessarily mean that any given country would be classified exclusively as a *doi tac* or a *doi tuong*. Instead, the application scope of the concepts would be narrowly based on specific areas of the bilateral relationship, whereby a partner country may be considered as a *doi tac* in areas of common interests, and a *doi tuong* in areas of discrepancies. Accordingly, Vietnam has viewed its relations with China (as well as other countries, especially the United States) as containing elements of both cooperation and struggle (Thayer 2011*b*, p. 351).

The dichotomies of *hop tac* versus *dau tranh*, and *doi tac* versus *doi tuong* have since served as a major strategic approach guiding Vietnam's foreign relations. Especially, the approach has great implications for Vietnam's relationship with China, which undoubtedly highlights the relevance of the dichotomies more clearly than any other of Vietnam's bilateral relationships. On the one hand, Vietnam seeks to exploit conditions conducive to bilateral cooperation, especially in the economic sphere, to promote its domestic development. On the other hand, competing claims in the South China Sea and China's increasingly threatening posture dictate that Vietnam must "struggle" with China in this aspect to best protect its national interests. The dichotomies, therefore, inform a hedging strategy vis-à-vis China. In effect, since normalization, Vietnam has been developing the strategy with four major components in mind:

1. Economic pragmatism, i.e. deepening bilateral economic cooperation to facilitate domestic development;
2. Direct engagement, i.e. expanding and deepening various bilateral mechanisms to build mutual trust and nurture cooperation, thereby shaping China's behaviour;
3. Hard balancing, i.e. pursuing military modernization to deter China from aggressive actions; and
4. Soft balancing, i.e. promoting participation in multilateral institutions and deepening relations with major partners to counter against undue pressure from China.

Figure 7.1 illustrates the components and operational mechanisms of Vietnam's hedging strategy vis-à-vis China. It's obvious that the first two components — namely economic pragmatism and direct engagement — tend to slide towards the bandwagoning end of the bandwagoning–balancing continuum, while the remaining two components are situated towards the opposite end.

FIGURE 7.1
Vietnam's Hedging Strategy against China

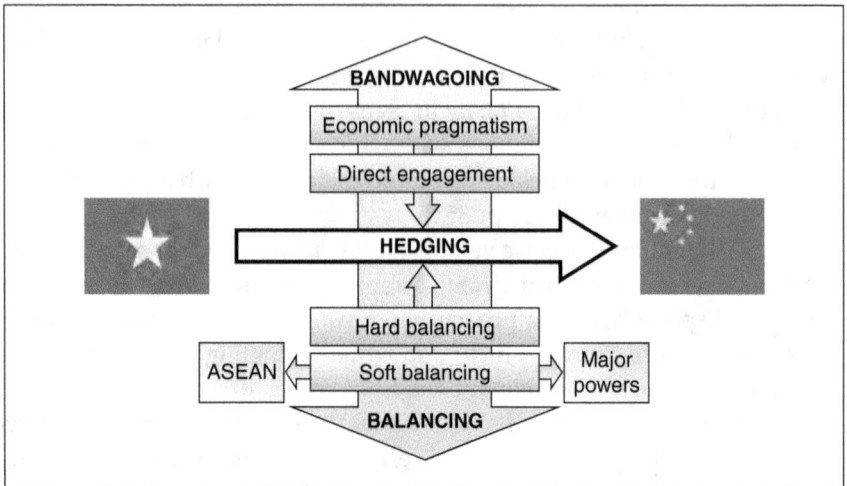

Source: Author's own compilation.

The individual components of the strategy will now be analysed to highlight how Vietnam has been putting the strategy into practice. It should be noted that as both Vietnam's political engagement and economic pragmatism with China have been examined elsewhere in the book (Chapter 4 and Chapter 5, respectively), this section only revisits these two aspects of bilateral relations from a security perspective, by which hedging as a security strategy vis-à-vis China is justified.

Economic Pragmatism

With economic development as the central task in its domestic agenda, Vietnam has every reason to seek a peaceful relationship with China. Such a relationship will not only help to reinforce a stable regional environment favourable for Vietnam's internal development, but also enable it to take advantage of opportunities offered by China's rise for its own interests. In fact, Vietnam's economic ties with China have witnessed unprecedented growth since bilateral normalization (see Chapter 5 for more details). As such, Vietnam's efforts to promote economic ties with China may be purely motivated by economic reasons. However, stronger and deeper economic ties with China also have important security implications for the country.

First and foremost, trade and investment ties with China have undeniably contributed to the economic growth of Vietnam over the last two decades. As economic capacity constitutes a major element of national power (Morgenthau 1948, pp. 86–88), stronger economic foundations achieved through deepened economic ties with China obviously help to strengthen Vietnam's security posture vis-à-vis China. This security rationale behind Vietnam's efforts to promote bilateral economic ties also resonates in the CPV's identification of "lagging behind other countries economically" as the most serious threat to national as well as regime security (CPV 2010, p. 524; Tung 2010, pp. 109–10). In effect, Vietnam's enhanced national security and defence capabilities achieved through its ongoing military modernization programme would have been impossible without the country's significant economic development under *Doi Moi*, for which expanded economic ties with China partly account.

Second, despite their asymmetric nature, bilateral economic ties obviously thicken the network of bilateral interactions, which serves as a cushion to absorb tensions arising from other domains of the bilateral relationship, including those related to the South China Sea disputes. Although Vietnam cannot rely on the growing economic interdependence with China to constrain its aggressive actions in the South China Sea, Beijing cannot freely choose to use economic measures such as trade disruption to sanction Vietnam or elicit concessions from it over the disputes. This is simply because such actions also involve potential costs for China, which are increasing in tandem with the rising volume of bilateral trade and investment. More specifically, although Vietnam accounts for a minor fraction of China's total foreign trade and investment, the disruption or suspension of bilateral economic ties certainly do significant damage to the economies of China's southern provinces as well as those industries that have a large stake in maintaining their exports to Vietnam. It is also these provinces and industries that are likely to lobby the central government for favourable relations with Vietnam. In other words, China has the option to use its economic clout as a tool of coercion against Vietnam, the potential costs involved make it an unattractive choice. Instead, deepened bilateral economic ties tend to raise the stakes for all parties to the point that they may ultimately favour a cooperative and stable bilateral relationship rather than an antagonistic one. Therefore, such logic obviously still makes Vietnamese strategists consider economic pragmatism an important component of the country's hedging strategy against China.

Direct Engagement

As far as hedging is concerned, direct engagement, just like pragmatic economic cooperation, should be given a priority because it pays significant security dividends without requiring substantial resources as in the case of hard balancing. The key logic underlying engagement is the promotion of bilateral communication and mutual trust, thereby facilitating cooperation and providing effective avenues to address conflicts of interests that may otherwise do serious harm to the overall relationship. In effect, Vietnam has paid serious attention to building a network of engagement with China through three major channels, namely government-to-government, party-to-party, and people-to-people interactions. As explained below, these efforts have led to positive results.

In the first channel, which is also the most important, the key institution is the exchange of visits between high-ranking leaders. As summarized in Table 4.2, between 1991 and 2015, Vietnam and China exchanged thirty-eight visits by top party and state leaders. These visits normally witnessed the signing of various agreements to promote bilateral cooperation in various fields. More importantly, they helped set the larger political framework for bilateral relations, as demonstrated by the adoption of the "Joint Statement on Comprehensive Cooperation in the New Century" during President Tran Duc Luong's visit to China in December 2000 and the statement on the "comprehensive strategic cooperative partnership" between the two countries during CPV General Secretary Nong Duc Manh's visit to Beijing in May 2008.

The visits have also resulted in progress towards better managing bilateral problems. For example, during CPV General Secretary Do Muoi's official visit to China in July 1997, the leaders of the two countries agreed to conclude a treaty on land border demarcation and another on the maritime delineation in the Gulf of Tonkin before the end of 2000 (Thao 2000, pp. 88–89). This political commitment resulted in the conclusion of the two treaties in 1999 and 2000, respectively, thereby stabilizing Vietnam's northern border and removing a potential security threat to the country. Meanwhile, during CPV General Secretary Nong Duc Manh's visit to China in May 2008, the two sides agreed to establish a hot line between the two countries' top leaderships to handle emergency or crisis situations (Vietnam News Agency 2008). By improving communication at the top decision-making levels, the hot line may serve as an important tool for Vietnam to manage crises with China, especially in the South China Sea.

Apart from high-ranking visits, other important cooperation mechanisms between the two governments have also been established. Among these, the central mechanism has been the Steering Committee on Vietnam–China Bilateral Cooperation established in 2006. Under the Committee, ministries and agencies of the two countries have also set up direct links to promote cooperation in their respective portfolios, ranging from coordinated efforts against human trafficking to fishery cooperation and combined naval patrols in the Tonkin Gulf. Particularly important for Vietnam's security has been the establishment of cooperation mechanisms between the two defence ministries. In 2010, the two defence ministries launched their annual strategic defence dialogues, which have subsequently served as an important channel for the two armed forces to build mutual trust and develop cooperation. The dialogues have resulted in concrete measures to prevent potential conflicts in the South China Sea, such as the agreement to establish a hot line between the two ministries.[6] Other notable cooperation measures include exchange of visits by high-ranking military leaders, combined naval patrols and port calls, combined patrols along the land border, officer training programmes, and scientific cooperation between military research institutions (Vietnam News Agency 2013*a*; *VnEconomy* 2013).

As shown in Table 7.1, in addition to key mechanisms mentioned above, there are also other arrangements through which Vietnam and China engage each other in different aspects of their bilateral relationship. These engagements generate a network of frequent interactions, thereby improving bilateral communication and minimizing the risk of misunderstandings or misperceptions. The agreement to establish the three hot lines is a significant payoff, and a primary example of how direct engagement has been serving as an important tool for Vietnam to improve its security vis-à-vis China.

TABLE 7.1
Major Direct Engagement Mechanisms between Vietnam and China

Mechanism	Channel
High-ranking visits; Hot line between high-ranking leaders	Government-to-Government Party-to-Party
Steering Committee on Vietnam–China Bilateral Cooperation	Government-to-Government
Annual meetings between Central Departments of External Affairs/Propaganda of the two communist parties	Party-to-Party
Annual consultation meetings between the two Ministries of Foreign Affairs	Government-to-Government
Annual strategic dialogues and hot line between the two Ministries of Defence;	Government-to-Government
Annual anti-crime conferences between the Ministries of Public Security	Government-to-Government
Committee on Bilateral Economic and Trade Cooperation	Government-to-Government
Committee on Bilateral Scientific and Technological Cooperation	Government-to-Government
Joint Committee on Land Border, Joint Working Groups on the South China Sea	Government-to-Government
Agreement on Fishery Cooperation in the Tonkin Gulf; Hot line between the two Ministries of Agriculture on fishery incidents	Government-to-Government
Annual meetings between border provincial governments	Government-to-Government People-to-People
Vietnam–China Youth Festivals, Vietnam–China Youth Friendship Meetings, Vietnam–China People's Forum	People-to-People

Source: Vietnam News Agency (2013*a*).

Hard Balancing

Although direct engagement is a useful tool for Vietnam to manage its relations with China, it does not provide enough assurance for the country in the South China Sea, especially given China's superior military capabilities. The rapid modernization of the Chinese navy is particularly worrisome for Vietnam, as many of its modernized naval capabilities are deployed in the South China Sea.[7] For example, in the early 2000s, China began construction of a naval base near Yalong Bay on Hainan island, which is capable of housing up to twenty submarines, including nuclear ballistic-missile submarines, as well as China's future aircraft carrier battle groups (AFP 2008). The base facilitates the Chinese navy's power projection into the South China Sea (Thayer 2010, p. 73). As the possibility of armed conflict over the land border diminished following the conclusion of the bilateral land border treaty in 1999, dealing with China's dominant and growing naval power in the South China Sea has become the focus of Vietnam's national defence policy as well as its China strategy. Against this backdrop, Vietnam has accelerated its military modernization efforts to address this concern.

Vietnam has sought to modernize its military capabilities through two key measures: acquiring modern hardware from foreign partners, and developing a domestic defence industry. Indeed, the country's 2009 National Defence White Paper stated that:

> in order to provide enough weapons and technological equipment for the armed forces, in addition to well maintaining and selectively upgrading existing items, Vietnam makes adequate investments to manufacture on its own certain weapons and equipment commensurate with its technological capabilities, while procuring a number of modern weapons and technological equipment to meet the requirements of enhancing the combat strength of its people's armed forces (Ministry of Defence, 2009, p. 91).

Vietnam began to modernize its armed forces soon after *Doi Moi* was initiated, and these efforts were accelerated in the mid-1990s due to China's increasing assertiveness in the South China Sea. In May 1995, CPV General Secretary Do Muoi called for the modernization of the country's navy and stated that "we must reinforce our defence capacity to defend our sovereignty, national interests and natural marine resources, while at the same time building a maritime economy" (cited in Thayer 1997, pp. 17–18). Since then, Vietnam's military modernization programme has made substantial progress, particularly in terms of naval power.

Vietnam's military modernization has been facilitated by the country's growing prosperity under *Doi Moi*, which has enabled the government to increase defence spending. In the early 1990s, the country's defence budget was still very limited. Commenting on the report on defence budget presented to the National Assembly in late 1991, the *Quan doi Nhan dan* (People's Army) lamented that "the projected expenditures cannot meet even the bare minimum requirements of the Army" (cited in Thayer 1997, p. 5). According to figures compiled by the Stockholm International Peace Research Institute (SIPRI), an authoritative source on global defence statistics, Vietnam's defence budget in 1992 was a modest $745 million (in 2011 U.S. dollars). Yet, it accounted for 3.4 per cent of the country's GDP. About a decade later, economic growth achieved under *Doi Moi* gave the Vietnamese government more room to expand its defence budget, while constantly maintaining its share of the GDP within a range of 2 to 2.5 per cent. Figure 7.2 provides details of Vietnam's military expenditures from 2003 to 2014.

The figures show that from 2003 to 2014, Vietnam's military expenditure increased steadily at an annualized average rate of 8.8 per

FIGURE 7.2
Vietnam's Estimated Military Expenditure, 2003–14

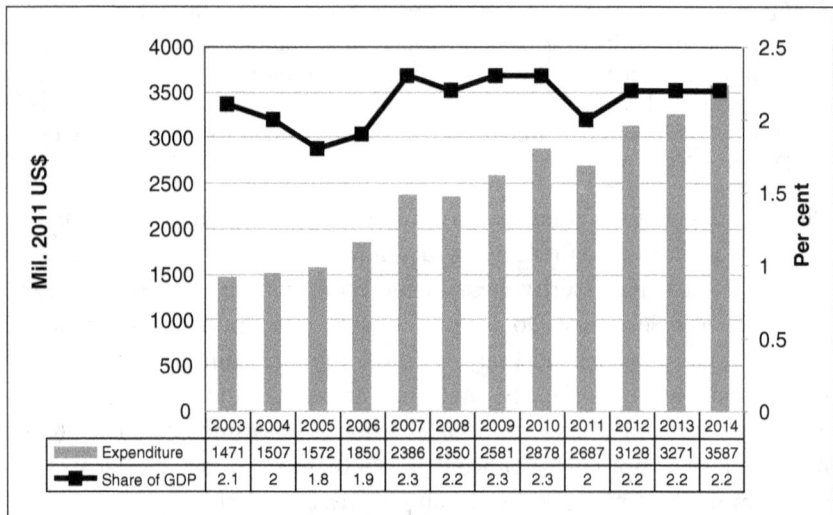

	2003	2004	2005	2006	2007	2008	2009	2010	2011	2012	2013	2014
Expenditure	1471	1507	1572	1850	2386	2350	2581	2878	2687	3128	3271	3587
Share of GDP	2.1	2	1.8	1.9	2.3	2.2	2.3	2.3	2	2.2	2.2	2.2

Source: SIPRI (2015). Data for 2012–15 are flagged by SIPRI as "highly uncertain".

cent (with the exception of 2008 and 2011). A significant share of the increased budget was dedicated to the procurement of advanced weapons systems. Against the backdrop of rising tensions in the South China Sea, it is not surprising that the navy and the air force have benefited most from rising defence spending and new acquisitions. Table 7.2 shows the most notable arms transfers that Vietnam has received or ordered from foreign partners since 1995.

As Table 7.2 shows, Vietnam's most notable arms procurement so far has been the order for six *Kilo*-class submarines worth approximately US$2 billion from Russia. The deal also entails Russian assistance in the training of Vietnamese submariners and refurbishment of submarine facilities at the Cam Ranh Bay naval base (BBC 2009). The first submarine was delivered in November 2013, and the sixth is scheduled for delivery in 2016. Other major naval acquisitions include two *Gerpard*-class frigates (two more to be delivered in 2014–16) and more than a dozen *Tarantul*-class corvettes and *Svetlyak*-class patrol vessels. Another significant deal has been the K-300P Bastion-P coastal defence systems and associated missiles worth US$300 million (*VnExpress* 2013). The systems' ability to strike naval warships within a range up to 300 kilometres not only strengthens Vietnam's Anti-Access/ Area Denial capabilities but also enables it to effectively cover parts of the Paracels and the Spratlys. Meanwhile, Vietnam's fleet of Su-30MK fighter craft can also provide air cover over the South China Sea. Since April 2013, Vietnam has employed Su-30 fighters to conduct regular patrols over the Spratlys (Nguyen Dinh Quan 2013). Undeniably, these enhanced naval and air capabilities provide Vietnam with a considerable level of deterrence against China in the South China Sea.

In addition to arms imports, Vietnam is also developing its own defence industry. In the early 1990s, following the termination of Soviet military aid, Vietnam identified the need for an indigenous arms industry as a priority for the country's defence policy (Thayer 1997, p. 7). In 1991, a report by the Central Military Party Commission stated "We should consolidate and step by step develop the network of national defence industries relevant to the development of the national economy" (cited in Thayer 1997, p. 8). More than a decade later, Vietnam's 2004 National Defence White Paper stated that the country's "R&D and application programs of military technologies as well as defence industry establishments have satisfied the requirements of repairing, upgrading, and manufacturing weapons and equipment for the armed

TABLE 7.2
Vietnam's Major Arms Acquisitions since 1995

Source Country	Item	Year of Order/ Licence	Year of Delivery	Notes
Belarus	7 Vostok-E radar systems	N/A	2005	
	20 Stoke-E radar systems	2013	N/A	
Canada	6 DHC-6 Twin Otter transport aircrafts	2010	2012–14	
Romania	12 Yak-52 trainer aircrafts	(1997)	1997	
	10 Yak-52 Trainer aircrafts	2008	2009–11	
Russia	2 Project-1241/Tarantul corvettes	1994	1996	
	6 Su-27S/Flanker-B aircrafts	1994	1995	
	6 Su-27S/Flanker-B aircrafts	1996	1997–98	
	2 Project-1241/Tarantul corvettes	1998	1999	
	2 Project-10412/Svetlyak patrol crafts	2001	2002	
	(75) 48N6/SA-10D Grumble SAM	2003	2005–06	
	2 S-300PMU-1/SA-20A SAM systems	2003	2005	
	4 Su-30MK/Flanker aircrafts	2003	2004	
	(20) Kh-31A1/AS-17 anti-ship missiles	2004	2004	For Su-30 combat aircrafts
	(400) Kh-35 Uran/SS-N-25 anti-ship missiles	2004	2008–2012	
	2 Gepard-3 Frigates	2006	2011	
	2 K-300P Bastion-P coastal defence systems	2007	2009–11	
	(40) Yakhont/SS-N-26 anti-ship missiles	2007	2009–11	For Bastion coastal defence systems
	6 Project-10412/Svetlyak patrol crafts	2007	2011–12	
	6 Project-636E/Kilo Submarines	2009	2013–16	

	8 Su-30MK/Flanker aircrafts	2009	2010–11	
	12 Su-30MK/Flanker aircrafts	2010	2011–12	
	2 Gepard-3 frigates	2012	2014–16	
	12 Su-30MK aircrafts	2013	2014–15	US$600 million deal
	10 Project-1241/Tarantul corvettes (1241.8/ Molniya version)	(2004)	2008–16	Licensed to be produced in Vietnam
Spain	3 CASA - 212-400	N/A	2012–13	For Vietnam Coast Guard
Ukraine	(6) MiG-21PFM/Fishbed-F fighter aircrafts	(1995)	1996	Second-hand
	(8) Su-22/Fitter-H/J/K FGA aircraft	2004	2005–06	Second-hand
	4 Kolchuga air search systems	(2009)	2012	

Note: Information concerning the year of order, year(s) of deliveries are in brackets if the accuracy of the data is uncertain.
Source: Author's own compilation based on SIPRI (2013) and various media sources.

forces" (Ministry of Defence 2004, p. 20). In 2008 the National Assembly Standing Committee enacted the Ordinance on Defence Industry which provided a legal framework for the industry's development.[8]

So far, Vietnam has been capable of producing a range of weapons and equipment, such as small arms, mortars, automatic grenade launchers, fuel component for Scud missiles, radar-absorbent paint, military-grade communication equipment, and basic unmanned aerial vehicles (UAVs) (*Tien Phong* 2013). In 2012 the Vietnam People's Navy commissioned two TT-400TP gunships locally built by Hong Ha Shipyard. The ships — which are capable of anti-ship missions, protecting bases against amphibious assaults and escorting civil ships and naval patrols — were praised as a "breakthrough" for the national defence industry (My Lang 2011). It should be noted that the ships' preliminary designs were purchased from an undisclosed country.

Vietnam has been active in seeking technology transfers from foreign partners in order to speed up the development of its domestic defence industry. For example, Vietnam obtained a licence from Russia's Vympel Shipyard to assemble 6 Project 1241.8 *Molniya*-class missile boats, with the option of producing 4 more by 2015 (RusNavy 2010). Another major deal with Russia has been an agreement to jointly produce anti-ship missiles in Vietnam in 2012 (Kate 2012). But Russia is not the only country from which Vietnam seeks to promote the transfer of military technologies. Other important partners include Belarus, India, the Netherlands, Israel, and the Ukraine. For example, in 2011, Vietnam started negotiating with the Netherlands to acquire 4 *Sigma*-class corvettes. The deal included the possible provision for two of them to be constructed at Vietnamese shipyards.[9] Through cooperation with the Netherland's Damen Shipyards Group, Vietnam also completed the construction of the *DN 2000*-class patrol vessel in 2012, which later became the Vietnam Coast Guard's largest patrol vessel (Xuan Tung 2013).

In sum, Vietnam has invested significantly in improving the capabilities of its armed forces, especially the navy and air force in order to safeguard its maritime interests in the South China Sea. Although China's military capabilities far exceed Vietnam's, the modernization of the Vietnamese armed forces provides that country with a credible deterrence and, in the worst case scenario, the ability to strike back against China.

Soft Balancing

Vietnam's soft balancing against China is conducted through two main channels: deepened bilateral ties with major powers, and more effective participation in regional multilateral arrangements to pursue a specific agenda. These efforts are generally in line with Vietnam's policy of "diversification and multilateralization" of its foreign relations. However, there are indications showing that Vietnam is trying to use these channels as important tools to soft-balance China. Before examining the role of the China factor in these efforts, however, it's important to review how Vietnam has deepened its ties with major powers and turned multilateral arrangements to its advantage.

By 1995 Vietnam had successfully established diplomatic ties with all major powers, including the United States. Since the early 2000s, Hanoi has endeavoured to deepen bilateral ties through the establishment of "strategic partnerships". By the end of 2015, Vietnam had established strategic partnerships with Russia (2001), Japan (2006), India (2007), China (2008), South Korea, Spain (2009), the United Kingdom (2010), Germany (2011), Italy, Thailand, Indonesia, Singapore, France (2013), Malaysia and the Philippines (2015). Among these, the partnerships with Russia and China have been upgraded to the "comprehensive strategic" level. Meanwhile, Vietnam has also entered into "comprehensive partnerships" with Australia (2009) and the United States (2013). Although Vietnam has never clarified what criteria is for these partnerships, it seems comprehensive partnerships and the two variants are generally the designations Vietnam use to label relationships which it deems important and wishes to develop further.

These countries generally fall into one or more of four major categories:

1. Political powers (e.g. members of the UN Security Council, key members of ASEAN, and/or influential regional middle powers);
2. Economic powerhouses (e.g. G-20 members, and/or countries with which Vietnam maintains significant economic ties);
3. Military powers (e.g. major strategic players and/or countries that are important sources of arms and military technology transfer for Vietnam); and
4. Countries that play significant roles in the management of the South China Sea disputes.

By deepening ties with these countries, Vietnam hopes to improve its international diplomatic status, facilitate its domestic economic development, strengthen its military capabilities, and better defend its interests in the South China Sea.

Among these bilateral ties, some are more significant than others, especially with regards to Vietnam's relations with China. For example, Russia has been the biggest source of Vietnam's arms imports, while India has also emerged as an important partner in terms of military cooperation.[10] These two countries are also active partners of Vietnam in its oil exploration and exploitation activities in the South China Sea. Japan is not only an important economic partner, but has also become an increasingly significant political and strategic partner for Vietnam. As both countries have ongoing maritime disputes with China and shared concerns over China's growing assertiveness, they find common ground to strengthen their strategic ties. In early August 2014, for example, Japan announced that it would provide Vietnam with six patrol boats to support the country's maritime defence activities in the South China Sea (*The Asahi Shimbun* 2014). Meanwhile, the strategic partnerships with Indonesia, Singapore and Thailand — influential ASEAN members but non-claimants in the South China Sea — are likely to facilitate Vietnam's efforts to forge an intra-ASEAN consensus on the disputes.

Above all, as far as Vietnam's efforts to balance China are concerned, its improved relationship with the United States is the most challenging, but also the most promising one. Since 1995, bilateral ties — especially in economic realms — have been developing at a pace that has surprised many observers. After a bilateral trade agreement was concluded in 1999, trade ties developed quickly, and in 2002 the United States became Vietnam's largest export market (GSO 2006a, p. 428). In 2008, Vietnam also joined the United States and other regional countries to negotiate the Trans-Pacific Partnership (TPP), which if successful will further integrate the two economies. In the political sphere, the two countries currently hold annual political, security, and defence dialogues in addition to those on human rights issues. The erstwhile enemies have also strengthened military ties through visits by high-ranking military officials, port calls by U.S. naval ships, training programmes and non-combat military exercises (Barta 2011). After Washington announced its "pivot" or "rebalance" towards Asia in 2011 — interpreted by some in China as part of a wider strategy to "contain" the country (see, e.g., Swaine 2012) — bilateral relations were promoted further, culminating in the establishment of the bilateral comprehensive partnership during President Truong Tan Sang's trip to Washington in July 2013 (The White House 2013). In July 2015, CPV General Secretary Nguyen Phu Trong paid a historic visit to Washington, further strengthening the rapprochement between the two former enemies.

Although Vietnam has repeatedly emphasized that its improved relationships with foreign powers are not directed against a third country,[11] it is clear that one of the major drivers behind Hanoi's efforts to forge closer ties with the United States is related to its growing rivalry with Beijing in the South China Sea. Indeed, the United States is currently the only power capable of effectively challenging and constraining China's military ambitions, including in the South China Sea. Closer ties with America therefore provide Vietnam with greater confidence and more options in dealing with China, especially when Washington itself is also seeking strong friends and allies to support its rebalancing strategy. Vietnam's intention has been reflected in its efforts to strengthen military ties with the America and mobilize U.S. diplomatic support regarding the South China Sea disputes. For example, in the very first item of the joint communiqué announcing the establishment of the bilateral comprehensive partnership in July 2013, the two countries "reaffirmed their support for the settlement of disputes by peaceful means in accordance with international law" and "the principle of non-use of force or threat-of-force in resolving territorial and maritime disputes" (White House 2013).

In sum, a major approach in Vietnam's efforts to soft-balance China has been the deepening of its relations with major powers, especially regional ones. At the same time, Vietnam has supplemented this bilateral approach with a multilateral one that involves mainly the rallying of international diplomatic support through multilateral arrangements to resist pressure from China, and to engage it into patterns of cooperative interactions.

The primary focus of Vietnam's multilateral approach is ASEAN. Hanoi's desire to use ASEAN as a diplomatic tool in its disputes with China has been demonstrated by its continuous efforts to make sure that the South China Sea is placed high in the Association's political and security agenda. This effort is opposed by China — which prefers the disputes to be dealt with bilaterally — but is shared by some regional countries, especially the other claimant states. At the 17th ARF in Hanoi in July 2010, for example, Vietnam was encouraged when representatives of more than half of its twenty-seven member states addressed the South China Sea disputes in their official speeches (Duong 2010). Notably, U.S. Secretary of State Hillary Clinton stated that "the United States, like every nation, has a national interest in freedom of navigation, open access to Asia's maritime commons, and respect for international law in the South China Sea" (U.S. Department of State 2010). In what was generally interpreted as an attack on the vague legal basis of China's expansive claims in the South China Sea, Clinton added that "legitimate claims to maritime space in the South China Sea should be derived solely from legitimate claims to land features". Clinton's speech was well received in Vietnam.

However, Vietnam's efforts to manage the South China Sea disputes through ASEAN has its limitations. At the 45th ASEAN Ministerial Meeting (AMM) hosted by Cambodia in July 2012, for example, despite the insistence of Vietnam and the Philippines, Cambodia refused — allegedly under China's pressure — to include references to incidents in the South China Sea in the final communiqué. Cambodia's intransigence ultimately led to the AMM's failure to issue a joint statement for the first time in its forty-five-year history.[12] Vietnamese Foreign Minister Pham Binh Minh's statement that he was "very disappointed" over the incident (Thul and Grudgings 2012) further testified to Vietnam's consistent efforts to soft-balance China through ASEAN.

While the above two examples illustrate the successes as well as the limitations in Vietnam's efforts to soft-balance China through ASEAN, the 2002 ASEAN–China Declaration on the Conduct of Parties in the SCS (DOC) is a mixed bag. The Declaration — which Vietnam and the Philippines strongly advocated[13] — has arguably been the most tangible outcome of Vietnam's efforts to constrain China in the South China Sea through multilateral arrangements. Although non-binding, the DOC still subjects China to certain normative constraints, thereby limiting its freedom of action and providing Vietnam with legitimate grounds to condemn China's aggressive and illegal activities in the sea.[14] However, the DOC still falls short of Vietnam's expectations. For example, it does not explicitly include the Paracels in its geographical scope. Moreover, the normative constraints have not proven strong enough to preclude China's growing assertiveness in the South China

Sea. Consequently, Vietnam, together with its ASEAN partners, has begun consultations with China on a supposedly more legally binding Code of Conduct (COC) to replace the DOC. The outcome of these talks remains to be seen. The bumpy road to the COC highlights the fact that the effectiveness of soft-balancing as an approach for Vietnam to handle China is heavily conditioned by external factors that Vietnam cannot control.

Conclusion

Facing a far more powerful China, Vietnam has employed a multi-tiered omni-directional hedging strategy to handle its relations with its northern neighbour. The strategy was a rational choice for the country given its historical experience of failed experiments with balancing and bandwagoning as alternative China strategies as well as the dominant domestic and bilateral conditions after normalization, such as Vietnam's economic reform under *Doi Moi* and persistent bilateral tensions in the South China Sea. In addition, Vietnam's expanded external relations, and changes in regional strategic setting since the late 1980s, also played important roles in shaping this strategy. These conditions not only turned hedging into a rational choice for Vietnam, but also made it feasible for the country to put the strategy into practice with the lowest strategic costs possible.

Vietnam's hedging strategy against China gradually emerged in the 1990s as a result of Vietnam's evolving strategic thinking. Accordingly, Vietnamese strategists departed from the rigid Cold War-style strategic thinking based on ideology and a clear division between friends and enemies to embrace a more pragmatic and flexible one derived first and foremost from the perceived interests of the nation as well as the CPV regime. Accordingly, they started to view foreign relations to be inherently composed of both cooperative and competing elements, which was well manifested in the emergence of the dichotomies of *hop tac* (cooperation) versus *dau tranh* (struggle) and *doi tac* (object of cooperation) versus *doi tuong* (object of struggle) in their strategic vocabulary. These dichotomies, in turn, best manifested themselves in Vietnam's China strategy since normalization.

Vietnam's current China strategy is composed of four major components, namely economic pragmatism, direct engagement, hard balancing, and soft balancing. These components reflect the essence of the hedging strategy, providing Vietnam with the opportunities to maintain a peaceful, stable and cooperative relationship with China for the sake of its domestic development, while enabling it to counter undue pressure from China and deter Chinese aggression.

So far, Vietnam's operationalization of this strategy has proved to be effective. It has managed to continuously promote economic ties with China and foster a greater level of economic interdependence, which may act as a cushion to absorb tensions arising from the South China Sea disputes. It has also developed a dense network of bilateral engagement with China through various avenues and at various levels to improve communication, thereby enhancing mutual trust. At the same time, Vietnam has also pursued efforts to hard-balance China by modernizing its armed forces, particularly the navy and air force. Finally, efforts to soft-balance China has also achieved considerable results, illustrated by the establishment of more than a dozen strategic partnerships with major powers and regional countries as well as Vietnam's purposeful utilization of regional multilateral arrangements, especially ASEAN, to counter China's assertiveness.

Nevertheless, Vietnam still faces certain challenges in effectively maintaining the strategy. First, although economic pragmatism and direct engagement serve as key mechanisms for Hanoi to foster a stable and cooperative relationship with Beijing and to handle the South China Sea disputes peacefully, they are subject to uncertainties caused by the disputes themselves. If, for some reason, the disputes escalate, then economic exchanges may be disrupted and bilateral engagements may be frozen. Second, Vietnam's hard balancing against China is largely dependent on the size of its defence budget, which is directly tied to the economic performance of the country. Vietnam's military modernization programme is therefore likely to be negatively affected by the economic hardship that the country experienced in the late 2000s and early 2010s. Third, the soft-balancing component of the strategy mainly relies on Vietnam's external ties with regional powers and institutions. This also exposes the strategy to a number of operational risks, including shifts in regional and global power dynamics and Beijing's counter-measures. In this connection, the U.S. rebalancing to East Asia, and China's responses as well as its efforts in fragmenting ASEAN over the South China Sea, are two important variables that may impact the effectiveness of Vietnam's hedging strategy against China in the future.

NOTES

1. For useful discussions of the two concepts, see also Paul (2005) and Pape (2005).

2. My argument is limited to individual states' efforts only. The sources cited also refer to engagement/enmeshment as a collective strategy of institutions/groups of states (such as ASEAN) to use "economic incentives and disincentives to extract desirable behaviours" and to "tie down" great powers by common norms and practices (Roy 1996, p. 766). In addition to multilateral platforms, small states can also engage greater powers in bilateral mechanisms, such as security dialogues, exchanges of visits by high-ranking leaders, or various sectoral cooperation arrangements.

3. For example, hedging has been defined as "a behaviour in which a country seeks to offset risks by pursuing multiple policy options that are intended to produce mutually counteracting effects, under the situation of high-uncertainties and high-stakes" (Cheng-Chwee 2008, p. 163); "a set of strategies aimed at avoiding ... a situation in which states cannot decide upon more straightforward alternatives such as balancing, bandwagoning, or neutrality" (Goh 2006); and "keeping open more than one strategic option against the possibility of a future security threat" (Roy 2005, p. 306). Meanwhile, using U.S.–China relations as an example, Medeiros (2005, p. 145) indirectly defines hedging as a strategy whereby states pursue "policies that, on the one hand, stress engagement and integration mechanisms and, on the other, emphasize realist-style balancing in the form of external security cooperation" with other states and "national military modernization programs".

4. This means the hedging strategy used here covers such elements as "accommodation", "engagement", "enmeshment", etc., which some scholars consider as separate strategies different from hedging. See, for example, Acharya (1999), Cheng-Chwee (2008), Goh (2005), McDougall (2012), Medeiros (2005), Mochizuki (2007), Roy (2005), Shekhar (2012), and Thayer (2008, 2011*b*).

5. Mutual trust between Vietnam and China during this time was relatively high. For example, following the 1954 Geneva Conference, Vietnam asked China to take over Bach Long Vi island in the Tonkin Gulf on its behalf. The Chinese did and returned the island to Vietnam in 1957. See Loi (1995, Chapter 5).

6. However, by October 2014, the hot line had not been in operation yet. In July 2013, the two countries also agreed to establish another hot line between their fishery authorities to handle the rising number of incidents related to fishermen, but it was unknown when the hot line would be activated.

7. For recent accounts of China's naval modernization, see O'Rourke (2013), Chang (2012), and Cole (2010).

8. Full text of the ordinance is available at <http://www.moj.gov.vn/vbpq/Lists/Vn%20bn%20php%20lut/View_Detail.aspx?ItemID=26116> (accessed 20 August 2015).

9. By August 2013, it had become clear that Vietnam would acquire 2 rather than 4 corvettes from the Netherlands. The deal, which was reported to be worth US$660 million, provided for one of the corvettes to be built in the Netherlands, the other in Vietnam (*Dat Viet* 2013).

10. For example, Vietnam was reportedly interested in acquiring Brahmos supersonic missiles from India. In 2013, India also offered Vietnam a US$100 million credit line to purchase four patrol boats (*The Hindu* 2013).

11. See various interviews with Deputy Minister of Defence Nguyen Chi Vinh, e.g.: <http://vnexpress.net/tin-tuc/xa-hoi/vn-quan-he-voi-my-khong-phai-de-can-bang-suc-manh-tai-bien-dong-2172881.html>, <http://vnexpress.net/tin-tuc/xa-hoi/viet-nam-khong-chap-nhan-nen-hoa-binh-le-thuoc-2184972.html>, and <http://vnexpress.net/tin-tuc/xa-hoi/viet-nam-khong-chap-nhan-su-can-du-xam-hai-chu-quyen-2660487.html>.

12. For useful insights into this incident, see Thayer (2012*a*, 2013).

13. In March 1999, the ARF assigned the Philippines and Vietnam the task of drafting the DOC. For more information about the DOC as well as the role of Vietnam in its emergence, see Thao (2001, 2003).

14. A survey of statements by Vietnam MOFA spokesperson shows that the DOC is constantly invoked in Vietnam's diplomatic protests against Chinese activities in the SCS. An archive of statements by the MOFA spokesperson is available at <http://www.mofa.gov.vn/vi/tt_baochi/pbnfn>.

8

The Prospects of Democratization in Vietnam and China and Implications for Bilateral Relations

Introduction

Thirty years of development under *Doi Moi* have not only transformed Vietnam economically, but also generated important political implications for the country. Significant socio-economic development achieved under *Doi Moi*, according to modernization theory, will contribute to the prospect of Vietnam transitioning itself into a liberal democracy in the long run. Such a prospect is not only consequential for Vietnam's domestic politics, but also carries important implications for Vietnam's foreign relations, including those with China. As China itself may ultimately undertake democratic transition as well, internal political developments in each country will open up a number of different possible directions in which future bilateral relations could evolve.

In effect, there are four major scenarios in which domestic conditions in both Vietnam and China could shape the future trajectory of bilateral relations. The first is more or less the same as the current situation in which both Vietnam and China remain authoritarian states with the CPV and CCP maintaining their firm grip on power. The second and third scenarios involve the possibility of one of the two countries democratizing while the other remains authoritarian. Finally, under the fourth scenario, both Vietnam and China transform themselves into liberal democracies. As such, the domestic political transformations of each of the above scenarios will inevitably add further nuances to the already complicated relationship. The prospects of democratization in both countries and their implications for bilateral relations therefore merit serious examination.

The current chapter looks into future political prospects of Vietnam and China and investigate their implications for bilateral relations. Accordingly, the chapter adopts the theoretical tenets of modernization theory to argue that as both Vietnam and China achieve further progress in their socio-economic development, they will move closer towards political democratization. However, the exact timing of such a transformation in each country is unknown, making it necessary to consider all four possible scenarios mentioned above. By analysing these scenarios and taking into account other independent variables, most notably the ongoing South China Sea disputes and the regional strategic environment, this chapter argues that contrary to expectations of liberal peace theorists, the first scenario in which both countries remain authoritarian tends to be more favourable for a stable bilateral relationship than the other three scenarios.

Modernization Theory: Key Tenets and Debates

Although political scientists may disagree on the relative weight of particular preconditions of democracy, they tend to share a consensus on what those preconditions are. These preconditions generally fall into three broad categories.

First, democracy is more likely to triumph in societies which have undergone modernization and accumulated a certain level of wealth. Such a modernization process, among other things, transforms the social structure of the society, breeding and nurturing modern classes that are receptive to democratic values, such as the middle classes, industrial bourgeoisie and workers, while marginalizing those who tend to reject it, such as traditional landowners (see, for example, Berger 1986; Dahl 1971; Huntington 1984; Lipset 1959; Papaioannou and Siourounis 2008; Schumpeter 1950; Skocpol 1979; Sørensen 2008). In Seymour M. Lipset's (1959, p. 75) words, "the more well-to-do a nation, the greater chances that it will sustain democracy."

The second major precondition concerning the emergence of democracy is the political culture and religious traditions of the societies in question. Certain cultures and religions tend to be more conducive to democracy than others. For example, many scholars have argued that while Protestantism is favourable to the growth of democracy, Islam, Confucianism, as well as Catholicism in many cases, are less so (see, for example, Bernard 1993; Huntington 1991; Lipset 1981, pp. 57–58; 1994, pp. 3–7; Sørensen 2008, pp. 30–31; Zakaria 2004). This seems to be an important factor accounting for the proliferation of democracy in Europe and America on the one hand, and its absence or fragile presence in the Middle East, Africa, and Asia on the other.

Finally, external factors also impact on the transition to democracy in particular countries. Accordingly, the economic, political and ideological environment of the international system can either facilitate or hinder the spread of democracy. For example, following World War II, the United States and victorious allies imposed democracy on Japan and Germany, while most Central and Eastern European countries rejected liberal values during the Cold War due to Soviet influences. Another relevant and more recent example is the Arab Spring in 2011, in which revolution and democratic transition in Tunisia inspired the same processes in neighbouring countries.

Among these three sets of preconditions, the modernization process is arguably the most important one for not only the advent but also the consolidation of democracy. Although the link between modernization and social change has been contemplated by various scholars since the Age of Enlightenment (Inglehart and Welzel 2005, p. 17), it was not until the latter half of the twentieth century that serious efforts to test empirically the hypothetical link began to gain momentum. One of the earliest and most-cited studies of this type was Lipset (1959), in which the author examined empirical data from forty-eight countries in Europe and America and found strong evidence that four important conditions generated by the modernization process, namely, wealth, industrialization, urbanization, and education, made the emergence of democracy more likely. In another influential work, Robert Dahl (1971, p. 65) also concurred with Lipset, concluding that the positive correlation between a country's socio-economic development level and its embrace of democracy is "pretty much beyond dispute".

In the 1960s and 1970s, the findings of Lipset and his supporters were contested by a number of scholars. For example, Andre Gunder Frank (1970) criticized Lipset on the grounds that his conclusions were strictly based on the history of Western countries and neglected Third World's experiences. Meanwhile, using some South American countries as case-studies, Guillermo O'Donnell (1973) turned Lipset's thesis on its head. According to O'Donnell, experiences in such countries as Argentine and Brazil showed that modernization tended to breed authoritarianism rather than democracy. In order to pursue industrial modernization effectively, the ruling elite in these countries needed an authoritarian system. O'Donnell's argument was supported by two notable cases in East Asia, where South Korea and Taiwan by then had maintained authoritarian systems despite their high speed of economic development.

Since the late 1970s, however, with the advent of the "Third Wave of Democratization", Lipset's thesis has gained further support as numerous studies, both theoretical and empirical, have reaffirmed its validity. In effect, by the 1990s, most countries that critics of modernization theory cited to support their case, including Argentine, Brazil, South Korea, and Taiwan, had undergone democratization. The level of socio-economic development was again identified as an important condition that enhanced the probability of democratization. For example, in the "Third Wave", Huntington (1991, p. 63) found that "twenty-seven out of thirty-one countries that liberalized or democratized were in the middle-income range". The Third Wave also spurred researchers to identify a development benchmark above which countries are likely to transition into democracy.

Accordingly, scholars have argued that a country enters a "transition zone" when it reaches a certain level of GDP per capita. For example, Huntington (1991, pp. 61–62) identified the entry point to be US$1,000 (in 1976 dollars, or US$3,116 in 2011 dollars) in per capita income.[1] Meanwhile, the UNDP's *Human Development Report 2002* cited the dataset provided by Michael Alvarez and his collaborators to show that the probability of a country undergoing democratization in a given year doubles as its per capita GDP (calculated in PPP) grows from US$1,001 to US$6,000 (in 1985 dollars, or US$1,802 to US$10,805 in 2011 dollars) (UNDP 2002, p. 58). The UNDP's report conforms with the findings by Adam Przeworski and Fernando Limongi (1997, pp. 159–60), who stated that the GDP per capita range of US$1,000–US$6,000 (in 1985 U.S. dollars) is the "transition zone", in which democratic transitions are "increasingly likely" as per capita income of the dictatorships rises.[2]

The rising level of income, which is obviously a key indicator of a country' modernization and development, facilitates the advent of democracy in several ways. Huntington (1984, p. 199) argues that wealth provides the resources needed to ease the tensions that social and political conflicts produce, thus facilitating the peaceful transition into democracy. Meanwhile, Lipset (1959, pp. 83–85) points out several positive effects of the higher national income level on the acceptance of democratic norms and institutions. For example, increased wealth changes the social conditions of workers, making them less prone to extreme ideologies and increasingly receptive to democracy. Similarly, greater prosperity also changes the society's stratification structure with a larger proportion of the middle class, which serves to moderate social conflicts as "it is able to reward moderate and democratic parties while penalize extremist groups" (p. 83). Moreover, greater wealth also brings about the proliferation of the "mass society" composed of organizations and institutions more or less independent of the state which can help disseminate democratic values and norms throughout the society.

The rising level of income is also normally accompanied by other social changes conducive to the emergence of democracy, such as the higher rate of urbanization and a higher level of educational attainment among the population. The latter factor is especially emphasized by Lipset as a very important condition for democracy, even "far more significant" than the role of income and occupation. Lipset observes that "education presumably broadens men's outlooks, enables them to understand the need for norms of tolerance, restrains them from

FIGURE 8.1

The Correlation between Income Level and Democratic Transition

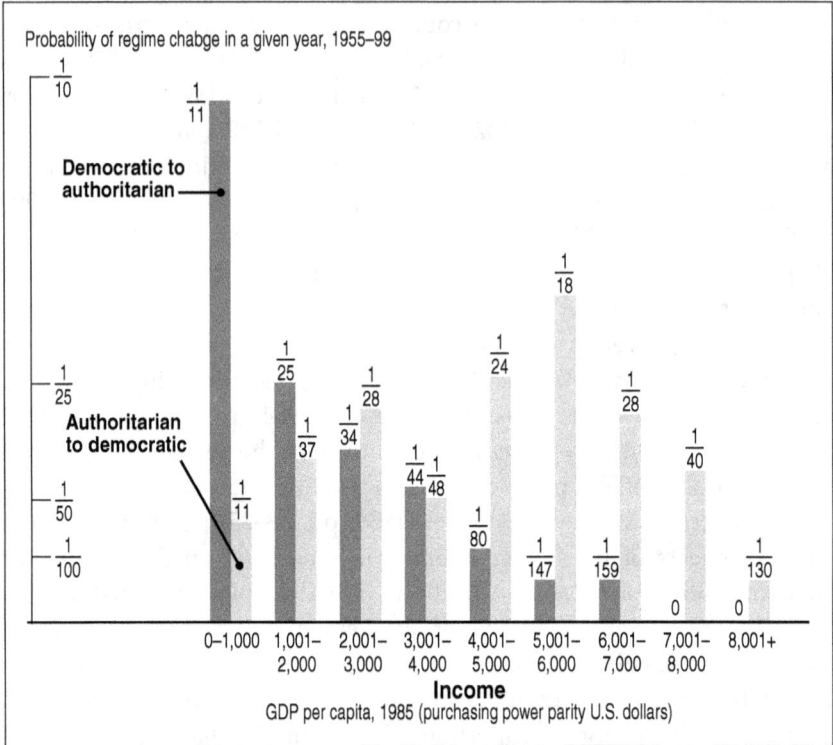

Probability of regime chabge in a given year, 1955–99

Income
GDP per capita, 1985 (purchasing power parity U.S. dollars)

Source: UNDP (2002, p. 58).

adhering to extremist and monistic doctrines, and increases their capacity to make rational electoral choices". He therefore concludes that "the higher one's education, the more likely one is to believe in democratic values and support democratic practices" (Lipset 1959, p. 79). Lipset's arguments have been strongly supported by various empirical works (see, for example, Barro 1999; Glaeser et al., 2004; Papaioannou and Siourounis, 2008; Przeworski et al. 2000).

In sum, there is a strong positive correlation between a country's level of socio-economic development and its probability to adopt a democratic political system. However, it should be noted that this correlation is still being disputed by some researchers, who base their argument on cases in the Middle East and elsewhere to show that a country's socio-economic development, especially in terms of high per capita national income, does not always signify that it is, or is likely to become, a liberal democracy. This puzzling fact has been predominantly explained as an effect of the "resource curse". According to these scholars, the authoritarian governments of these countries can use multiple tools made available by their resource abundance to relieve the pressure for democratization (see, for example, Friedman 2006; Jensen and Wantchekon 2004; Papaioannou and Siourounis 2008; Ross 2001; Wantchekon 2002). For example, Michael Ross, a key proponent of this thesis, argues that resource-rich governments can buy off political opposition by using low tax and patronage to relieve democratic pressures; spending money earned from resource exports to fund their oppressive internal security apparatus at their discretion, and maintaining a growth model based on resource exports that fails to produce social and cultural changes conducive to democratic transition (Ross 2001). Meanwhile, some other scholars have also explained the Middle East's democracy deficit in religious and cultural terms. Their argument is that Islam and its hierarchical, patrimonial culture make Middle Eastern countries largely incompatible with democratic systems (see, for example, Fish 2002; Karatnycky 2002; Kedourie 1994; Pipes 1983; Waterbury 1994). It should be noted, however, that these alternative views on the lack of democracy despite high per capita income are still discussed and contested by scholars from different disciplines.[3]

Given all these ongoing debates, although development has been proven empirically to be a major factor driving certain non-democratic countries into the democratization process, one should be vigilant to not turn a blind eye to other variables that may hinder or facilitate the advent of democracy. After all, there appears to be no universal formula or process which can explain the democratic transformation in all countries. Instead, one should take into account each country's historical context as well as its political, cultural and socio-economic characteristics to have a more in-depth understanding of its actual or potential democratization. Against this backdrop, Vietnam and China, both of which have experienced significant socio-economic developments over the past three decades but remain authoritarian regimes, present intriguing cases for scholarly examination.

Socio-economic Developments vs. Authoritarian Persistence in Vietnam and China

In the 1980s and 1990s, the "third wave of democratization" swept through Asia to bring about democratic transitions in nine countries: Bangladesh (1990), Indonesia (1998), Mongolia (1990), Nepal (1990), Pakistan (1988), the Philippines (1986), South Korea (1987), Taiwan (1987), and Thailand (1992). Yet, when it comes to accounting for these transitions, modernization theory seems to become weaker in comparison with other settings in the world. As summarized by Lee (2002, p. 823), seven out of the nine countries were low- or middle-income economies, and only two of them were upper-middle or high-income ones, namely South Korea and Taiwan. The fact that some of these countries transitioned into democracy when they were still low- or middle-income economies suggests that there are factors other than socio-economic development that can nudge a country into the democratization process.

A number of Southeast Asian countries also seem to challenge the central tenets of modernization theory. Brunei, Singapore and Malaysia, for example, remain authoritarian or semi-democratic states despite their high levels of economic development and per capita income. These divergent cases have prompted scholars as well as policymakers to look for explanations, in which the most notable one is the "Asian values" thesis.[4] Prominent proponents of the thesis — such as former Malaysian Prime Minister Mahathir Mohamad and his Singaporean counterpart Lee Kuan Yew — contend that "Asian values" make Western model of liberal democracy undesirable, if not detrimental, to the stability and prosperity of East Asian societies. As neatly summarized by Robison (1996, p. 311),

> At the heart of the "Asian values" perspective is an organic view of society in which the state embodies and is the guardian of the general interests of society, above and against the contest of vested interest. The notion of society consisting of contending interests is replaced with that of a society comprising a range of functional elements. In such a harmonious organism, political competition is replaced with service to the common interest. Opposition becomes deviance and dysfunction.

Nevertheless, the "Asian values" thesis tends to be promoted as an argument to defend the authoritarian/semi-democratic rule in certain countries. At the broader regional level, however, the thesis becomes an inadequate intellectual endeavour to explain the dynamics of political democratization in this region. Certain East Asian societies such as South Korea and Taiwan did transition successfully into liberal democracy despite their long-standing embedded traditions of "Asian values". These two are textbook cases supporting modernization theory, as both started their democratization process after reaching upper-middle or high levels of per capita income following decades of robust economic development. These observations from Asia and elsewhere in the world lend support to the argument that a single theoretical formulation cannot account for the diverse circumstances under which regional regimes operate, as well as their embrace or rejection of liberal democracy. While the level of a country's socio-economic development may offer an important indicator as to how and/or whether it will democratize or remain undemocratic, the most plausible answer can more likely be found in each country's specific political, historical, socio-economic and cultural conditions.

As far as Vietnam and China are concerned, the economic reforms that the two countries have pursued over the last thirty years or so have significantly improved their citizens' living standards in general and per capita income in particular. Table 8.1 provides some key democratization-related development indicators as identified by modernization theorists, especially Lipset (1959) that are likely to have benefited from these reforms.

As seen in Table 8.1, these key "social requisites" for democracy in both China and Vietnam have been strengthened over the last thirty years. These include the growing levels of wealth (indicator 1), industrialization (indicator 2), education (indicators 3 and 4), and urbanization (indicator 5). In other words, in undertaking their economic reforms, China and Vietnam are moving closer to the type of democratic transition depicted by classical modernization theory. Together with these socio-economic developments, the political environments in the two countries have also become significantly more relaxed. Individuals now enjoy a much greater level of civilian liberty and the two ruling communist parties are also experimenting with certain political reforms in reaction to pressures for democratization that are slowly building up from within their respective societies. As such, Vietnam and China now stand out as the most likely candidates for the next "wave of democratization" in the region, although how it

TABLE 8.1
Some Key Development Indicators of China and Vietnam

Year	China	Vietnam
1. GDP per Capita (PPP in current U.S. dollars)		
1991	890	792
2001	2,612	1,709
2011	8,322	3,574
2. Total Share of Industry and Services in GDP (%)		
1991	75.5	59.5
2001	85.6	78.5
2011	90	79.9
3. Literacy Rate, Adult Total (% of people ages 15 and above)		
1990	77.8	87.6 (1989)
2000	90.9	90.2
2010	95.1	93.4 (2011)
4. School Enrolment, Tertiary (% gross)		
1991	3.0	1.9
2001	9.8	9.4
2011	24.3	24.4
5. Urban Population (% of total)		
1991	27.3	20.6
2001	37.2	25
2011	50.5	31

Source: World Bank's World Development Indicators database <http://data.worldbank.org/data-catalog/world-development-indicators>, accessed 26 February 2014.

will happen and how long the process will take are issues that are more likely speculative rather than definitive at this juncture.

Among the four above-mentioned indicators, the level of wealth expressed in terms of GDP per capita is often used by researchers as a major predictor of democratic transition. As both Vietnam and China have not democratized yet, looking into the growth of GDP per capita and its possible future movements in both countries can provide some useful clues on the possibility of this future scenario. Figure 8.2 shows the two countries' GDP per capita in 2011 and its projections up to 2030.

FIGURE 8.2
GDP per capita (PPP, in 2011 U.S. dollar) of Vietnam and China, 2011–30

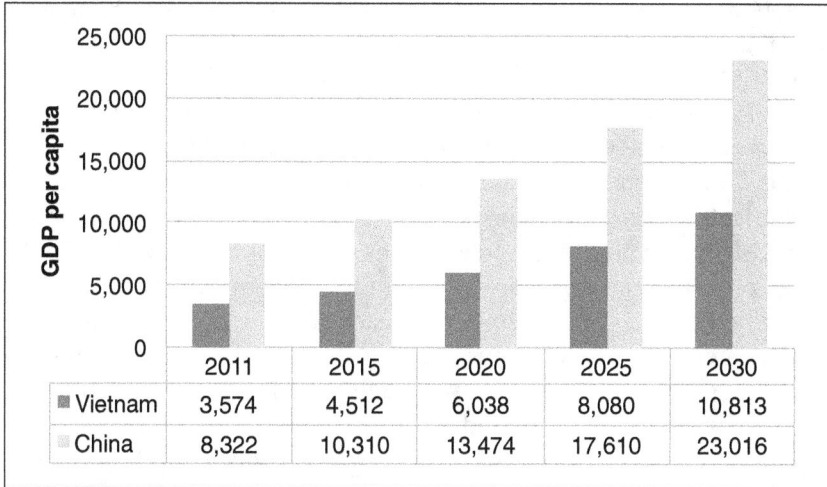

	2011	2015	2020	2025	2030
Vietnam	3,574	4,512	6,038	8,080	10,813
China	8,322	10,310	13,474	17,610	23,016

Source: The 2011 figures were retrieved from the World Bank's World Development Indicators database <http://data.worldbank.org/data-catalog/world-development-indicators>, accessed 26 February 2015. The projected figures are the author's own estimation based on the assumption that, ceteris paribus, the average annual GDP growth rates of China and Vietnam during the 2011–30 period are 5.5 and 6 per cent, respectively.

It should be noted that the projected figures are based on a rather conservative estimation that during the period of 2011–30, Vietnam's and China's GDP will grow at annual average rates of 6 per cent and 5.5 per cent, respectively. The actual growth rates may be higher if the structural reforms introduced in the two economies lead to expected or better performance outcomes.

If we adopt the GDP per capita range of US$1,802 to US$10,805 (PPP, in 2011 U.S. dollars) to be the transition zone as proposed by the UNDP (2002) and Przeworski and Limongi (1997), we can see that both Vietnam and China are now progressing through that zone. China is expected to exit this zone by around 2016 and Vietnam in the late 2020s. This prospect has prompted a number of scholars to predict that the present form of government in the two countries, especially China, will not be able to survive.

For example, in a controversial book published in 2001, Gordon Chang predicted that the People's Republic of China would collapse within a matter of five to ten years, bringing down with it communist rule (G.G. Chang 2001). Although Chang's arguments are mainly based on economic grounds, such as the inefficiency of state-owned enterprises and the problems embedded in the country's financial system, they also imply that modernization can contribute in various ways to the country's democratization process. Meanwhile, in his 2007 article, Rowen predicts that if China's economy and the educational attainments of its population keep growing, China will be "correctly classed as belonging to the free nations of the earth" by 2025 (Rowen 2007, p. 38). Drawing more directly on modernization theory, Liu and Chen (2012) also argue that reasons rooted in the economic development trajectory, cultural change, political leadership trends, and the global environment will cause China to embark on the democratization process around 2020.

These predictions, however, are over-optimistic at least under current conditions. So far, there have been no credible signs that either China or Vietnam is going to democratize any time soon. China, in particular, is presenting a serious test to the modernization hypothesis as it will have exited the purported democratic "transition zone" with no prospect of a regime change within the next five years. Nevertheless, the divergence of China from the general trend proposed by modernization theory may not necessarily invalidate the theory. In the long run, after exiting the zone, there's little ground to believe that China will revert to a stricter form of authoritarian rule. Instead, it is likely that the communist regime will have to embrace further political reforms, both to facilitate economic development and to respond to mounting democratic pressures generated by the economic reforms themselves. All these developments, in turn, may yet pave the way for the ultimate advent of democratization. The same could also be true for Vietnam.

In this connection, the persistence of communist rule in China has been widely discussed by scholars (see, for example, A. Miller 2008; Nathan 2003; Shambaugh 2008). While China's robust economic growth since the late 1970s is obviously a key factor sustaining communist rule, the country's "authoritarian resilience" can also be attributed to the CCP's ability to adapt itself to the changing environment by introducing limited and well-tailored political reforms aimed at promoting good governance and the efficiency of the state apparatus, such as the institutionalization of succession politics; the emphasis on meritocratic rather than factional considerations in the promotion of political leaders; the differentiation and functional specialization of institutions within the regime, and the establishment of institutions for political participation (Nathan 2003). In particular, the introduction of direct village committee elections since the late 1980s can be seen as a strategy to boost "grass-root democracy", thereby easing pressures for democratization at higher levels.[5]

Similarly, the persistence of the communist one-party state in Vietnam has also been examined by various scholars (see, for example, Gainsborough 2012; London 2009; Thayer 2009a, 2009b, 2011a; T. Vu 2012). Explanations have focused on the CPV's claims of legitimacy based on its historical role in liberating and unifying the country as well as the successful economic reforms under *Doi Moi* which have significantly improved the living standards of large segments of the population. These factors have provided the CPV with grounds to justify its monopoly of power. Gainsborough (2012) also attributed the CPV's resistance to liberal political reforms to the country's political culture based on elitism and paternalism. Such a political culture tends to encourage authoritarianism and reject reforms that may pave the way for the political participation of the masses. As elitism and paternalism are deeply rooted in Confucianism, this cultural prism can also be applied to account for the CCP's unwillingness to undertake liberal political reforms.

Furthermore, when examining China's "socialism with Chinese characteristics" or Vietnam's "socialist-oriented market economy", one finds that rent-seeking has become a dominant behaviour in both regimes through which the elites take advantage of economic reforms to enrich themselves as well as their families and cronies.[6] As extraction of rents would be impossible without exclusive access to power, they have a vested interest in safeguarding their monopoly on power. This rent-seeking impulse not only accounts for the widespread corruption in both regimes, but also underscores their resistance to liberal reforms that may deprive them of political and economic privileges.

The two regimes' ability to effectively repress opposition movements plays an equally important role in the durability of their rule. In China, the repression of the 1989 Tiananmen Square pro-democracy demonstrations highlights the importance of the army and security forces in protecting the CCP's rule. In 2012, China's budget for internal "stability maintenance", code words for regime security, even exceeded its budget for national defence (C. Li 2013, p. 44).[7] In Vietnam, there is no disclosure of the budget for internal security, but there are indications that the CPV is highly reliant on the police and the army for regime protection. A significant number of seats in the CPV Central Committee are always reserved for representatives from the Ministry of National Defence and the Ministry of Public Security. For example, as of late 2013, 26 out of 175 full members, or 14.8 per cent, of the CPV Central Committee elected at the Party's 11th Congress in 2011 came from or were associated with these two ministries.[8] In revising the Constitution in 2013, the CPV even made a proposed amendment that the Vietnam People's Army would place absolute loyalty to the Party before its loyalty to the nation and the people. Although the proposal was finally rejected, it showed the Party's increasing reliance on the army to protect its rule.

Due to the reasons discussed above, there hardly exists any significant organized opposition movement in both China and Vietnam. Political dissidents and pro-democracy activists are routinely isolated, harassed, prosecuted, or pushed into exile.[9] Although such practices subject the two countries to international criticism regarding their human rights records, they certainly help maintain the two regimes' grip on power. Therefore, even if socio-economic developments generate democratic pressures, the two regimes may well survive as long as they can maintain an effective strategy to respond to these pressures. Such a strategy includes both hard and soft aspects. Hard aspects include such measures as isolating or persecuting outstanding dissidents, preventing organized opposition movements from being established or being able to operate effectively inside the country, or even using security forces to crack down on mass pro-democracy demonstrations when necessary as showcased by the Tiananmen Square incident. Meanwhile, soft aspects primarily include the strict censorship of the Internet and the mass media, the co-optation of potential political opponents,[10] and the implementation of restricted — if not cosmetic — political reforms to dissipate democratic pressures.

In addition, whether the two regimes can continue to maintain a positive socio-economic performance in the future will play no less a significant role in sustaining their rule, at least in the short run.

Robust economic growth, while unlikely to eliminate democratic pressures altogether, may forestall the eruption of social discontent into revolutions that may bring down the two regimes. In the long run, maintaining healthy socio-economic development will not be a magic bullet that can help the two regimes stay in power forever. In pursuing performance-based legitimation strategy, the two communist parties are indeed facing a dilemma. On the one hand, positive economic development is necessary to boost the regimes' legitimacy and stability. If the economy is stagnant or in crisis, they will face higher risks of vertical opposition in the form of street demonstrations and riots as well as horizontal challenges in the form of cleavages within the ruling elites (Tanneberg, Stefes and Merkel 2013). On the other hand, continued and robust economic development will create further conditions that are conducive to democratization, such as a wealthier society with a larger middle class, a better educated population with greater political awareness, and a more dynamic and autonomous civil society.[11] In other words, although continued socio-economic development is desired for the two regimes' survival, it unavoidably sows the seeds of their self-destruction.

Democratization Prospects and Their Implications for Bilateral Relations

The above analysis suggests that the ultimate democratization of both China and Vietnam is a question of when and how rather than whether or not. Accordingly, there are four hypothetical scenarios in which the future domestic political trajectory of China and Vietnam will play out. In Scenario 1, in the near future, possibly up to 2025, it is highly likely that the two communist regimes will remain securely in power. In Scenario 2, if modernization theory holds for the two countries and all other things being equal, China is likely to democratize before Vietnam as the former's current GDP per capita as well as other socio-economic development indicators are significantly higher than those of the latter. In Scenario 3, however, if other things are taken into account, there is a possibility that Vietnam may embark on democratization before China. Finally, in Scenario 4, both China and Vietnam will become democracies, either at roughly the same time in a cascade of regional regime change, or one after another. The four scenarios are summarized in Table 8.2.

TABLE 8.2
Four Scenarios of Democratization in China and Vietnam

	China	Vietnam
Scenario 1	Authoritarian	Authoritarian
Scenario 2	Democratic	Authoritarian
Scenario 3	Authoritarian	Democratic
Scenario 4	Democratic	Democratic

Source: Author's own compilation.

Given the rich literature on the domestic–foreign policy nexus in general and the democratic peace theory in particular,[12] the four scenarios offer a useful framework to analyse the implications of future political developments in Vietnam and China for bilateral relations. For analytical purposes of this chapter, it should be noted that these scenarios have been simplified to highlight the possible democratization in Vietnam and China as a key variable shaping the future trajectory of their relations. Future bilateral relations, however, will be much more nuanced and complex than what any single theoretical formulation or independent variable can capture. One should therefore be careful not to make over-simplified assessments based solely on the theoretical grounds offered by the democratic peace theory, or to treat regime type in Vietnam and China as the sole determinant of bilateral relations. In order to gain a more comprehensive and balanced insight into the future relationship between the two countries, the interference of other relevant variables, most notably the South China Sea disputes as well as the dynamics of the regional strategic environment, should also be taken into consideration. With this in mind, the section will now evaluate and compare the trajectories of future bilateral relations in the four above scenarios.

Scenario 1: Authoritarian Vietnam vs. Authoritarian China

In this scenario, the domestic political status quo in both Vietnam and China will remain unchanged, possibly at least for the next ten years. The two communist parties will stay firmly in power and sustained socio-economic development will continue to be their key source of legitimacy, although it is likely that both will attempt to experiment with some further yet well-designed political reforms to respond to criticisms against their authoritarian rules. In terms of foreign policy, the stable domestic conditions will enable China to continue its pursuit of global power status. At the regional level, it will continue to assert its territorial and maritime claims in the South China Sea, especially through its increased military power. Meanwhile, Vietnam will likely continue its current foreign policy of "diversification and multilateralization" and its hedging strategy against China will likely be maintained.

Therefore, in essence, the current trajectory of bilateral relations will be extended. As such, the sporadic bursts of tensions due to the South China Sea disputes will be carefully managed through bilateral mechanisms (see Chapter 7 for more detail) in order to maintain the overall stability of the relationship. Despite differences, especially regarding the South China Sea disputes, the two communist parties obviously share an interest in keeping the relationship peaceful and stable in order to stay focused on more important priorities, especially regime maintenance and domestic development. On the part of China, although Beijing will likely continue to press its claims in the South China Sea, it will try not to push them to the point of armed clashes. Vietnam, on its part, will continue to resist Chinese pressures through both its military modernization programme and its deepened relationships with foreign partners as well as regional institutions. While ASEAN will continue to provide Vietnam with the central avenue to address its "China problem", Vietnam's relations with the United States will also be further consolidated but not to an official level further than the "comprehensive partnership" established in July 2013. Joint efforts, however, will be made behind the scene to deal with China if its coercion in the South China Sea intensifies.

The key element in this scenario is the political affinity between the two regimes and their authoritarian nature. The former minimizes the impact of ideological differences as seen in Scenarios 2 and 3, thereby facilitating their cooperation in managing the South China Sea disputes. Meanwhile, the latter enables them to relatively isolate bilateral relations from domestic pressures, which is also helpful for the management of bilateral ties. In this scenario, the party-to-party communication and interaction is highly relevant for the handling of bilateral problems. This is also a key factor explaining the largely peaceful and stable relationship between the two countries since normalization in 1991.

However, as the crisis around the Chinese placement of the oil rig *Haiyang Shiyou* 981 in Vietnam's EEZ in May 2014 shows, the political affinity between the two regimes will become less relevant as a facilitator of bilateral relations when their territorial and maritime disputes come to the fore. In such cases, the two regimes' ability to isolate the management of bilateral relations from domestic pressures will also be seriously undermined. Leaders of both countries will be subject to enormous popular pressures to take strong actions in defence of national interests. Therefore, in this scenario, although the relatively peaceful and stable bilateral relationship since normalization will stand a good chance to be extended, the South China Sea disputes, if intensified, are likely to offset any stabilizing effects that the political affinity between the two regimes may generate on bilateral relations.

Scenario 2: Democratic China vs. Authoritarian Vietnam

In this scenario, China will democratize either from a top-down reform led by the CCP, or through a bottom-up revolution.[13] The former possibility will most likely occur when Chinese society transforms under the impact of the modernization process to a point that the CCP finds it impossible to withhold the country's transition into democracy without risking its dominant position in the political system. In this scenario orchestrated by the CCP itself, the party will embrace a more pluralistic and democratic political system characterized by the establishment of opposition parties and the organization of multi-party, competitive elections. However, the party will likely manipulate the transition in such a way that ensures its continued rule or overwhelming position for at least some time after the transition. Under these circumstances, China will evolve at best into an electoral democracy, but on the positive side, the transition will be rolled out peacefully and internal stability generally will be maintained. Meanwhile, the second possibility could happen when the CCP decays from within due to rampant corruption and inefficient governance, while poor economic performance coupled with rising social discontents encourages the people to take to the streets to demand democratic change. In this case, a democracy may eventually emerge but the nation as a whole will likely suffer from chaos and instability.

In both possibilities, China's conduct of foreign policy may be distracted for some time as domestic developments dominate the country's political agenda. In the South China Sea, China may keep a rather low-profile posture during the transitional period, but assertive actions may return as political parties will soon start to appeal to nationalist sentiments to garner popular support.

Meanwhile, in Vietnam, the CPV's rule is likely to be deeply shaken by developments in China but the party will manage to maintain its grip on power, possibly through stepped-up repression against any concerted attempts to take advantage of transformations in China to pressure the party into democratization. In terms of foreign policy, the CPV will feel somehow less confident but the foundations of its foreign policy will likely be maintained. Its relations with ASEAN and major powers will not suffer heavily from developments in China. However, Western powers, especially the United States, may again direct heavy criticism against the communist regime if its stepped-up repression against pro-democracy movements does occur. Meanwhile, Vietnam's relations with China will undergo a major transformation.

As China becomes democratic, the ideological affinity between the two countries will dissipate. This presents a new challenge for the two countries as the traditional communication channel between the two communist parties, which used to serve as major tool for the management of bilateral relations as discussed above, will have been eroded. Even when a new party-to-party channel is established, it will not function effectively due to ideological differences. The long-standing distrust between the two countries is likely to deepen, causing tensions over the South China Sea to become harder to contain. These tensions may also happen more frequently due to the fact that a democratic China is likely to become more responsive to domestic nationalist sentiments, forcing its policy makers to consider in certain cases extreme measures to assert China's territorial and maritime claims in the South China Sea.

At the broader strategic level, a democratic China is likely to have a more accommodating posture towards the United States, which encourages cooperation rather than competition between the two superpowers. This does not automatically present a major obstacle to Vietnam's relations with the United States as the latter still wants to maintain a healthy relationship with the former in case strategic competition between the two superpowers persists (as seen in the case of U.S.–Russia relations following the democratization of Russia in the early 1990s). Nevertheless, Vietnam will still find itself in a more vulnerable position as the ideological differences between the two superpowers will decrease, enhancing the possibility for them to reach compromises regarding the South China Sea at the expense of Vietnam.

Therefore, in this scenario, a democratic China is likely to enjoy a more favourable strategic position vis-à-vis an authoritarian Vietnam. The latter may find itself in a disadvantaged position and a more hostile strategic environment, at least in its relations with its northern neighbour. This will likely encourage pro-democracy attitudes among both the Vietnamese public as well as CPV elites, who may think that, other benefits notwithstanding, democratization will also improve Vietnam's strategic position in the regional order and reset its relations with China to a more balanced, favourable posture. In the meantime, given the above-mentioned reasons, it is likely that the bilateral relationship will generally become less stable than it is in Scenario 1.

Scenario 3: Democratic Vietnam vs. Authoritarian China

This scenario is the reverse image of Scenario 2. Based on the level of socio-economic development in both countries, modernization theory predicts that, if other things are equal, China should undertake democratization well before Vietnam due to its much higher level of development. However, if other things are taken into account, there is still a possibility that Vietnam will transition to democracy before China. As mentioned in the second section, in certain cases, low-income countries can democratize before those of higher income due to the interference of variables other than socio-economic development.

In the case of Vietnam, this prospect is underwritten by certain factors, such as Vietnam's smaller size which makes its democratization process easier to be managed, as well as its relatively more open domestic politics.[14] These conditions may make democratization more appealing and acceptable to certain segments of the CPV leadership. The emergence of a radical, reform-minded leadership, as seen in the Soviet Union in the late 1980s for example, will make a CPV-led democratization process more likely. In an alternative possibility, the domestic pressures for democratization in Vietnam may quickly build up if the CPV cannot maintain positive economic growth, or fails to address its legitimacy deficits such as corruption, income inequality, or its repeated denial of meaningful political reforms to accommodate an expanding, better educated and more politically-aware middle class. As such, although a bottom-up revolution that forces the CPV out of power is an undesirable outcome, it cannot completely be ruled out.

In this scenario, democratization in Vietnam may not generate a large impact on the CCP's rule as long as the CCP can firmly control its internal security apparatus. In addition, with a much larger territory and some separatist movements active in certain regions, such as Tibet and Xinjiang, risks associated with the democratization process, including the breakup of the nation, will provide the CCP with a legitimate excuse to resist democratization, even through harsh repression. Moreover, as long as the CCP succeeds in maintaining a relatively robust rate of economic development, its democratic pressures may be contained for an extended period of time. Therefore, China's potential democratization will be more likely shaped by its domestic factors rather than external ones, including developments in Vietnam.

In this scenario, it is likely that China's current trajectory of foreign policy will generally be maintained. Specifically, Beijing is likely to continue its pursuit of global power status through its economic and military modernization programme. Against this backdrop, its increased power projection capabilities will likely harden its stance over territorial and maritime disputes. As a consequence, tensions between Hanoi and Beijing over the South China Sea are due to occur more frequently, especially when Vietnam becomes a democracy. This judgement is based on a number of highly possible developments. First, as in Scenario 2, the direct communication channel between the two communist parties erodes, making it harder to manage crisis situations. Second, the democratization of Vietnam will unleash nationalist and anti-China sentiments. These sentiments are almost certain to be exploited by Vietnamese politicians for electoral advantages[15] and may be translated into official policies if they get elected. Third, a democratic Vietnam will likely strengthen relationships with regional democracies that share concerns regarding China's territorial and maritime designs, such as the Philippines and Japan. In particular, Vietnam's relations with the United Sates will likely be promoted to the point that the two countries may even become *de facto* allies. This is particularly the case if China maintains an aggressive posture in the South China Sea and strategic competition between China and the United States deepens. A closer relationship with Washington, while boosting Hanoi's confidence in its handling of Beijing, is likely to irritate the latter and generate destabilizing effects on bilateral relations.

Scenario 4: Democratic China vs. Democratic Vietnam

This scenario is the extension of developments described in Scenarios 2 and 3, in which the undemocratic country in the dyad will sooner or later transition into democracy. The triumph of democracy in both countries will be a major landmark in bilateral relations, as they will be guided for the first time in history by democratic governments on both sides. This may raise the hope long cherished by proponents of democratic peace theory that the two countries will finally find themselves in a "perpetual peace". However, is such an optimistic view warranted?

On the positive side, if both Vietnam and China become democracies, they will have basically a shared ideological framework. This might encourage cooperation between the two countries to manage their relations. The embrace of democratic institutions, norms and practices by both countries are also conducive to peace.[16] On the downside, however, the emergence of democracy in both countries will subject bilateral relations to the influence of a greater range of domestic actors, such as political parties, activist groups, the media, and public opinion. In other words, unlike the current communist parties, the ruling parties in the two countries cannot relatively insulate the management of bilateral relations from domestic pressures, thereby exposing them to greater risks of instability. Against this backdrop, the South China Sea disputes will be a key factor determining the state of bilateral relations. If the disputes undergo negative developments, they will undermine the pacifying effects that the two countries' joint democracy may generate on bilateral relations. This is particularly the case given the fact that a country's territorial and maritime claims normally persist despite regime changes or the nature of the regime itself.[17] A democratic China will likely pursue an assertive stance regarding the South China Sea as an authoritarian China. Its relations with Vietnam will therefore suffer as a consequence.

Furthermore, one should take into consideration a related possibility that in the early period following democratization, China may retain certain authoritarian traits of a communist regime rather than developing into a fully liberal Western-style democracy. In this case, the experience of democratization in other major countries, especially Russia, indicates that the strategic competition between China and the United States may not evaporate overnight. Instead, the two superpowers may again find themselves locked in enduring competition, which has a negative impact on the regional strategic environment. In this scenario, national interests, especially in terms of security, may override regime type in determining how countries treat each other. Consequently, if U.S.–China strategic competition deepens and Vietnam–China disputes over the South China Sea persist, Hanoi may be tempted to forge closer ties, even an explicit alliance, with Washington to counter Beijing's pressures. However, given Vietnam's geographical proximity to China and the power asymmetry between the two countries, such a strategy is undesirable for Vietnam. Under any circumstances, it should be in Vietnam's best national interests to maintain a healthy and stable relationship with China regardless of who is in power in Hanoi or Beijing.

In sum, although Scenario 4 opens up the possibility that Vietnam and China will enjoy a more peaceful and stable relationship once both have become democracies, there are still other factors at work that may undermine such a tendency. In particular, the South China Sea disputes and the regional strategic environment will also play important roles in shaping the trajectory of the two democracies' relations. As such, the dynamics of bilateral relations in Scenario 4 will be rather similar to those in Scenario 1, except for the fact that in the latter scenario, the two communist parties can more or less insulate the management of bilateral relations from domestic pressures as they see fit to preserve peace and stability, while it will be much harder for the governments in Hanoi and Beijing to do the same in the former scenario.

Conclusion

The significant socio-economic developments that Vietnam and China have achieved under their respective economic reform programmes over the last thirty years have brought about increasingly mature conditions for their democratic transition. As identified by modernization theorists, the most important conditions are related to the increased levels of wealth, industrialization, urbanization and education. Among these, the increasing level of GDP per capita is the most powerful indicator showing both countries' greater readiness for democratization.

Currently, however, the two communist parties still maintain a firm grip on power and there are no credible indications that they will go down the democratization path any time soon. The persistence of authoritarian rule in the two countries can be explained by a number of factors related to their specific historical, cultural, socio-economic as well as political conditions. Among these, the two ruling parties' effective strategies to deal with democratic pressures — as well as their ability to maintain generally positive, uninterrupted socio-economic development — prove to be the most important ones. In the long run, however, democratization tends to be highly likely given two important trends. First, a wealthier, better-educated population with greater political awareness will naturally generate more pressures for democratization. Second, the two communist parties tend to strengthen the first trend by pursuing performance-based legitimation strategy. Democratization therefore seems to be an inescapable prospect for both countries. The more important question that remains is when and how it will happen.

The uncertainty around when and how the two countries will democratize therefore presents four scenarios in which each country's internal political developments can shape future bilateral relations. These include: authoritarian Vietnam vs. authoritarian China (Scenario 1); democratic China vs. authoritarian Vietnam (Scenario 2); democratic Vietnam vs. authoritarian China (Scenario 3); and democratic China vs. democratic Vietnam (Scenario 4).

Among these four scenarios, Scenario 1 tends to be the most conducive to a stable bilateral relationship. This is mainly due to the two communist parties' ability to insulate the management of bilateral relations from domestic pressures as well as the political affinity that may, to some extent, facilitate their cooperation to address bilateral problems. Scenario 4 may be the second most peaceful scenario, as the democratic nature of the two governments encourages them to manage their relations in a peaceful manner. However, this prospect is undermined by the fact that bilateral relations will now be subject to greater domestic pressures, which are much harder to control in democracies than in authoritarian regimes. Meanwhile, Scenarios 2 and 3 tend to be the least favourable for a stable relationship as political differences will likely exacerbate the mutual historical distrust and undermine efforts to peacefully manage bilateral tensions.

Apart from regime type, future developments in the South China Sea and U.S.–China relations will also have important implications for bilateral relations. In all cases, bilateral relations will become much more peaceful and stable if the South China Sea disputes are resolved. However, given the current status of the disputes, this is an unlikely prospect even in the long run. Therefore, how the two countries manage the disputes will be an important factor that shapes the overall relationship. No matter which regime is in power in Hanoi and Beijing, aggressive actions in the South China Sea by either side will most likely undermine bilateral relations.

Meanwhile, the future trajectory of U.S.–China relations will also affect how Vietnam is perceived by the two superpowers, which necessarily generates important implications for Vietnam–China relations. The preceding analyses suggest that regardless of the nature of Hanoi and Beijing regimes, Vietnam will be at a disadvantaged position vis-à-vis China if U.S.–China relations become either too warm or too cold. In the former case, Vietnam is likely to be marginalized in U.S. strategic calculations, which makes it more vulnerable to China's pressures. In the latter case, Vietnam's efforts to balance its relations with the two superpowers will be at risk. While bandwagoning with China will be almost impossible due to various reasons such as historical experiences and the persistence of the South China Sea disputes, moving closer to the United States will turn the country into a hostile target in Beijing's eyes. Therefore, it will be in the best interest of Vietnam, whether it be authoritarian or democratic, to witness a U.S.–China relationship that has both competitive and cooperative elements. Furthermore, unless China becomes too aggressive in the South China Sea, maintaining a hedging strategy against Beijing will best serve Hanoi's broad national interests, especially when it comes to addressing strategic risks arising from the uncertainty around future U.S.–China relations.

NOTES

1. The conversion into 2011 dollars here and elsewhere in this chapter is done by Areppim's Mathematics & Financial Calculators, available at <http://stats.areppim.com/calc/calc_usdlrxdeflator.php>.

2. Nevertheless, it should be noted that Przeworski and Limongi (1997, pp. 159–60) also argue that above the threshold of US$6,000, dictatorships become more stable, and transitions to democracy become less likely. However, Boix and Stokes (2003) have found that this conclusion is ill-founded and misleading due to errors in the authors' methodology.

3. For example, the "resource curse" thesis has been contested by authors such as Dunning (2008), Haber and Menaldo (2011), and Herb (2005). Meanwhile, the explanation for the lack of democracy in the Middle East in religious and cultural terms has been challenged by, among others, Diamond (2010), Esposito and Voll (2001), Hefner (2011), and Kurzman (1998).

4. Although there is no consensus on the definition of the term, its core tenets include: the central role of family as the focal point of social organization; the precedence of community interests over individual ones; the preference for consensus rather than confrontation through representative systems in making political decisions; the emphasis on social cohesion and harmony achieved through moral principles and strong government, which in turn produces economic growth and development (Robison 1996, pp. 310–11).

5. For analyses on the implications of village elections for China's domestic politics, see Epstein (1997), Shi (1999), O'Brien and Li (2000), and Pastor and Tan (2000).

6. For accounts of rent-seeking in China, see, for example, Lu (1999), Che (2002), Chen, Li and Su (2005), and Ngo (2008). For recent analyses of the behaviour and its implications in Vietnam, see Jandl (2013) and Vuving (2013).

7. Specifically, in 2012, the regime spent 679 billion yuan on defence and 702 billion on "stability maintenance".

8. To put it in perspective, the Ministry of Foreign Affairs has only three seats, the Ministry of Planning and Investment and Ministry of Finance one seat each. Data taken from the list of Central Committee members found at <http://vneconomy.vn/thoi-su/danh-sach-uy-vien-ban-chap-hanh-trung-uong-dang-khoa-xi-20110118023313750.htm>

9. Reports on the repression of political dissidents, democracy and human rights activists in China and Vietnam can be retrieved from Human Rights Watch's website at <http://www.hrw.org/asia/china> and <http://www.hrw.org/asia/vietnam>, respectively.

10. In China, the most relevant example for this is the CPC's decision in the early 2000s to allow private business people to join the Party.
11. Some useful discussions on the role of the civil society in the domestic politics of China and Vietnam can be found in Tang and Zhan (2008) and Thayer (2009b).
12. The liberal peace theory's central thesis, which is strongly supported by empirical evidence, is that liberal democracies do not go to war against each other (see, e.g., Michael W. Doyle, 1983a; Michael W. Doyle, 1983b; Jack S. Levy, 1988; Mesquita, et al., 1999; J.L. Ray, 1998; Rummel, 1983; Russett, 1993). A useful review of the theory and debates around it can be found in Ray (1998).
13. A assessment of the two possibilities can be found in Li (2013).
14. Some other authors share the same observation. For example, London (2009, p. 376) contends that "despite many undemocratic aspects, Vietnam's political regime has been more substantively progressive than China's, devoting proportionately more attention to the aspirations and interests of the general population." Meanwhile, Cheng (2011, p. 401) also observes that "in recent years, Vietnam's political reforms have been more progressive than those in China, which have largely been stagnant since the Tiananmen Square Incident in 1989". This observation is further buttressed by recent political developments in Vietnam, such as the revision of the 1992 Constitution which includes more provisions on human rights, or the introduction of confidence vote on key public office holders at both national and local levels.
15. An illuminating parallel is the exploitation of anti-Vietnamese sentiments by Cambodian politician Sam Rainsy and his Cambodia National Rescue Party in national elections.
16. For analyses of how democratic institutions, norms and practices help promote international peace, see Russett (1993), Doyle (1997), Owen (2000), De Mesquita et al. (1999). For counter-arguments, see Rosato (2003).
17. The Philippines' claims to the Spratlys and Argentina's claims to the Falklands/Malvinas islands are cases in point.

9

Conclusion: The Lessons of *Doi Moi* for Vietnam's China Policy

In March 2014, a news article in *Dat Viet* reported that Chinese textile producer Yulun Jiangsu received a licence to invest US$68 million into a textile plant in Nam Dinh province, 50 km south of Hanoi (Thu Phuong 2014). The article cited provincial authorities as saying that an unnamed investor from Hong Kong was also planning to set up a 1,000-hectare textile processing complex in Nghia Hung District of the same province. It went on to quote experts as explaining that the new wave of Chinese investment into the country's textile industry was due to Chinese investors' expectation to take advantage of the Trans-Pacific Partnership (TPP) Agreement that Vietnam and other partners, including the United States but not China, were going to conclude. These experts also voiced their concern that such developments could lead to the domination and manipulation of the country's economy by Chinese companies. One of the experts even referred to concerns raised by netizens that the concentration of Chinese labourers working for a multi-billion steel project by Taiwanese company Formosa in Vung Ang Economic Zone of the central province of Ha Tinh might make Vietnam vulnerable in the event of a Chinese attack.[1] The expert emphasized that the large presence of Chinese nationals in the area therefore generated more challenges than just social and economic ones (Thu Phuong 2014).

In the same month, a flurry of news stories commemorating the naval clash on 14 March 1988 between Vietnam and China in the Spratlys also appeared in most major Vietnamese news websites. Almost one month before that, a wide range of news articles and stories commemorating the thirty-fifth anniversary of the Vietnam–China border war, which broke out on 17 February 1979, were also published in numerous newspapers and websites, including state-sanctioned ones. These moves came as a surprise as the 1979 border war as well as the 1988 naval clash had always been considered "sensitive issues" by Vietnamese authorities. They were even hardly mentioned in official textbooks and the media were previously restricted from covering the issues. The Vietnamese government's decision to relax the censorship on these two events in 2014 therefore, to a certain extent, reflects a shift in its attitude towards these two issues.

Broadly speaking, the above stories are just two among the various examples of the increasingly complex relationship between Vietnam and China and how it has evolved through both continuity and change over the last three decades. The first example shows that as economic interactions between the two countries deepen, they have now been enmeshed into a dense network of trade and investment ties which serve to meet their economic needs but, in certain cases, also heighten the sense of vulnerability on the part of Vietnam due to the asymmetrical nature of the bilateral economic relations. Meanwhile, the second example highlights the politics of memory through which deep-seated historical animosity keeps casting a shadow on current ties. The simmering disputes over the South China Sea, in particular, are providing an important impetus for Vietnam to become increasingly wary of China's rise. With its own power growing after three decades of economic development, Vietnam is now in a much better position to defy China's power when necessary to protect its interests. To a certain extent, Hanoi's decision to relax censorship of the two above-mentioned events reflects its growing confidence as well as its wish to deal with Beijing on a more equal footing.

The Changing Structure of Vietnam–China Relations

Although Vietnam's current relations with China still reflect the traditional pattern of deference and defiance, they have proven to be more complex and nuanced than before. Specifically, the structure of bilateral relations, especially since normalization in 1991, has expanded both horizontally and vertically due to the emergence of new layers and dimensions in the relationship. Horizontally, bilateral relations have expanded beyond the traditional realms of diplomacy and trade to embrace new areas of interactions. The traditional ones, such as political or economic ties, have also been deepened or expanded to unprecedented levels. Vertically, the bilateral relations are now composed of not only the national level, but also those of sub-national and regional nature. The current structure of Vietnam–China relations is depicted in Figure 9.1.

At the horizontal dimension, for thousands of years, the traditional agenda of Vietnam–China relations was dominated by diplomatic interactions and limited economic exchanges through the China-centred tributary system. Since the two countries became independent states in the 1940s until the late 1970s, bilateral interactions thickened but remained largely limited to political ties, while economic ones were dominated by China's aid to assist Vietnam's war efforts. However, since normalization in 1991, bilateral relations have been expanded

FIGURE 9.1
The Structure of Contemporary Vietnam–China Relations

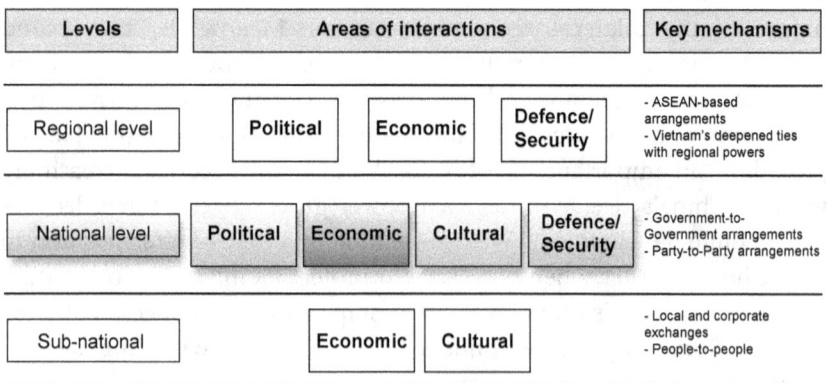

Source: Author's own compilation.

beyond the traditional diplomatic and economic realms. Economic ties, especially in terms of trade and investment, have now been strengthened to an unprecedented level and have become a defining feature of contemporary bilateral relations. As such, economic considerations now form a key factor in the policy-making process of each country towards the other. Other pillars of the relationship, such as political ties, defence and security, and cultural exchanges, have also been strengthened and diversified to significant levels that were unseen in previous historical periods.

At the vertical dimension, traditional bilateral relations were restricted to interactions at the national level. In the Cold War era, an international dimension was added to the relationship as both countries also interacted with each other within the communist bloc. Such multilateral interactions, however, were neither broad nor deep as the communist camp itself was small and divided. Since normalization in 1991, although the national level remains the core channel of interactions, bilateral relations have expanded to include much more significant levels of regional and sub-national interactions. At the regional level, the integration of both Vietnam and China into regional institutions and arrangements, especially ASEAN-centred ones such as the ARF, ASEAN+3, AFTA, is arguably a game changer, especially for Vietnam. The rules and norms of these institutions and arrangements have played an increasingly important role in shaping both sides' expectations and behaviour towards each other. At the same time, Vietnam's expanded and deepened foreign relations, especially with major powers, have also indirectly shaped the working environment of bilateral relations, in which both sides' interests are entangled with those of regional powers. At the sub-national level, the people-to-people interactions have been intensified due to the two countries' opening of their borders to flows of goods and people. The enhanced economic exchanges have also created a dense network of interactions between businesses of the two countries, which serves as a new important foundation for the bilateral relationship.

In effect, since normalization, Vietnam–China relations have been developing continuously and comprehensively. Politically, the two countries settled their land border disputes by concluding a land border treaty in late 1999, followed by the actual demarcation process that was completed in 2008. The two neighbours also settled part of their South China Sea disputes by concluding an agreement on the delimitation of the Tonkin Gulf in 2000. In 2008, they officially declared the establishment of a "comprehensive strategic cooperative partnership". Economically, trade ties expanded exponentially, turning China into Vietnam's largest trade partner in 2004. In 2013, for example, Vietnam's exports to and imports from China accounted for 10 per cent and 28 per cent of its respective total. China's investment in Vietnam, although remaining relatively limited, has also increased steadily over the last ten years. By the end of 2013, for example, there had been 992 Chinese FDI projects in Vietnam with the total registered capital reaching over US$7.5 billion. These significant developments have contributed to the horizontal expansion of bilateral relations as well as the growing role of economic interactions as a key pillar of bilateral relations.

Domestic Transformation and External Relations: The Lessons of *Doi Moi*

Observable throughout the changes in the structure of the bilateral relations is the role of the economic reform that Vietnam has been undertaking under *Doi Moi,* through which various newly emergent political and economic factors have been interacting to shape the current trajectory of the relationship. As documented and analysed in the preceding chapters, the impacts of *Doi Moi* on Vietnam's relations with China can be tracked in five major developments: (1) the normalization of bilateral relations in 1991; (2) the growing economic interdependence between the two countries; (3) the intensifying disputes over the South China Sea; (4) Vietnam's hedging strategy vis-à-vis China since normalization; and (5) the future trajectory of bilateral relations under the prospect of political democratization in both countries.

Although the persistence of traditional constraints such as power asymmetry and geographical proximity means that China will remain a major security threat for Vietnam, Hanoi today is in a better position to deal with Beijing than it was at any point during past history. Vietnam's newfound position vis-à-vis China comes from its enhanced national strength achieved under *Doi Moi* as well as its increased network of mutually beneficial interactions with China. Moreover, Vietnam's ability to capitalize on its expanded and deepened foreign relations to hedge against China through both bilateral and multilateral channels is of no less importance. The combination of the above factors has generated a strategic setting in which bilateral cooperation is encouraged while conflict is increasingly constrained, even disfavoured.

That said, given China's overwhelming power as well as the ongoing South China Sea disputes, Vietnam should keep a constant wary eye on its northern neighbour and look for initiatives to maintain the foundations of its current relatively successful China policy. The key foundations of Vietnam's China policy as well as its overall security posture will remain embedded in its domestic transformations, which in turn will dictate its overall foreign policy orientation. In this regard, Vietnam's experience over the past three decades of *Doi Moi* offers some vital lessons to be contemplated by itself as well as other small and medium countries which are facing their own dilemmas in dealing with greater powers.

First, external posture is built on internal strength. Without a significant level of economic development under *Doi Moi* over the past three decades, Vietnam's vulnerabilities vis-à-vis China would have been exacerbated. Vietnam's economic development not only results in increased wealth, which is in turn translated into more credible military capabilities over time, but also creates a network of economic interdependence between Vietnam and China that tends to have some moderating effects on their relations. Therefore, in order for Vietnam to extend its enhanced posture vis-à-vis China, it is essential for Vietnam to maintain the momentum of economic development under *Doi Moi*. Against this backdrop, the current economic problems that the country has been facing since 2008 should be seen as not only a domestic challenge, but also a foreign and security policy one. On the one hand, extended economic stagnation may cause budget constraints on the military modernization programme.[2] On the other hand, economic difficulties tend to distract the government from activities to support its diplomacy and foreign policy agenda.[3] More broadly speaking, a weakened economy will also tend to create unfavourable domestic conditions, which further disadvantages Vietnam in its dealings with China. Therefore, it is essential for Hanoi to overcome the current economic challenges, and the revitalization of *Doi Moi* should be seen as a task of utmost importance for both the domestic and foreign policy agendas of the country.

Second, maintaining an open and diversified foreign policy based on both bilateral and multilateral approaches is a prerequisite for the country's successful handling of pressures from China. In dire realist terms, a credible military modernization programme may serve Vietnam well, but it is not enough. Even when Vietnam's military capabilities keep growing, they will never be able to match those of China. Moreover, defence upgrades will inevitably gobble up investments for other essential areas of the country's social and economic life. Therefore, diplomacy offers a less expensive, yet effective, supplementary option for Vietnam to counter Chinese pressures. The current trajectory of Vietnam's foreign policy needs to be maintained at all cost, as a reversion to the international isolationism of the 1980s would be disastrous for both its economic development and security posture, especially vis-à-vis China. Although such a prospect is now largely unthinkable, certain developments at the broader regional and global level may generate strategic challenges for the country's foreign policy in the long run. In this regard, the possibility of a renewed Cold War between great powers, especially the United States and China, will probably be the greatest risk. Despite the significant economic interdependence between the two great powers and their recent call for a "new type of great power relationship", the prospect of a new Cold War is not totally out of question as long as China's power keeps growing to threaten the U.S. strategic primacy. In such a case, Vietnam needs to be careful to maintain its independent and neutral foreign policy to stay out of any collision between the two superpowers. The lessons of the twentieth century Cold War show that to ensure such an outcome, Vietnam needs to calibrate its foreign policy in accordance with its national interests rather than ideological inclinations or regime interests.

Third, Vietnam needs to maintain its view of China as the most important foreign partner and its relations with China the most important foreign relationship. The importance of China to Vietnam is derived from both the opportunities and threats that China presents Vietnam. Nevertheless, the opportunities that China's rise as a global growth engine, from which Vietnam's economic performance under *Doi Moi* has benefited, are only part of the picture. Far more important and central to Vietnam's current relations with China are the security implications of China's rise as a global political and military power. Historical lessons, including those from the Cold War era, have made clear to Vietnam that even when China is weak and vulnerable, its sheer size and the condition of geographic proximity can still make China a major security threat to Vietnam. Now with China's resurgence, the threat is even more formidable. Therefore, under no circumstance should Vietnam incite hostility from China. Vietnam should consistently maintain its diplomatic and legal approach to the handling of the South China Sea disputes at least to preserve the status quo and to prevent the occurrence of any incident that may spark a Chinese invasion. Although the possible resort to force in the South China Sea is more at the discretion of China than Vietnam, the latter can still minimize such a probability by exercising self-constraint, developing a credible deterrence capability, and utilizing diplomatic tools, especially its membership in ASEAN-led institutions and arrangements as well as its enhanced relations with regional powers, to shape China's behaviour.

Fourth, Vietnam should not expect to rely exclusively on any other external powers to counter China. Historical lessons from the 1974 and 1988 incidents in the South China Sea, for example, have shown that it is wishful thinking to expect other powers to sacrifice their ties with China just to protect Vietnam's interests. And even if they do, Vietnam's geographical proximity to China and the power asymmetry between the two countries mean that Vietnam will be exposed to constant pressures from China. Therefore, although external ties will be important to Vietnam's China strategy, Vietnam should be careful not to go to extremes by over-relying on them to counter Beijing. Instead, a nuanced approach which combines both internal strengths and external support, and balances between China and other powers, will be a wiser option for Vietnam to pursue. However, should China keep resorting to coercive measures to push its claims in the South China Sea, Vietnam should consider a shift towards "alliance politics", or efforts to forge close security and defence ties short of formal, treaty-bound alliances with key partners, to deal with the new situation.

Future Questions

This book has focused strictly on the political economy of Vietnam's relations with China under *Doi Moi* up to 2013. Several aspects of bilateral relations as well as their international implications have been left unexplored or under-investigated. Therefore, further studies should be conducted to shed more light on the relationship, especially given recent significant changes in the regional strategic environment as well as each country's domestic conditions. A number of topics and approaches appear to be particularly relevant.

First, a comprehensive study on the relationship using Chinese sources and focusing on Beijing's perceptions of Vietnam will be valuable as it will supplement this book to produce a more complete picture of the relationship. Such a study may help to clarify important yet under-investigated questions, such as China's motives in normalizing its relations with Vietnam; the role of ideological versus economic and strategic considerations in Beijing's handling of its relations with Hanoi, China's perception of Vietnam's hedging strategy, especially its hard and soft balancing approaches; China's view of Vietnam and its role in the regional order envisioned by Beijing; and the drivers behind China's increasing assertiveness, especially vis-à-vis Vietnam, in the South China Sea.

Second, although it is in Vietnam's best interest to maintain a balance between China and other regional powers, especially the United States, whether it can do so in face of an increasingly aggressive China in the South China Sea is quite a different question. In case China's aggression in the South China Sea seriously threatens Vietnam's core interests, for which Beijing's placement of the oil rig *Haiyang Shiyou 981* in Vietnam's EEZ in May 2014 is a relevant example, the rationality of Hanoi's current approach towards Beijing can be questioned. In any case, no matter how much Hanoi appreciates stable and friendly ties with Beijing, it will not be willing to trade its national sovereignty and territorial integrity for such a relationship. Against this backdrop, whether and under what conditions Vietnam will abandon its current non-aligned foreign policy in favour of alliance politics to deal with China is an interesting question that merits thorough examination. A study on this topic should also assess the potential costs and benefits for Vietnam if it adopts alliances to deal with China, the feasibility of such an approach, as well as its international ramifications.

Third, a number of researchers have posited that Vietnam's relations with China have been driven by the pull and push of the pro-Chinese versus pro-Western factions within the CPV. However, whether this is true, and if so, how much factional politics impact on the transformation of bilateral relations remains unknown as most studies on this topic are based on suppositions rather than concrete evidence. Therefore, research on this topic which bases its investigation on first-hand accounts, especially through access to key figures in the two camps and published as well as unpublished memoirs, will be a significant contribution to the literature on bilateral relations.

Finally, at the broader international level, the political economy of Vietnam's relations with China under *Doi Moi* may offer some valuable lessons to other countries, especially those that are experiencing both difficult domestic conditions and troubled relations with external powers. The two most relevant countries that may benefit from Vietnam's experiences are Cuba and North Korea. Both are one-party communist states that are facing harsh economic conditions as Vietnam did in the 1980s. They are also having troubled relations with external powers, especially the United States, as Vietnam did with China prior to bilateral normalization. Therefore, although the two countries' domestic and foreign policy options are shaped by conditions specific to themselves, they can still look to Vietnam for relevant lessons. Against this backdrop, studies that compare Vietnam's experience with China under *Doi Moi* and these two countries' experience with the United States over the past three decades may be useful contributions to the study of international relations, especially the literature on the domestic–foreign policy nexus.

In sum, Vietnam's relations with China have undergone significant changes under *Doi Moi*. Although traditional patterns of interactions persist, bilateral ties have become more complicated due to the expansion and deepening of cross-border interactions. Various political and economic factors both within each country and the regional setting have contributed to the dynamics of bilateral relations. While the two countries are increasingly interconnected, they are now also integrated more deeply into regional political, economic and security structures. This tendency poses greater challenges for students of Vietnam–China relations. Further studies from different perspectives and on various aspects of bilateral ties are therefore necessary to provide a better understanding of this interesting and important relationship as well as its regional implications.

NOTES

1. The argument made by critics was that as Vung Ang is close to the Ngang Pass and the narrowest part of the country (around 50 km) in the nearby Quang Binh province, Chinese workers could act to cut the country into two parts in the event of a Chinese attack. The critics also referred to the upgrade of the Vung Ang Border Station into Vung Ang Border Command in early 2014 as an indication that the Ministry of National Defence might have been aware of the risk and took steps to mitigate it. However, it should be noted that these threats may be exaggerated by critics of the government, who frequently exploit issues in Vietnam–China relations to discredit the government's policies and to undermine the CPV's legitimacy.

2. In 2013, for example, Vietnam suffered significant budget constraints due to a contracted tax base, causing the government to ask the National Assembly to approve an increase in the budget deficit ceiling from 4.8 per cent of GDP in 2013 to 5.3 per cent in 2014. See Anh Vu (2013).

3. For example, in 2012, Prime Minister Nguyen Tan Dung called on government officials, especially heads of government agencies, to cut foreign trips to save budget. See Kieu Trinh (2012).

Bibliography

Acharya, A. "Containment, Engagement, or Counter-Dominance? Malaysia's Response to the Rise of Chinese Power". In *Engaging China: The Management of a Rising Power*, edited by R. Ross and I. Johnson, pp. 129–51. London: Routledge, 1999.

————. "Will Asia's Past Be its Future?". *International Security* 28, no. 3 (2004): 149–64.

AFP. "China's new naval base triggers US concerns". 12 May 2008 <http://www.google.com/hostednews/afp/article/ALeqM5gRqO2xhQzglbp4 Cums3qh3MO07Yw> (accessed 14 August 2013).

Aitken, B.J. and A.E. Harrison. "Do domestic firms benefit from direct foreign investment? Evidence from Venezuela". *American Economic Review* 89, no. 3 (1999): 605–18.

Alden, C. "China in Africa". *Survival* 47, no. 3 (2005): 147–64.

Amer, R. "The Territorial Disputes Between China and Vietnam and Regional Stability". *Contemporary Southeast Asia* 19, no. 1 (1997): 86–113.

Amighini, A. "China in the international fragmentation of production: Evidence from the ICT industry". *European Journal of Comparative Economics* 2, no. 2 (2005): 203–19.

Anh, D.D. *Dat nuoc Viet Nam qua cac doi: Nghien cuu dia ly hoc lich su Viet Nam* [Vietnamese Territory in History: A Study of Vietnam's Historical Geography]. Ha Noi: NXB Khoa hoc (Science Publishing House), 1964.

Anh, N.N. and N. Thang. "Foreign direct investment in Vietnam: An overview and analysis the determinants of spatial distribution across provinces". MPRA Paper No. 1921 (2007).

Anh Vu. "Government demands higher budget deficit cap". *ThanhnienNews*, 3 October 2013 <http://www.thanhniennews.com/business/government-demands-higher-budget-deficit-cap-1032.html> (accessed 23 April 2013).

Anwar, S. and L.P. Nguyen. "Foreign direct investment and economic growth in Vietnam". *Asia Pacific Business Review* 16, nos 1-2 (2010): 183-202 <doi: 10.1080/10438590802511031>.

—— and L.P. Nguyen. "Foreign direct investment and export spillovers: Evidence from Vietnam". *International Business Review* 20, no. 2 (2011*a*): 177–93. <doi: 10.1016/j.ibusrev.2010.11.002>.

—— and L.P. Nguyen. "Foreign direct investment and trade: The case of Vietnam". *Research in International Business and Finance* 25, no. 1 (2011*b*): 39–52 <doi: 10.1016/j.ribaf.2010.05.004>.

Asahi Shimbun, The. "Japan to give patrol boats to Vietnam to keep China in check". 1 August 2014 <http://ajw.asahi.com/article/behind_news/politics/AJ201408020031> (accessed 11 February 2015).

Asia Times. "China, Vietnam find love". 21 July 2005 <http://www.atimes.com/atimes/Southeast_Asia/GG21Ae01.html> (accessed 22 November 2012).

Associated Press. "Vietnam PM says China used force to occupy islands". 25 November 2011 <http://www.philstar.com/breaking-news/751619/vietnam-pm-says-china-used-force-occupy-islands> (accessed 2 July 2014).

——."China travel agencies suspend trips to Philippines". 10 May 2012 <http://globalnation.inquirer.net/36217/china-travel-agencies-suspend-trips-to-philippines> (accessed 2 July 2014).

Ba, H.C. *Lich su tu tuong Viet Nam* [A History of Vietnamese Ideologies]. Hue: NXB Thuan Hoa [Thuan Hoa Publishing House], 2006.

Bao Anh. "Kien nghi han che nha thau Trung Quoc vao cac du an dien" [Chinese contractors proposed to be restricted from power plant projects]. *VnEconomy*, 16 September 2011 <http://vneconomy.vn/201109160936479P0C9920/kien-nghi-han-che-nha-thau-trung-quoc-vao-cac-du-an-dien.htm> (accessed 8 December 2012).

Barbieri, K. "Economic Interdependence: A Path to Peace or a Source of Interstate Conflict?". *Journal of Peace Research* 33, no. 1 (1996): 29–49.

Barro, R. "Determinants of Democracy". *Journal of Political Economy* 107, no. 6 (1999): 158–83.

Barta, P. "U.S., Vietnam in Exercises Amid Tensions With China". *Wall Street Journal*, 16 July 2011 <http://online.wsj.com/article/SB10001424052702304223804576447412748465574.html> (accessed 28 August 2013).

BBC. "Hoi dam ve ngoai cua vinh Bac Bo" [Talk starts on the sea area beyond the mouth of Tonkin Gulf], 20 January 2006 <http://www.bbc.co.uk/vietnamese/vietnam/story/2006/01/060120_vietchinaborder.shtml> (accessed 28 October 2012).

——. "Viet Nam ky hop dong mua tau ngam cua Nga" [Vietnam seals submarine purchasing contract with Russia], 16 December 2009 <http://www.bbc.co.uk/vietnamese/vietnam/2009/12/091216_russia_viet_contracts.shtml> (accessed 19 August 2013).

————. "Gan 100 ngu dan Quang Ngai con bi giu" [Nearly 100 Quang Ngai fishermen are still detained], 7 October 2010*a* <http://www.bbc.co.uk/vietnamese/vietnam/2010/10/101007_fishermen_update.shtml> (accessed 25 April 2013).

————. "Nhieu tau ca TQ vao lanh hai Viet Nam" [Many Chinese fishing boats intrude into Vietnam's territorial water], 6 February 2010*b* <http://www.bbc.co.uk/vietnamese/vietnam/2010/02/100206_china_fishing.shtml> (accessed 25 April 2013).

Beckman, R. "South China Sea: Worsening Dispute or Growing Clarity in Claims?". *RSIS Commentaries, 90/2010* (2010).

Beijing Review. "China's Outward FDI in 2012", 16 September 2013 <http://www.bjreview.com.cn/Cover_Stories_Series_2013/2013-09/16/content_568457.htm> (accessed 30 June 2014).

Beresford, M. and D. Phong *Economic Transition in Vietnam: Trade and Aid in the Demise of a Centrally Planned Economy.* Cheltenham: Edward Elgar, 2000.

Berger, P. *The Capitalist Revolution.* New York: Basic Books, 1986.

Bernard, L. "Islam and Liberal Democracy". *Atlantic Monthly* 27, no. 2 (1993): 89–98.

Bich Ngoc. "Trung Quoc thue dat trong rung: Dung cac du an 'nhay cam'" [China leases land for growing trees: "Sensitive projects" to be cancelled]. *Bao Dat Viet,* 18 June 2014 <http://baodatviet.vn/chinh-tri-xa-hoi/tin-tuc-thoi-su/trung-quoc-thue-dat-trong-rungdung-cac-du-an-nhay-cam-3042767/> (accessed 30 June 2014).

Bielenstein, H. *Diplomacy and Trade in the Chinese World, 589–1276.* Leiden & Boston: Brill, 2005.

Bien, N.T. "Thuong mai Viet-Trung: Ba lan kim ngach vuot chi tieu lien Chinh phu" [Vietnam-China trade: Two-way turnover exceeds inter-governmental targets for three times]. *VnEconomy,* 1 October 2009 <http://vneconomy.vn/20091001082441835P19C9931/thuong-mai-viet-trung-ba-lan-kim-ngach-vuot-chi-tieu-lien-chinh-phu.htm> (accessed 4 November 2012).

Blomström, M. and F. Sjöholm. "Technology transfer and spillovers: Does local participation with multinationals matter?". *European Economic Review* 43, no. 4-6 (1999): 915–23.

————, A. Kokko and M. Zejan. *Foreign Direct Investment: Firm and Host Country Strategies.* Hampshire & New York: Palgrave Macmillan, 2000.

Bloomberg. "Vietnam Says China Must Avoid Trade Weapon in Maritime Spat", 3 December 2012 <http://www.bloomberg.com/news/2012-12-02/vietnam-says-china-must-avoid-trade-weapon-in-maritime-disputes.html> (accessed 2 May 2013).

Boix, C. and S.C. Stokes. "Endogenous Democratization". *World Politics* 55, no. 4 (2003): 517–49.

Borensztein, E., J. De Gregorio and J.W. Lee. "How does foreign direct investment affect economic growth?". *Journal of International Economics* 45, no. 1 (1998): 115–35 <doi: 10.1016/s0022-1996(97)00033-0>.

Boukhars, A. "A Two-level Game Analysis of the Complexities of Interstate Rivalries in the Maghreb". *Columbia International Affairs Online Working Papers*, May 2001 <http://www.ciaonet.org/access/boa02/index.html> (accessed 10 January 2011).

BP. *BP Statistical Review of World Energy June 2012*. London: BP p.l.c., 2012.

Brautigam, D. *The Dragon's Gift: The Real Story of China in Africa*. Oxford, England & New York: Oxford University Press, 2009.

———. "China, Africa and the International Aid Architecture". *African Development Bank Working Papers Series, No. 107* (2010).

Brule, D. and A. Mintz. "Blank Check or Marching Orders? Public Opinion and Presidential Use of Force". In *Approaches, Levels and Methods of Analysis in International Politics: Crossing Boundaries*, edited by H. Starr, pp. 157–72. New York: Palgrave Macmillan, 2006.

Buckley, P.J., L.J. Clegg, A.R. Cross, X. Liu, H. Voss and P. Zheng. "The Determinants of Chinese Outward Foreign Direct Investment". *Journal of International Business Studies* 38, no. 4 (2007): 499–518.

Business Monitor International Ltd. *Vietnam: Annual Report on Government, Economy, the Business Environment and Industry, with Forecasts Through End-1994*. London: Business Monitor International Limited, 1993.

Buszynski, L. "The South China Sea: Oil, Maritime Claims, and U.S.–China Strategic Rivalry". *Washington Quarterly* 35, no. 2 (2012): 139–56.

——— and I. Sazlan. "Maritime Claims and Energy Cooperation in the South China Sea". *Contemporary Southeast Asia* 29, no. 1 (2007): 143–71.

Butterfield, A.A. "Vietnamese Strategic Culture and the Coming Struggle for the South China Sea". Master thesis, Naval Postgraduate School, Monterey, 1996 <http://archive.org/details/vietnamesestrate00butt>.

Cao, D. and Y. Sun. *China's History* (Di 1 ban. ed.). Singapore: Cengage Learning, 2011.

Chang, F.K. "China's Naval Rise and the South China Sea: An Operational Assessment". *Orbis* 56, no. 1 (2012): 19–38.

Chang, G.G. *The Coming Collapse of China*. New York: Random House, 2001.

Che, J. "Rent Seeking and Government Ownership of Firms: An Application to China's Township–Village Enterprises". *Journal of Comparative Economics* 30, no. 4 (2002): 787–811.

Chen, C., Z. Li and X. Su. "Rent Seeking Incentives, Political Connections and Organizational Structure: Empirical Evidence from Listed Family Firms in China". *City University of Hong Kong Working Paper*, 2005.

Chen, K.C. *China's War with Vietnam, 1979: Issues, Decisions, and Implications*. Stanford: Hoover Institution Press, Stanford University, 1987.

Cheng-Chwee, K. "The Essence of Hedging: Malaysia and Singapore's Response to a Rising China". *Contemporary Southeast Asia* 30, no. 2 (2008): 159–85.

Cheng, J.Y.S. "Sino-Vietnamese Relations in the Early Twenty-first Century: Economics in Command?". *Asian Survey* 51, no. 2 (2011): 379–405.

Chi Hieu. "Ha tieu chuan Viet Nam de san pham dat yeu cau?" [Vietnam standards to be lowered for products to pass quality test?]. *Sai Gon Tiep thi*, 17 August 2011 <http://sgtt.vn/Thoi-su/151533/Ha-tieu-chuan-Viet-Nam-de-san-pham-dat-yeu-cau.html> (accessed 4 December 2012).

China Eximbank. "Chinese Government Concessional Loan and Preferential Export Buyer's Credit". 2012 <http://english.eximbank.gov.cn/businessarticle/activities/loan/200905/9398_1.html> (accessed 30 November 2012).

Claget, B. M. "Competing Claims of Vietnam and China in the Vanguard Bank and Blue Dragon Areas of the SCS". *Oil and Gas Law and Taxation Review*, no. 375 & 377 (1995).

Clark, H. R. *Community, Trade, and Networks: Southern Fujian Province from the Third to the Thirteenth Century*. Cambridge, U.K. & New York: Cambridge University Press, 1991.

Cline, R. S. *World Power Assessment 1977: A Calculus of Strategic Drift*. Boulder, CO: Westview Press, 1977.

Clymer, K. J. *The United States and Cambodia, 1969-2000: A Troubled Relationship*. London & New York: Routledge, 2004.

Co, T.Q. "Hoi uc va suy nghi: 1975-1991" [Memoir and Reflections: 1975-1991]. Unpublished manuscript, 2003.

Cole, B.D. *The Great Wall at Sea: China's Navy in the Twenty-first Century*. 2nd ed. Annapolis, MD: Naval Institute Press, 2010.

Cooke, N. and T. Li. *Water Frontier: Commerce and the Chinese in the Lower Mekong Region, 1750–1880*. Singapore: Singapore University Press, 2004.

Cooper, R.N. *The Economics of Interdependence: Economic Policy in the Atlantic Community*. New York: McGraw-Hill, 1968.

Copeland, D.C. "Economic Interdependence and War: A Theory of Trade Expectations". *International Security* 20, no. 4 (1996): 5–41.

Coser, L. *The Function of Social Conflict*. New York: Free Press, 1956.

CPV. *Van kien Dang toan tap* [Complete Collection of Party Documents]. Vol. 36 [1975]. Ha Noi: National Political Publishing House, 2004.

——. *Van kien Dang toan tap* [Complete Collection of Party Documents]. Vol. 47 [1986]. Ha Noi: National Political Publishing House, 2006*a*.

——. *Van kien Dang toan tap* [Complete Collection of Party Documents]. Vol. 49 [1988–89]. Ha Noi: National Political Publishing House, 2006*b*.

——. "Thong bao Hoi nghi lan thu tu Ban Chap hanh Trung uong Dang khoa X" [Communiqué of the fourth Plenum (tenth tenure) of the Party Central

Committee]. 25 January 2007*a* <http://www.xaydungdang.org.vn/Home/Lyluan-Thuctien-Kinhnghiem/2007/1136/Thong-Bao-Hoi-nghi-lan-thu-tu-Ban-Chap-hanh-Trung-uong.aspx> (accessed 15 April 2013).

———. *Van kien Dang toan tap* [Complete Collection of Party Documents]. Vol. 52 [1992–93]. Ha Noi: National Political Publishing House, 2007*b*.

———. *Van kien Dang toan tap* [Complete Collection of Party Documents]. Vol. 51 [Jun–Dec 1991]. Ha Noi: National Political Publishing House, 2007*c*.

———. *Van kien Dang toan tap* [Complete Collection of Party Documents]. Vol. 53 [1994]. Ha Noi: National Political Publishing House, 2007*d*.

———. *Van kien dai hoi dai bieu toan quoc thoi ky doi moi* [Documents of National Congresses in the Era of Doi Moi] (Vol. 1). Ha Noi: National Political Publishing House, 2010.

———. "Resolution No. 22/NQ-TW". 2013 <http://www.mofahcm.gov.vn/vi/mofa/nr091019080134/nr091019083649/ns140805203450/NQ22.ENG.doc/download> (accessed 16 October 2015).

Curtin, P.D. *Cross-cultural Trade in World History*. Cambridge & New York: Cambridge University Press, 1984.

Dahl, R.A. *Polyarchy: Participation and Opposition*. New Haven: Yale University Press, 1971.

Dahlman, C.J. and Aubert, J.-E. *China and the Knowledge Economy: Seizing the 21st Century*. Washington, D.C.: World Bank, 2001.

Dat Viet. "Viet Nam mua 2 tau ho ve tang hinh Sigma Ha Lan" [Vietnam to acquire 2 stealth Sigma-class corvettes from the Netherlands]. 23 August 2013 <http://baodatviet.vn/quoc-phong/toan-canh/bao-ha-lan-viet-nam-mua-2-tau-ho-ve-tang-hinh-sigma-ha-lan-2353145/> (accessed 24 August 2013).

Dau, N.D. *Viet Nam, Quoc hieu va cuong vuc qua cac thoi dai* [Vietnam: National Name and Territory in History]. Ho Chi Minh City: NXB Tre [Youth Publishing House], 1999.

De Mesquita, B.B., J.D. Morrow, R.M. Siverson and A. Smith. "An Institutional Explanation of the Democratic Peace". *American Political Science Review* 93 (December 1999): 791–807.

DeRouen Jr., K. *Politics, Economics and Presidential Use of Force Decision Making*. Lewiston, NY: Edwin, Mellen, 2001.

Diamond, L. "Why are There no Arab Democracies?". *Journal of Democracy* 21, no. 1 (2010): 93–112.

Diep, N.H. "Tiep tuc dua quan he Viet Nam - Trung Quoc phat trien" [Vietnam–China relations continue to be promoted]. *Vietnam Plus*, 17 June 2013 <http://www.vietnamplus.vn/Home/Tiep-tuc-dua-quan-he-Viet-NamTrung-Quoc-phat-trien/20136/202510.vnplus> (accessed 21 June 2013).

Directorate of Fisheries. *Bao cao tom tat Quy hoach tong the phat trien nganh thuy san Viet Nam den nam 2020, tam nhin 2030* [Summary of Master Plan for

Developing Vietnam's Fishery Industry until 2020, with a Vision to 2030]. Ha Noi: Directorate of Fisheries, 2012.

Doan Cuong. "Nha thau Trung Quoc 'thao than'" [The run-away Chinese contractors]. *Tuoi Tre*, 14 September 2012 <http://tuoitre.vn/Chinh-tri-Xa-hoi/511397/Nha-thau-Trung-Quoc-%E2%80%9Cthao-than%E2%80%9D.html> (accesed 8 December 2012).

Domke, W.K. *War and the Changing Global System*. New Haven: Yale University Press, 1988.

Doyle, M.W. "Kant, Liberal Legacies, and Foreign Affairs". *Philosophy & Public Affairs* 12, no. 3 (1983a): 205–35.

———. "Kant, Liberal Legacies, and Foreign Affairs (Part 2)". *Philosophy & Public Affairs* 12, no. 4 (1983b): 323–53.

———. *Ways of War and Peace*. New York: W.W. Norton, 1997.

Du, D. and H. Zhao, eds. *Yuenan Laowo Jianpuzhai shouce*. Beijing: Shishi chubanshe, 1988.

Duiker, W.J. "Looking beyond Cambodia: China and Vietnam". *Indochina Issues* 88 (1989): 1–6.

Dunning, T. *Crude Democracy: Natural Resource Wealth and Political Regimes*. Cambridge: Cambridge University Press, 2008.

Duong, N.N. "Du am ARF va quan he ASEAN - Trung Quoc tren bien Dong" [The ARF's resonance and ASEAN–China relations in the SCS]. *Vietnamnet*, 1 September 2010 <http://tuanvietnam.vietnamnet.vn/2010-08-31-du-am-arf-va-quan-he-asean-trung-quoc-tren-bien-dong> (accessed 5 September 2013).

Durand, J.D. "The Population Statistics of China, A.D. 2–1953". *Population Studies* 13, no. 3 (1960): 209–56.

Ebrey, P.B., A. Walthall and J.B. Palais. *East Asia: A Cultural, Social, and Political History*. Boston: Houghton Mifflin, 2006.

Economist, The. "Vietnam and China: Bauxite bashers". 23 April 2009 <http://www.economist.com/node/13527969> (accessed 7 February 2013).

EIA. "Country Analysis Briefs: Vietnam". 9 May 2012 <http://www.eia.gov/countries/cab.cfm?fips=VM> (accessed 14 April 2013).

———. "Analysis Briefs: South China Sea", 7 February 2013 <http://www.eia.gov/countries/regions-topics.cfm?fips=SCS> (accessed 14 April 2013).

Epstein, A.B. "Village Elections in China: Experimenting with Democracy". In *China's Economic Future: Challenges to US Policy*, edited by C. o. t. U. S. Joint Economic Committee, pp. 403–22. Armonk, NY: M.E. Sharpe, 1997.

Erickson, D.P. and J. Chen. "China, Taiwan, and the Battle for Latin America". *Fletcher Forum of World Affairs* 31 (2007): 69.

Esposito, J.L. and J.O. Voll. *Islam and Democracy*. Oxford: Oxford University Press, 2001.

FAO. *FAO Yearbook of Fishery and Aquaculture Statistics 2010*. Rome: FAO, 2012.

Ferris, W.H. *The Power Capabilities of Nation-states: International Conflict and War*. Lexington, MA: Lexington Books, 1973.

Findlay, T. *Cambodia: The Legacy and Lessons of UNTAC*. Oxford & New York: Oxford University Press, 1995.

Fish, M.S. "Islam and Authoritarianism". *World Politics* 55, no. 01 (2002): 4–37.

Franckx, E. "Fisheries in the South China Sea: A Centrifugal or Centripetal Force?". *Chinese Journal of International Law* 11, no. 4 (2012): 727–47.

Frank, A.G. *Latin America: Underdevelopment or Revolution*. New York: Monthly Review Press, 1970.

Fravel, M.T. "China's Strategy in the South China Sea". *Contemporary Southeast Asia* 33, no. 3 (2011): 292–319.

Friedberg, A.L. "Ripe for Rivalry: Prospects for Peace in a Multipolar Asia". *International Security* 18, no. 3 (1993): 5–33.

Friedman, T. "The First Law of Petropolitics". *Foreign Policy* 154 (2006): 28–36.

Gainsborough, M. "Vietnam II: A Turbulent Normalisation with China". *The World Today* 48, no. 11 (1992): 205–207.

———. "Elites vs. Reform in Laos, Cambodia, and Vietnam". *Journal of Democracy* 23, no. 2 (2012): 34–46

Gao, Z. "The South China Sea: From Conflict to Cooperation". *Ocean Development and International Law* 25, no. 3 (1994): 345–59.

Garrison, J.A. *China and the Energy Equation in Asia: The Determinants of Policy Choice*. Boulder, CO: FirstForumPress, 2009.

Gartner, S. "Deadly Pictures: An Experimental Analysis of Images of Death and the Casualty-Opinion Nexus". Paper presented at the Annual Meeting of the American Political Science Association, Boston, 2008.

Gartzke, E., Q. Li and C. Boehmer. "Investing in the Peace: Economic Interdependence and International Conflict". *International Organization* 55, no. 2 (2001): 391–438.

Gasiorowski, M.J. "Economic Interdependence and International Conflict: Some Cross-national Evidence". *International Studies Quarterly* 30, no. 1 (1986): 23–38.

——— and S. Polachek. "Conflict and Interdependence: East-West Trade and Linkages in the Era of Détente". *Journal of Conflict Resolution* 26, no. 4 (1982): 709–29.

Gaubatz, K.T. "Election Cycles and War". *Journal of Conflict Resolution* 35, no. 2 (1991): 212–44.

General Department of Customs. "Customs Statistics for 2012". 2013*a* <http://www.customs.gov.vn/DocLib/Forms/AllItems.aspx?RootFolder= %2FDocLib%2FCac%20Bieu%20Thong%20Ke%2FNam2012> (accessed 25 January 2012).

————. "Statistics of exports by country/territory — Main exports". December 2013*b* <http://www.customs.gov.vn/Lists/EnglishStatisticsCalendars/Attachments/116/2013-T12T-5X(EN-FN).pdf> (accessed 24 June 2014).

————. "Statistics of imports by country/territory — Main imports". December 2013*c* <http://www.customs.gov.vn/Lists/EnglishStatisticsCalendars/Attachments/117/2013-T12T-5N(EN-FN).pdf> (accessed 24 June 2014).

————. "Customs Trade Statistics". 2014 <http://www.customs.gov.vn/Lists/EnglishStatistics/ScheduledData.aspx?Group=Trade%20analysis&language=en-US> (accessed 27 June 2014).

Giang Linh. "Hai Phong tran ngap lao dong Trung Quoc" [Hai Phong crowded by Chinese workers]. *Dat Viet*, 11 June 2012 <http://baodatviet.vn/Home/chinhtrixahoi/Hai-Phong-tran-ngap-lao-dong-Trung-Quoc/20126/216160.datviet> (accessed 8 December 2012).

Glaeser, E.L., R. La Porta, F. Lopez-de-Silanes and A. Shleifer. "Do Institutions Cause Growth?". *Journal of Economic Growth* 9, no. 3 (2004): 271–303.

Global Times. "Vietnam underestimates China's will to protect sovereignty". 9 December 2012 <http://www.globaltimes.cn/content/749031.shtml> (accessed 14 April 2013).

————. "China will not be passive in sea disputes". 29 March 2013 <http://www.globaltimes.cn/content/771547.shtml#.UVYkTxeW_-Y> (accessed 30 March 2013).

Goh, E. "Meeting the China Challenge: The US in Southeast Asian Regional Security Strategies". *Policy Studies* 16 (2005) <http://scholarspace.manoa.hawaii.edu/handle/10125/3509>.

————. "Understanding 'Hedging' in Asia-Pacific Security". *PacNet* 43. 31 August 2006.

————. "Great Powers and Hierarchical Order in Southeast Asia: Analyzing Regional Security Strategies". *International Security* 32, no. 3 (2008): 113–57.

Goldstein, J.S. and J.R. Freeman. *Three-way Street: Strategic Reciprocity in World Politics*. Chicago: University of Chicago Press, 1990.

GSO. *Statistical Yearbook of Vietnam 2005*. Ha Noi: Statistical Publishing House, 2006*a*.

————. *The Vietnamese International Merchandise Trade for Twenty Years of Renovation*. Ha Noi: Statistical Publishing House, 2006*b*.

————. *Statistical Yearbook of Vietnam 2007*. Ha Noi: Statistical Publishing House, 2008.

————. *Statistical Yearbook of Vietnam 2009*. Ha Noi: Statistical Publishing House, 2010.

————. *Statistical Yearbook of Vietnam 2010*. Ha Noi: Statistical Publishing House, 2011.

————. *Statistical Yearbook of Vietnam 2011*. Ha Noi: Statistical Publishing House, 2012.

———. *Statistical Yearbook of Vietnam 2013*. Ha Noi: Statistical Publishing House, 2014*a*.

———. *Statistical Yearbook of Vietnam 2013 [Abridged version]*. Ha Noi: Statistical Publishing House. 2014*b*.

———. *Statistical Handbook of Vietnam 2014*. Ha Noi: Statistical Publishing House, 2015.

Haber, S. and V. Menaldo. "Do Natural Resources Fuel Authoritarianism? A Reappraisal of the Resource Curse". *American Political Science Review* 105, no. 1 (2011): 1–26.

Haddad, M. and A. Harrison. "Are there positive spillovers from direct foreign investment? Evidence from panel data for Morocco". *Journal of Development Economics* 42, no. 1 (1993): 51–74 <doi: 10.1016/0304-3878(93)90072-u>.

Hai, C. T. "Dien bien dia ly va lich su trong qua trinh tiep xuc va giao luu van hoa Viet - Hoa" [Geographical and Historical Happenings in the Process of Cultural Contacts and Exchanges between the Viet and Hoa]. In *Buoc dau tim hieu su tiep xuc va giao luu van hoa Viet - Hoa trong lich su* [Initial Examination of the Viet-Hoa Cultural Contacts and Exchanges in History], edited by P.D. Duong and C.T. Hai, pp. 11–30. Ha Noi: NXB The Gioi (The Gioi Publishers), 1998.

———. "Nguoi Hoa trong lich su Viet Nam" [Hoa Ethnic in Vietnam's History]. Paper presented at the international conference "Vietnam: Integration and Development", 5–7 December 2008, Ha Noi.

——— and P.D. Duong, eds. *Buoc dau tim hieu su tiep xuc va giao luu van hoa Viet - Hoa trong lich su* [Initial Examination of the Viet-Hoa Cultural Contacts and Exchanges in History]. Ha Noi: NXB The Gioi (The Gioi Publishers), 1998.

Han, X. "The Present Echoes of the Ancient Bronze Drum: Nationalism and Archeology in Modern Vietnam and China". *Explorations in Southeast Asian Studies* 2, no. 2 (1998).

Hefner, R.W. *Civil Islam: Muslims and Democratization in Indonesia*. Princeton, NJ: Princeton University Press, 2011.

Herb, M. "No Representation without Taxation? Rents, Development, and Democracy". *Comparative Politics* (2005): 297–316.

Hiep, L. H. "Performance-based Legitimacy: The Case of the Communist Party of Vietnam and *Doi Moi*". *Contemporary Southeast Asia* 34, no. 2 (2012): 145–72.

Hindu, The. "India offers Vietnam credit for military ware". 28 July 2013 <http://www.thehindu.com/news/national/india-offers-vietnam-credit-for-military-ware/article4960731.ece> (accessed 28 August 2013).

Hoang Lan. "Nguoi Trung Quoc nam nhieu du an trong diem cua VN" [Chinese contractors win many essential projects of Vietnam]. *VnExpress*, 7 August 2010 <http://vnexpress.net/gl/kinh-doanh/2010/08/3ba1ee8f/> (accessed 4 December 2012).

Holsti, K.J. *Peace and War: Armed Conflicts and International Order 1648-1989*. Cambridge: Cambridge University Press, 1991.

Hung, N.M. "Thuc hien nhat quan duong loi doi ngoai doc lap, tu chu, hoa binh, hop tac va phat trien" [Consistently Implementing the Foreign Policy of Independence, Autonomy, Peace, and Development]. *Tap chi Cong san* [Communist Review] 17 (2006): 14–18.

Huntington, S.P. "Will More Countries Become Democratic?". *Political Science Quarterly* 99, no. 2 (1984).

———. *The Third Wave: Democratization in the Late Twentieth Century*. Norman: University of Oklahoma Press, 1991.

Information Office of the State Council. "China's Foreign Aid". 21 April 2011 <http://news.xinhuanet.com/english2010/china/2011-04/21/c_13839683.htm> (accessed 19 November 2012).

Inglehart, R. and C. Welzel. *Modernization, Cultural Change, and Democracy: The Human Development Sequence*. Cambridge: Cambridge University Press, 2005.

Institute of History. *Lich su Viet Nam, Tap 1* [History of Vietnam, Vol. 1]. Ha Noi: NXB Khoa hoc xa hoi [Social Sciences Publishing House], 2001a.

———. *Lich su Viet Nam, Tap 3* [History of Vietnam, Vol. 3]. Ha Noi: NXB Khoa hoc xa hoi [Social Sciences Publishing House], 2001b.

Ishida, M. "Comparing Investment Climates among Major Cities in CLMV Countries". In *Investment Climates of Major Cities in CLMV Countries*, edited by M. Ishida. Bangkok: Institute of Developing Economies, Japan External Trade Organization, 2010.

Jandl, T. *Vietnam in the Global Economy: The Dynamics of Integration, Decentralization, and Contested Politics*. Plymouth: Lexington Books, 2013.

Jensen, N. and L. Wantchekon. "Resource Wealth and Political Regimes in Africa". *Comparative Political Studies* 37, no. 7 (2004): 816–41.

Johnston, A.I. and R.S. Ross. *Engaging China: The Management of an Emerging Power*. Vol. 10. London: Routledge, 1999.

Kang, D.C. "Getting Asia Wrong: The Need for New Analytical Frameworks". *International Security* 27, no. 4 (2003): 57–85.

Karatnycky, A. "Muslim Countries and the Democracy Gap". *Journal of Democracy* 13, no. 1 (2002): 99–112.

Kate, D.T. "Russia to Help Vietnam Produce Anti-Ship Missiles, RIA Says". *Bloomberg*, 16 February 2012 <http://www.bloomberg.com/news/2012-02-16/russia-to-help-vietnam-produce-anti-ship-missiles-ria-says-1-.html> (accessed 20 August 2013).

Kedourie, E. *Democracy and Arab Political Culture*. London: Frank Cass, 1994.

Keohane, R.O. and J.S. Nye. "World Politics and the International Economic System". In *The Future of the International Economic Order: An Agenda for Research*, edited by C.F. Bergsten. Lexington, MA: D.C. Heath, 1973.

——— and J.S. Nye. *Power and Interdependence*. Longman Publishing Group, 2001.

Khoo, N. *Collateral Damage: Sino-Soviet Rivalry and the Termination of the Sino-Vietnamese Alliance*. New York: Columbia University Press, 2011.

Kieu Trinh. "Thu tuong yeu cau han che di cong tac nuoc ngoai" [PM orders a cut in foreign trips]. *VnExpress*, 2 November 2012 <http://vnexpress.net/tin-tuc/xa-hoi/thu-tuong-yeu-cau-han-che-di-cong-tac-nuoc-ngoai-2354170.html> (accessed 23 April 2014).

Kim, T.T. *Viet Nam su luoc, Quyen II (A Historical Précis of Vietnam*. Vol. II. Sai Gon: Dai Nam, 1971.

Kolko, G. "Vietnam since 1975: Winning a war and losing the peace". *Journal of Contemporary Asia* 25, no. 1 (1995): 3–49 <doi: 10.1080/00472339580000021>.

Kolstad, I. and A. Wiig. "What determines Chinese outward FDI?". *Journal of World Business* 47 (2012): 26–34.

Kubny, J. and H. Voss. "The impact of Chinese outward investment: Evidence from Cambodia and Vietnam". *German Development Institute Discussion Paper 16/2010* (2010).

Kunmakara, M. "China to invest $9.6b in Cambodia". *Phnom Penh Post*, 1 January 2013 from <http://www.phnompenhpost.com/2013010160560/Business/china-to-invest-9-6b-in-cambodia.html> (accessed 7 February 2013).

Kurzman, C. *Liberal Islam: A Source Book*. Oxford: Oxford University Press, 1998.

Ky, V. "2.000 tan quang 'vuot bien' moi dem" [2000 tons of ore smuggled every night]. *Sai Gon Tiep thi*, 12 October 2011 <http://sgtt.vn/Thoi-su/154143/Bai-2-2000-tan-quang-%E2%80%9Cvuot-bien%E2%80%9D-moi-dem.html> (accessed 7 February 2013).

Lam, T.B., ed. *Borrowings and Adaptations in Vietnamese Culture*. Honolulu: Center for Southeast Asian Studies, School of Hawaiian, Asian and Pacific Studies, University of Hawaii at Manoa, 1987.

Le Thu and Van Thinh. "'Thot tim' du an nhiet dien tai Hai Phong" ["Thrills" at Hai Phong Thermal Power Plant]. *Cong an Nhan dan*, 26 August 2010 <http://www.cand.com.vn/vi-VN/kinhte/2010/8/135959.cand> (accessed 4 December 2012).

Le Viet. "TS. Nguyen Thanh Son: Xuat lau than - Con bo chui lot lo kim" [Smuggled Coal is Massive but Ignored: Dr. Nguyen Thanh Son]. *Phunu Today*, 18 July 2013 <http://phunutoday.vn/xi-nhan/trai-hay-phai/201307/ts-nguyen-thanh-son-xuat-lau-than-con-bo-chui-lot-lo-kim-2217397/> (accessed 20 July 2013).

Lee, J. "Primary Causes of Asian Democratization: Dispelling Conventional Myths". *Asian Survey* 42, no. 6 (2002): 821–37.

Leifer, M. "Chinese economic reform and security policy: The South China Sea connection". *Survival* 37, no. 2 (1995): 44–59 <doi: 10.1080/00396339508442789>.

Levy, J.S. "Domestic Politics and War". *Journal of Interdisciplinary History* 18, no. 4 (1988): 653–73.

———. "The Diversionary Theory of War". In *Handbook of War Studies*, edited by M. Midlarsky. Boston: Unwin Hyman, 1989.

——— and L.I. Vakili "Diversionary Action by Authoritarian Regimes: Argentina in the Falklands/Malvinas Case". In *The Internationalization of Communal Strife*, edited by M. Midlarsky, pp. 118–46. London: Routledge, 1992.

Li, C. "Top-Level Reform or Bottom-Up Revolution?". *Journal of Democracy* 24, no. 1 (2013): 41–48.

Li, J. and D. Li. "The Dotted Line on the Chinese Map of the South China Sea: A Note". *Ocean Development and International Law* 34, nos. 3-4 (2003): 287–95.

Li, Q. and G. Liang. "Political Relations and Chinese Outbound Direct Investment: Evidence from Firm- and Dyadic-Level Tests". *Research Center for Chinese Politics & Business (Indiana University) Working Paper Series*, No. 19 (2012).

Li, T. *Nguyen Cochinchina: Southern Vietnam in the Seventeenth and Eighteenth Centuries*. Ithaca, NY: Cornell Southeast Asia Program, 1998.

Lieberman, V.B. *Strange Parallels: Southeast Asia in Global Context, c 800–1830. Volume 1: Integration of the Mainland*. New York: Cambridge University Press, 2003.

Linh Chi. "Nha thau Trung Quoc i ach, be boi va gio chung" [Chinese contractors are slow, sloppy and badly-behaved]. *An ninh Thu do*, 22 July 2012 <http://www.anninhthudo.vn/Kinh-doanh/Nha-thau-Trung-Quoc-i-ach-be-boi-va-gio-chung/456737.antd> (accessed 8 December 2012).

Linh, N.P. and M. Martina. "South China Sea tensions rise as Vietnam says China rammed ships". Reuters, 7 May 2014 <http://www.reuters.com/article/2014/05/07/us-china-seas-fishermen-idUSBREA4603C20140507> (accessed 9 May 2014).

Lipset, S.M. "Some Social Requisites of Democracy: Economic Development and Political Legitimacy". *American Political Science Review* 53, no. 1 (1959): 69–105.

———. *Political Man: The Social Bases of Politics*. Baltimore, MD: Johns Hopkins University Press, 1981.

———. "The Social Requisites of Democracy Revisited". *American Sociological Science Review* 59, no. 1 (1994): 1–22.

Liu, Y. and D. Chen. "Why China Will Democratize". *Washington Quarterly* 35, no. 1 (2012): 41–63.

Lo, C.-k. *China's Policy towards Territorial Disputes: The Case of the South China Sea Islands*. London: Routledge, 1989.

Loi, L.V. *Cuoc tranh chap Viet - Trung ve hai quan dao Hoang Sa va Truong Sa* [The Sino-Vietnamese dispute over the Paracels and Spratlys]. Ha Noi: NXB Cong an Nhan dan [Police Publishing House], 1995.

————. *Ngoai giao Dai Viet* [Dai Viet Diplomacy]. Ha Noi: NXB Cong an Nhan dan [Police Publishing House], 2000.

————. *50 Years of Vietnamese Diplomacy, 1945–1995*. 2nd ed. Ha Noi: The Gioi Publishers, 2006.

London, J. "Viet Nam and the Making of Market-Leninism". *Pacific Review* 22, no. 3 (2009): 375–99.

Lu, X. "From Rank-seeking to Rent-seeking: Changing Administrative Ethos and Corruption in Reform China". *Crime, Law and Social Change* 32, no. 4 (1999): 347–70.

Ma, W. and J. Hookway. "Vietnam Spars With China Over Oil Plans". *Wall Street Journal*, 27 June 2012 <http://online.wsj.com/article/SB1000142405270 2303649504577491823837421842.html> (accessed 21 April 2012).

Maddison, A. *The World Economy: Historical Statistics*. Paris: Organisation for Economic Co-operation and Development, 2003.

Mai, P.H. "Regional Economic Development and Foreign Direct Investment Flows in Vietnam, 1988–98". *Journal of the Asia Pacific Economy* 7, no. 2 (2002): 182–202 <doi: 10.1080/13547860220134815>.

————. "The economic impact of foreign direct investment flows on Vietnam: 1988–98". *Asian Studies Review* 27, no. 1 (2003): 81–98 <doi: 10.1080/10357820308713367>.

Man-Cheong, I. *The class of 1761: Examinations, State, and Elites in Eighteenth-Century China*. Stanford, CA: Stanford University Press, 2004.

Manguin, P.-Y. "Trading Ships of the South China Sea. Shipbuilding Techniques and Their Role in the History of the Development of Asian Trade Networks". *Journal of the Economic and Social History of the Orient* 36, no. 3 (1993): 253–80.

Maoz, Z. "Realist and Cultural Critiques of the Democratic Peace: A Theoretical and Empirical Re-assessment". *International Interactions* 24 (1998): 3–89.

————. "The Effects of Strategic and Economic Interdependence on International Conflict Across Levels of Analysis". *American Journal of Political Science* 53, no. 1 (2009): 223–40.

Mariko, Y., P.D. Manh and B.C. Hoang. "Western Han bronze mirrors recently discovered in central Vietnam". *Bulletin of the Indo-pacific Prehistory Association* 21 (2001): 99–106.

Marston, H. "Bauxite Mining in Vietnam's Central Highlands: An Arena for Expanding Civil Society?". *Contemporary Southeast Asia* 34, no, 2 (2012): 173–96.

Mattlin, M. and M. Nojonen. "Conditionality in Chinese Bilateral Lending". *BOFIT Discussion Papers* 14 (2011).

McDougall, D. "Responses to 'Rising China' in the East Asian Region: Soft balancing with accommodation". *Journal of Contemporary China* 21, no. 73 (2012): 1–17.

Medeiros, E.S. "Strategic Hedging and the Future of Asia-Pacific Stability". *Washington Quarterly* 29, no. 1 (2005): 145–67.

Meernik, J. and P. Waterman. "The Myth of the Diversionary Use of Force by American Presidents". *Political Research Quarterly* 49, no. 3 (1996): 573–90.

Mesquita, B.B. d., J.D. Morrow, R.M. Siverson and A. Smith. "An Institutional Explanation of the Democratic Peace". *American Political Science Review* 93, no. 4 (1999): 791–807.

Miller, A. "Institutionalization and the Changing Dynamics of Chinese Leadership Politics". In *China's Changing Political Landscape: Prospects for Democracy*, edited by C. Lim, pp. 61–79. Washington, D.C.: Brookings Institution Press, 2008.

Miller, R.A. "Domestic Structures and the Diversionary Use of Force". *American Journal of Political Science* 39, no. 3 (1995): 760–85.

———. "Regime Type, Strategic Interaction, and the Diversionary Use of Force". *Journal of Conflict Resolution* 43, no. 3 (1999): 388–402.

Ministry of Commerce. "2009 年越南成为中国在东南亚最大的工程承包市场" [Vietnam became China's largest engineering contract market in Southeast Asia in 2009]. 2 March 2010 <http://vn.mofcom.gov.cn/aarticle/zxhz/tjsj/201003/20100306802009.html> (accessed 4 December 2012).

———. *2010 Statistical Bulletin of China's Outward Foreign Direct Investment*. Beijing: MOFCOM, 2011.

Ministry of Defence. *Quoc phong Viet Nam nhung nam dau the ky XXI* [Vietnam's national defence in the first years of the 21st century]. Ha Noi: Ministry of Defence, 2004.

———. *Quoc phong Viet Nam* [Vietnam's national defence]. Ha Noi: Ministry of Defence, 2009.

Ministry of Finance. "Statistics Tables 2006-2010". *External Debt Bulletin* 7 (2011).

Ministry of Planning and Investment. "China". 24 December 2009 <http://oda.mpi.gov.vn/LinkClick.aspx?fileticket=%2fYU7XCcnRKg%3d&tabid=176> (accessed 26 November 2012).

Mintz, A. and K.R. DeRouen. *Understanding Foreign Policy Decision Making*. Cambridge: Cambridge University Press, 2010.

Mitton, R. "Beijing Refuses Aid to Hanoi after Rebuff over Taiwan". *Straits Times*, 22 December 2006.

Mochizuki, M.M. "Japan's shifting strategy toward the rise of China". *Journal of Strategic Studies* 30, nos. 4–5 (2007): 739–76.

MOFA. *Su that ve quan he Viet Nam–Trung Quoc trong 30 nam qua* [The Truth about Vietnam–China Relations over the Last 30 Years]. Ha Noi: NXB Su that [The Truth Publishing House], 1979.

MOIT. "Quyet dinh phe duyet De an Phat trien xuat nhap khau hang hoa voi Trung Quoc giai doan 2007–2015" [Decision approving the Blueprint for promoting trade in goods with China in the period of 2007–2015], 2007 <http://www.moit.gov.vn/Images/Upload/QD%20023-2007-BTM.doc> (accessed 28 January 2013).

Morgan, T.C. and C.J. Anderson. "Domestic Support and Diversionary External Conflict in Great Britain, 1950-1992". *Journal of Politics* 61. no. 3 (1999): 799–814.

—— and K. Bickers. "Domestic Discontent and the External Use of Force". *Journal of Conflict Resolution* 36, no. 1 (1992): 25–52.

—— and S. Campbell. "Domestic Structure, Decisional Constraints, and War". *Journal of Conflict Resolution* 35, no. 2 (1991): 187–211.

Morgenthau, H.J. *Politics among Nations: The Struggle for Power and Peace.* New York: A.A. Knopf, 1948.

Morrison, W.M. *China's Economic Conditions.* Washington, D.C.: Congressional Research Service, 2012.

My Lang. "Tau chien 'made in Viet Nam'" ["Made in Vietnam" warships]. *Tuoi Tre*, 3 October 2011 <http://tuoitre.vn/chinh-tri-xa-hoi/phong-su-ky-su/458636/tau-chien-%E2%80%9Cmade-in-viet-nam%E2%80%9D.html> (accessed 20 August 2013).

Nam Cuong and Nguyen Thanh. "Cong nhan Trung Quoc, nhung he luy buon" [Chinese workers and sad consequences]. *Tien Phong*, 27 August 2011 <http://www.tienphong.vn/xa-hoi/549935/Cong-nhan-Trung-Quoc-nhung-he-luy-buon-tpp.html> (accessed 8 December 2012).

Nam, P.D. "Ngoai giao Viet Nam sau 20 nam doi moi" [Vietnam's Diplomacy after 20 years of Renovation]. *Tap chi Cong san* [Commusit Review] 14 (2006): 26–30.

Nathan, A.J. "China's Changing of the Guard: Authoritarian Resilience". *Journal of Democracy* 14, no. 1 (2003): 6–17.

Nghiep, L.T. and L.H. Quy. "Measuring the Impact of Doi Moi on Vietnam's Gross Domestic Product". *Asian Economic Journal* 14, no. 3 (2000): 317–32.

Ngo, T.-W. "Rent-seeking and Economic Governance in the Structural Nexus of Corruption in China". *Crime, Law and Social Change* 49, no. 1 (2008): 27–44.

Nguoi Lao Dong. "Tap doan Dau khi Viet nam dat tong doanh thu 745.500 ti dong" [PetroVietnam's revenue reached 145.5 trillion dongs], 4 January 2015 <http://nld.com.vn/kinh-te/tap-doan-dau-khi-viet-nam-dat-tong-doanh-thu-745500-ti-dong-20150104190818334.htm> (accessed 20 August 2015).

Nguyen, D.H. "Vietnamese Creativity in Borrowing Foreign Elements". In *Borrowings and Adaptations in Vietnamese Culture*, edited by T.B. Lâm, pp. 22–40. Honolulu: Center for Southeast Asian Studies, School of Hawaiian, Asian and Pacific Studies, University of Hawaii at Manoa, 1987.

Nguyen Dinh Quan. "Tiem kich SU-30 tuan tra tai Truong Sa" [SU-30 aircrafts patrol the Spratlys]. *Tien Phong*, 28 April 2013 <http://www.tienphong.vn/

xa-hoi/624786/Tiem-kich-SU-30-tuan-tra-tai-Truong-Sa-tpov.html> (accessed 19 August 2013).

Nguyen, H.T. "Vietnam's Position on the Sovereignty over the Paracels & the Spratlys: Its Maritime Claims". *Journal of East Asia and International Law* 5, no. 1 (2012): 165–211.

Nguyen, L.-H.T. "The Sino-Vietnamese Split and the Indochina War, 1968–1975". In *The Third Indochina War: Conflict between China, Vietnam and Cambodia, 1972-79*, edited by O.A. Westad and S. Quinn-Judge, pp. 12–32. New York: Routledge, 2006.

Nguyen, N.H., V.T. Ta and V.L. Tran. *The Le Code: Law in Traditional Vietnam: A Comparative Sino-Vietnamese Legal Study with Historical-Juridical Analysis and Annotations*. Athens, Ohio: Ohio University Press, 1987.

Nhat Minh. "Viet Nam ngay mot thua thiet khi buon ban voi Trung Quoc" [Vietnam suffers increasing disadvantages in trade with China]. *VnExpress*, 13 August 2012 <http://vnexpress.net/gl/kinh-doanh/2012/08/viet-nam-ngay-mot-thua-thiet-khi-buon-ban-voi-trung-quoc/> (accessed 4 December 2012).

Ninh, K. "Vietnam: Struggle and Cooperation". In *Asian Security Practice: Material and Ideational Influences*, edited by M. Alagappa, pp. 445–76. Stanford, CA: Stanford University Press, 1998.

O'Brien, K.J. and L. Li. "Accommodating 'Democracy' in a One-party State: Introducing Village Elections in China". *China Quarterly* 162 (2000): 465–89.

O'Donnell, G. *Modernization and Bureaucratic-Authoritarianism: Studies in South American Politics*. Berkeley: University of California, Institute of International Studies, 1973.

OECD. *OECD Investment Policy Reviews: Viet Nam 2009 — Policy Framework for Investment Assessment*. OECD Publishing, 2010.

Oneal, J.R., F.H. Oneal, Z. Maoz and B.M. Russett. "The Liberal Peace: Interdependence, Democracy, and International Conflict, 1950–85". *Journal of Peace Research* 33, no. 1 (1996): 11–28.

———— and J.L. Ray. "New Tests of the Democratic Peace: Controlling for Economic Interdependence, 1950–85". *Political Research Quarterly* 50, no. 4 (1997): 751–75.

———— and B.M. Russett. "The Classical Liberals Were Right: Democracy, Interdependence, and Conflict, 1950–1985". *International Studies Quarterly* 41, no. 2 (1997): 267–95.

———— and B.M. Russett. "The Kantian Peace: The Pacific Benefits of Democracy, Interdependence, and International Organizations, 1885–1992". *World Politics* 52, no. 1 (1999): 1–37.

O'Rourke, R. *China Naval Modernization: Implications for US Navy Capabilities: Background and Issues for Congress*. Washington, D.C.: Congressional Research Service, 2013.

Owen, J.M. *Liberal Peace, Liberal War: American Politics and International Security*. New York: Cornell University Press, 2000.

Owen, N.A. and C.H. Schofield. "Disputed South China Sea Hydrocarbons in Perspective". *Marine Policy* 36, no. 3 (2012): 809–22 <doi: http://dx.doi.org/10.1016/j.marpol.2011.11.010>.

Papaioannou, E. and G. Siourounis. "Economic and Social Factors Driving the Third Wave of Democratization". *Journal of Comparative Economics* 36, no. 3 (2008): 365–87.

Pape, R.A. "Soft Balancing against the United States". *International Security* 30, no. 1 (2005): 7–45.

Pastor, R.A. and Q. Tan. "The Meaning of China's Village Elections". *China Quarterly* 162, no. 1 (2000): 490–512.

Paul, T.V. "Introduction: The Enduring Axioms of Balance of Power Theory and Their Contemporary Relevance". In *Balance of Power: Theory and Practice in the 21st Century*, edited by T.V. Paul, J.J. Wirtz and M. Fortmann, pp. 1–25. Stanford: Stanford University Press, 2004.

———. "Soft Balancing in the Age of US Primacy". *International Security* 30, no. 1 (2005): 46–71.

Perlez, J. and Gladstone, R. "China Flexes Its Muscles in Dispute With Vietnam". *New York Times*, 8 May 2014 <http://www.nytimes.com/2014/05/09/world/asia/china-and-vietnam.html?ref=world> (accessed 9 June 2014).

PetroVietnam. *Lich su nganh dau khi Viet Nam (den nam 2010)* [History of Vietnam's Oil and Gas Industry (up to 2010)], Vol. 1. Ha Noi: National Political Publishing House, 2011a.

———. *Lich su nganh dau khi Viet Nam (den nam 2010)* [History of Vietnam's Oil and Gas Industry (up to 2010)], Vol. 3. Ha Noi: National Political Publishing House, 2011b.

———. "Bao cao thuong nien 2011" [Annual Report 2011]. 2012 <http://www.pvn.vn/cms/data/files/file/03_2013/03_2013_88.pdf> (accessed 5 May 2014).

Pham Huyen. "Tap doan Than cung 'to' kho vi nha thau Trung Quoc" [Vinacomin denouces Chinese contractors]. *Vietnam Economic Forum*, 24 September 2010 <http://vef.vn/2010-09-24-tap-doan-than-cung-to-kho-vi-nha-thau-trung-quoc> (accessed 8 December 2012).

———. "Xuat sieu 'duoc tieng khong duoc mieng'" [Trade surplus: Not much true value]. *Vietnamnet*, 26 December 2012 <http://vietnamnet.vn/vn/kinh-te/102573/xuat-sieu--duoc-tieng-khong-duoc-mieng-.html> (accessed 10 January 2013).

Pham Tuyen. "Kien nghi xem lai chat luong nha thau Trung Quoc" [Quality of Chinese contractors proposed to be reconsidered]. *Tien Phong*, 15 September 2011 <http://www.tienphong.vn/Kinh-Te/551770/Kien-nghi-xem-lai-chat-luong-nha-thau-Trung-Quoc-tpp.html> (accessed 4 December 2012).

Phan Le. "Viet Nam phan doi cam danh bat ca tren Bien Dong" [Vietnam protests fishing moratorium in East Sea]. *VnExpress*, 15 May 2012 <http://vnexpress.net/gl/the-gioi/2012/05/viet-nam-phan-doi-cam-danh-bat-ca-tren-bien-dong/> (accessed 25 April 2013).

Phong Cam. "Hon ba van lao dong ngoai 'chui' o Viet Nam" [More than 30,000 illegal foreign workers in Vietnam]. *Tien Phong*, 10 January 2012 <http://www.tienphong.vn/kinh-te/563833/hon-ba-van-lao-dong-ngoai-chui-o-viet-nam-tpp.html> (accessed 8 December 2012).

Phong, P.C. "Quan he kinh te - thuong mai Viet - Trung tu nam 1991 den nay va trien vong" [Sino-Vietnam economic and trade relations from 1991 to date and prospects]. In *Quan he kinh te - van hoa Viet Nam–Trung Quoc: Hien trang va Trien vong* [Vietnam–China economic and Cultural Relations: Current Conditions and Prospects], edited by National Center of Social Sciences and Humanity, pp. 49–70. Ha Noi: Social Sciences Publishing House, 2001.

Phuong Linh. "GDP co the giam 10% neu thuong mai Viet-Trung ngung tre" [GDP may contract 10% if Sino-Vietnamese trade stops]. *VnExpress*, 28 June 2014 <http://kinhdoanh.vnexpress.net/tin-tuc/doanh-nghiep/gdp-co-the-giam-10-neu-thuong-mai-viet-trung-ngung-tre-3010195.html> (accessed 28 June 2014).

Pipes, D. *In the Path of God: Islam and Political Power*. New York: Basic Books, 1983.

Polachek, S. "Conflict and Trade". *Journal of Conflict Resolution* 24, no. 1 (1980): 55–78.

———. "Conflict and Trade: An Economics Approach to Political International Interactions". In *Economics of Arms Reduction and the Peace Process*, edited by W. Isard and C.H. Anderton, pp. 89–120. Amsterdam: North Holland, 1992.

——— and J. McDonald. "Strategic Trade and the Incentive for Cooperation". In *Disarmament, Economic Conversion, and Peace Management*, edited by M. Chatterji and L.R. Forcey. New York: Praeger, 1992.

Porter, G. "The Transformation of Vietnam's World-view: From Two Camps to Interdependence". *Contemporary Southeast Asia* 12, no. 1 (1990): 1–19.

PRC Permanent Mission to the UN. "Note Verbale CML/17/2009". United Nations website, 7 May 2009 <http://www.un.org/depts/los/clcs_new/submissions_files/mysvnm33_09/chn_2009re_mys_vnm_e.pdfw> (accessed 28 October 2014).

Przeworski, A. and F. Limongi. "Modernization: Theories and Facts". *World Politics* 49, no. 2 (1997): 155–83.

———, M. Alvarez, J.A. Cheibub and F. Limongi. *Democracy and Development: Political Institutions and Well-being in the World, 1950–1990*. Vol. 3. New York: Cambridge University Press, 2000.

Putnam, R.D. "Diplomacy and Domestic Politics: The Logic of Two-Level Games". *International Organization*, 42, no. 3 (1988): 427–60.

Quoc Dung. "Nha thau Trung Quoc bi phat tren 120 ti dong" [Chinese contractor fined over VND120 billion]. *Vietnam Economic Forum*, 16 August 2011 <http://vef.vn/2011-08-16-nha-thau-trung-quoc-bi-phat-hon-120-ti-do-ng> (accessed 8 December 2012).

Radio Free Asia. "Dong thai trich thuong cua Trung Quoc" [China's arrogant move]. 8 July 2009 <http://www.rfa.org/vietnamese/in_depth/China-to-keep-harrasing-Vietnam-media-by-criticize-the-articles-written-about-China-commodities-07082009111748.html> (accessed 29 January 2013).

———. "Tay chay hang Trung Quoc - duoc phep hay khong?" [Boycotting Chinese products: Is it allowed?]. 10 December 2012 <http://www.rfa.org/vietnamese/in_depth/boycot-cn-produc-12102012102902.html> (accessed 29 January 2013).

Ray, H.P. "Early Maritime Contacts between South and Southeast Asia". *Journal of Southeast Asian Studies* 20, no. 1 (1989): 42–54.

Ray, J.L. *Democracy and International Conflict: An Evaluation of the Democratic Peace Proposition.* Columbia: University of South Carolina Press, 1995.

———. "Does Democracy Cause Peace?". *Annual Review of Political Science* 1, no. 1 (1998): 27–46.

Robison, R. "The Politics of 'Asian values'". *Pacific Review* 9, no. 3 (1996): 309–27.

Rosato, S. "The Flawed Logic of Democratic Peace Theory". *American Political Science Review* 97. no. 4 (2003): 585–602.

Ross, M. "Does Oil Hinder Democracy?". *World Politics* 53 (2001): 325–61.

Rotberg, R.I., ed. *China into Africa: Trade, Aid, and Influence.* Washington, D.C.: Brookings Institution Press, 2008.

Rowen, H.S. "When Will the Chinese People be Free?". *Journal of Democracy* 18, no. 3 (2007): 38–52.

Roy, D. "The 'China Threat' Issue: Major Arguments". *Asian Survey* 36, no. 8 (1996): 758–71.

———. "Southeast Asia and China: Balancing or Bandwagoning?". *Contemporary Southeast Asia* 27, no. 2 (2005): 305–22.

Rummel, R.J. "Libertarianism and International Violence". *Journal of Conflict Resolution* 27, no. 1 (1983): 27–71.

RusNavy. "Vympel Shipyard to assist Vietnam in building Russian missile boats". 28 October 2010 <http://rusnavy.com/news/navy/index.php?ELEMENT_ID=10648&print=Y> (accessed 20 August 2013).

Russett, B. *Peace, War, and Numbers.* Beverly Hills, CA: Sage Publications, 1972.

———. *Grasping the Democratic Peace: Principles for a Post Cold War World.* Princeton, NJ: Princeton University Press, 1993.

Sai Gon Giai Phong. "Nong bong buon lau bien gioi phia Bac" [Rampant smuggling along northern border]. 17 December 2012 <http://www.sggp.org.vn/thongtincanuoc/2012/12/306902/> (accessed 26 January 2013).

Sang, H.T., H.T.M. Hanh, N.T.T. Uyen and N.L.T. Xinh. *Nhan thuc va thai do ve Trung Quoc cua sinh vien Dai hoc Quoc gia TP.HCM* [Perception of and attitude toward China among students of VNU-HCM]. Faculty of International Relations, VNU-HCM, HCM City, 2011.

Schumpeter, J. *Capitalism, Socialism, and Democracy*. 3rd ed. New York: Harper and Row, 1950.

Schweller, R.L. "Bandwagoning for Profit: Bringing the Revisionist State Back In". *International Security* 19, no. 1 (1994): 72–107.

Shambaugh, D. "Containment or Engagement of China? Calculating Beijing's Responses". *International Security* 21, no. 2 (1996): 180–209.

———. *China's Communist Party: Atrophy and Adaptation*. Washington, D.C.: Woodrow Wilson Center Press, 2008.

Shekhar, V. "ASEAN's Response to the Rise of China: Deploying a Hedging Strategy". *China Report* 48, no. 3 (2012): 253–68.

Shi, T. "Village Committee Elections in China: Institutionalist Tactics for Democracy". *World Politics* 51, no. 3 (1999): 385–412.

Shiro, M. "Dai Viet and the South China Sea Trade: from the 10th to the 15th Century". *Crossroads: An Interdisciplinary Journal of Southeast Asian Studies* 12, no. 1 (1998): 1–34.

Simmel, G. "The Persistence of Social Groups". *American Journal of Sociology* 3, no. 5 (1898): 662–98.

Singer, J.D. *The Correlates of War: Testing Some Realpolitik Models*. New York: Free Press, 1980.

SIPRI. "The SIPRI Arms Transfers Database". 9 August 2013 <http://www.sipri.org/contents/armstrad/at_data.html> (accessed 17 August 2013).

———. "SIPRI Military Expenditure Database 2015". 2015 <http://www.sipri.org/research/armaments/milex/milex_database> (accessed 17 August 2015).

Skocpol, T. *States and Social Revolutions*. Cambridge: Cambridge University Press, 1979.

Smith, A. "Diversionary Foreign Policy in Democratic Systems". *International Studies Quarterly* 40, no. 1 (1996): 133–54.

Snyder, J. *The Soviet Strategic Culture: Implications for Limited Nuclear Operations*. Santa Monica: RAND Corporation, 1977.

Sørensen, G. *Democracy and Democratization: Processes and Prospects in a Changing World*. 3rd ed. Boulder, CO: Westview Press, 2008.

Storey, I. J. "Creeping Assertiveness: China, the Philippines and the South China Sea Dispute". *Contemporary Southeast Asia* 21, no. 1 (1999): 95–118.

——— and C.A. Thayer. "Cam Ranh Bay: Past Imperfect, Future Conditional". *Contemporary Southeast Asia* 23, no. 3 (2001): 452–73.

Sun, L. "Chinese Military Technology and Dai Viet: c1390–1497". *Asia Research Institute Working Paper Series*, No. 11, 2003.

Swaine, M.D. "Chinese Leadership and Elite Responses to the US Pacific Pivot". *China Leadership Monitor* 38 (2012): 1–26.

Taagepera, R. "Expansion and Contraction Patterns of Large Polities: Context for Russia". *International Studies Quarterly* 41, no. 3 (1997): 475–504.

Tang, J. *Heavy Storm and Gentle Breeze: A Memoir of China's Diplomacy*. New York: HarperCollins Publishers, 2011.

Tang, S.-Y. and X. Zhan. "Civic Environmental NGOs, Civil Society, and Democratisation in China". *Journal of Development Studies* 44, no. 3 (2008): 425–48.

Tanneberg, D., C. Stefes and W. Merkel. "Hard Times and Regime Failure: Autocratic Responses to Economic Downturns". *Contemporary Politics* 19, no. 1 (2013): 115–29 <doi: 10.1080/13569775.2013.773206>.

Taylor, I. "China's Foreign Policy towards Africa in the 1990s". *Journal of Modern African Studies* 36, no. 3 (1998): 443–60.

Taylor, K.W. *The Birth of Vietnam*. Berkeley: University of California Press, 1983.

Telegraph, The. "China blocked exports of rare earth metals to Japan, traders claim". 24 September 2010 <http://www.telegraph.co.uk/finance/china-business/8022484/China-blocked-exports-of-rare-earth-metals-to-Japan-traders-claim.html> (accessed 2 July 2014).

Thach, N.C. "Statement of H.E. Nguyen Co Thach, Vice-Chairman of the Council of Ministers, Minister of Foreign Affairs of the S.R. Vietnam at the International Conference on Cambodia (Paris, July 31, 1989)". In *Cambodia — The 1989 Paris Peace Conference: Background Analysis and Documents*, edited by A. Acharya, P. Lizee and S. Peou, pp. 43–50. New York: Kraus International Publications, 1991.

Thakur, R.C. and C.A. Thayer. *The Soviet Union as an Asian Pacific Power: Implications of Gorbachev's 1986 Vladivostok Initiative*. Boulder, CO: Westview Press, 1987.

Thang, N.D. and N.T.T. Ha. "The Code of Conduct in the South China Sea: The International Law Perspective". Paper presented at the Manila Conference on the South China Sea: Toward a Region of Peace, Cooperation and Progress, Manila, 5–6 July 2011.

——— and N.H. Thao. "China's Nine Dotted Lines in the South China Sea: The 2011 Exchange of Diplomatic Notes Between the Philippines and China". *Ocean Development & International Law* 43, no. 1 (2012): 35–56 <doi: 10.1080/00908320.2012.647490>.

Thanh Huy. "Bao ve tham do tai nguyen dau khi tren vung vien Viet Nam la trach nhiem cua moi nganh" [Protecting oil and gas exploration activities in Vietnam's waters is the common task of all forces]. *Petrotimes*, 28 July 2011 <http://petrotimes.vn/news/vn/xa-hoi/bao-ve-tham-do-tai-nguyen-dau-

khi-tren-vung-bien-viet-nam-la-trach-nhiem-cua-moi-nganh.html> (accessed 22 April 2013).

Thanh Mai. "Viet - Trung dam phan ve bien" [Vietnam and China starts talks on maritime issues]. *VnExpress*, 24 May 2012 <http://vnexpress.net/gl/the-gioi/2012/05/viet-trung-dam-phan-ve-bien/> (accessed 28 March 2013).

Thanh Phong. "'Bay' dau thau gia re" [The low-priced tender "trap"]. *Thanh Nien*, 19 August 2010 <http://www.thanhnien.com.vn/pages/20100819/bay-dau-thau-gia-re.aspx> (accessed 8 December 2012).

Thanh Tung. "Nha thau Trung Quoc va nhung du an quoc te tai tieng" [Chinese contractors and infamous international projects]. *Dan Tri*, 24 July 2012 <http://dantri.com.vn/kinh-doanh/nha-thau-trung-quoc-va-nhung-du-an-quoc-te-tai-tieng-622365.htm> (accessed 8 December 2012).

Thao, N.H. "The China-Vietnam Border Delimitation Treaty of 30 December 1999". *Boundary & Security Bulletin* 8, no. 1 (2000): 87–90.

————. "Vietnam and the Code of Conduct for the South China Sea". *Ocean Development & International Law* 32, no. 2 (2001): 105–30.

————. "The 2002 Declaration on the Conduct of Parties in the South China Sea: A Note". *Ocean Development & International Law* 34, nos. 3–4 (2003): 279–85.

————. "Maritime Delimitation and Fishery Cooperation in the Tonkin Gulf". *Ocean Development & International Law* 36 (2005): 25–44.

———— and R. Amer. "Managing Vietnam's Maritime Boundary Disputes". *Ocean Development & International Law* 38, no. 3 (2007): 305–24 <doi: 10.1080/00908320701530482>.

Thayer, C.A. "Security Issues in Southeast Asia: The Third Indochina War". Paper delivered to Conference on "Security and Arms Control in the North Pacific", co-sponsored by the Peace Research Centre, Strategic and Defence Studies Centre and the Department of International Relations, Research School of Pacific Studies, The Australian National University, Canberra, 12–14 August 1987.

————. "Sino-Vietnamese Relations: The Interplay of Ideology and National Interest". *Asian Survey* 34, no. 6 (1994*a*): 513–28.

————. *The Vietnam People's Army under Doi Moi*. Pacific Strategic Paper no. 7. Singapore: Institute of Southeast Asian Studies, 1994*b*.

————. "Force Modernization: The Case of the Vietnam People's Army. *Contemporary Southeast Asia* 19, no. 1 (1997): 1–28.

————. "Vietnamese Perspectives of the 'China Threat'". In *The China Threat: Perceptions, Myths and Reality*, edited by H.S.S. Yee and Ian Storey, pp. 270–92. London & New York: Routledge, 2002.

————. "China's 'New Security Concept' and Southeast Asia". In *Asia-Pacific Security: Policy Challenges*, edited by D.W. Lovell, pp. 89–107. Singapore: Institute of Southeast Asian Studies, 2003.

————. "Vietnam: The Tenth Party Congress and After". In *Southeast Asian Affairs 2007*, edited by D. Singh and L.C. Salazar, pp. 379–97. Singapore: Institute of Southeast Asian Studies, 2007.

————. "The Structure of Vietnam-China Relations, 1991–2008". Paper presented at the 3rd International Conference on Vietnamese Studies, Hanoi, 4–7 December 2008.

————. "Political Legitimacy of Vietnam's One Party-State: Challenges and Responses". *Journal of Current Southeast Asian Affairs* 28, no. 4 (2009*a*): 47–70.

————. "Vietnam and the Challenge of Political Civil Society". *Contemporary Southeast Asia* 31, no. 1 (2009*b*): 1–27.

————. *Vietnam People's Army: Development and Modernization*. Bandar Seri Begawan: Sultan Haji Bolkiah Institute of Defence and Strategic Studies, 2009*c*.

————. "The United States and Chinese Assertiveness in the South China Sea". *Security Challenges* 6, no. 2 (2010): 69–84.

————. "Political Legitimacy in Vietnam Under Challenge". In *Political Legitimacy in Asia: New Leadership Challenges*, edited by H. Patapan, J. Kane and L.H. Chieh, pp. 39–59. London: Palgrave, 2011*a*.

————. "The Tyranny of Geography: Vietnamese Strategies to Constrain China in the South China Sea". *Contemporary Southeast Asia* 33, no. 3 (2011*b*): 348–69.

————. "ASEAN's Code of Conduct in the South China Sea: A Litmus Test for Community-Building?". *Asia-Pacific Journal* 10, no. 4 (2012*a*): 1–23.

————. "Vietnam's regional growth tied to renewed Russian relations". *Global Times*, 24 September 2012*b* <http://www.globaltimes.cn/content/735031.shtml>.

————. "ASEAN, China and the Code of Conduct in the South China Sea". *SAIS Review of International Affairs* 33, no. 2 (2013): 75–84.

The Dung. "Thanh lap luc luong kiem ngu" [Fishery patrol force to be established]. *Nguoi Lao dong*, 4 December 2012 <http://nld.com.vn/20121204101220165p0c1002/thanh-lap-luc-luong-kiem-ngu.htm> (accessed 25 April 2013).

Them, T.N. *Co so van hoa Viet Nam [The Foundation of Vietnamese Culture]*. HCM City: NXB Giao duc [Education Publishing House], 1999.

Thien Phuoc. "1.000 lao dong Trung Quoc lam viec khong phep tai Ca Mau" [1,000 Chinese workers have no working permit in Ca Mau]. *VnExpress*, 10 August 2011 <http://vnexpress.net/gl/xa-hoi/2011/08/1-000-lao-dong-trung-quoc-lam-viec-khong-phep-tai-ca-mau/> (accessed 8 December 2012).

Thirlwall, A.P. *Growth and Development: With Special Reference to Developing Economies*. Macmillan, 1994.

Thu Phuong. "Trung Quoc dau tu nghin ti vao Nam Dinh: Them lo?" [China to invest trillions of dongs into Nam Dinh: More reasons for concern?]. *Dat*

Viet, 11 March 2014 <http://www.baodatviet.vn/kinh-te/doanh-nghiep/trung-quoc-dau-tu-nghin-ty-vao-nam-dinh-them-lo-3003226/> (accessed 12 March 2014).

Thul, P.C. and S. Grudgings. "SE Asia meeting in disarray over sea dispute with China". Reuters, 13 July 2012 <http://www.reuters.com/article/2012/07/13/us-asean-summit-idUSBRE86C0BD20120713> (accessed 5 September 2013).

Tianran, X. "Deep-water drilling starts". *Global Times*, 9 May 2012 <http://www.globaltimes.cn/NEWS/tabid/99/ID/708511/Deep-water-drilling-starts.aspx> (accessed 25 April 2013).

Tien Phong. "'Diem mat' vu khi moi cua quan doi Viet Nam" [New weapons of Vietnamese army]. 30 May 2013 <http://www.tienphong.vn/hanh-trang-nguoi-linh/628314/Diem-mat-vu-khi-moi-cua-quan-doi-Viet-Nam-tpot.html> (accessed 19 August 2013).

Tien, T.D. "Nang quan he Viet - Trung len tam cao moi" [Elevating Vietnam–China relations to a New Height]. Communist Party of Vietnam Website, 30 October 2005 <http://www.cpv.org.vn/cpv/Modules/Preview/PrintPreview.aspx?co_id=30569&cn_id=96243> (accessed 25 November 2012).

Tonnesson, S. "Vietnam's Objective in the South China Sea: National or Regional Security?". *Contemporary Southeast Asia* 22, no. 1 (2000): 199–220.

Tran, N.V. "Our gratitude for China's generous and unselfish aid". *Nhan Dan (People's Daily)*, 28 September 1959 <http://www.dtic.mil/cgi-bin/GetTRDoc?Location=U2&doc=GetTRDoc.pdf&AD=ADA367409>.

Trung, N. "Phai chan dung nguy co tai dien kich ban Thanh Do 1990" [The threat of repeating the 1990 Chengdu disaster must be stopped]. *Viet-studies*, 10 August 2012 <http://www.viet-studies.info/NguyenTrung/NguyenTrung_ChanDungThanhDo.htm> (accessed 10 November 2012).

Tull, D.M. "China's Engagement in Africa: Scope, Significance and Consequences". *Journal of Modern African Studies* 44, no. 3 (2006): 459–79.

Tung, N.V. "Vietnam's Security Challenges: Ha Noi's New Approach to National Security and Implications to Defense and Foreign Policies". In *Asia Pacific Countries' Security Outlook and Its Implications for the Defense Sector*, edited by National Institute for Defense Studies, pp. 107–22. Tokyo: National Institute for Defense Studies, 2010.

Tuoitrenews. "Work starts on first thermal plant in southern Vietnam". 9 August 2010 <http://www.tuoitrenews.vn/cmlink/tuoitrenews/business/work-starts-on-first-thermal-plant-in-southern-vietnam-1.8718/7.13994> (accessed 8 December 2012).

Turchin, P., T.D. Hall and J.M. Adams. "East-West Orientation of Historical Empires". *Journal of World-Systems Research* 12, no. 2 (2006): 219–29.

UNCTAD. "FDI outward stock, by region and economy, 1990–2014". 24 June 2015 <http://unctad.org/Sections/dite_dir/docs/WIR2015/WIR15_tab04.xls> (accessed 10 October 2015).

UNDP. *Human Development Report 2002: Deepening Democracy in a Fragmented World*. New York: UNDP, 2002.

United Nations. *Treaty Series* (Vol. 2336). New York, 2007.

U.S. Department of State. "Secretary of State Hillary Rodham Clinton Remarks" at Press Availability, National Convention Center, Hanoi, 23 July 2010 <http://www.state.gov/secretary/rm/2010/07/145095.htm> (accessed 5 September 2013).

U.S. Embassy in Hanoi. "2008 Recap of the Sino-Vietnamese South China Sea Territorial Dispute". *Wikileaks*, 20 January 2009*a* <https://www.wikileaks.org/plusd/cables/09HANOI52_a.html> (accessed 9 July 2014).

———. "Bauxite Controversy Produces Leadership Divisions, Vibrant National Assembly Debate". *Wikileaks*, 11 June 2009*b* <https://wikileaks.org/cable/2009/06/09HANOI537.html> (accessed 9 July 2014).

———. "In Vietnam, China and Bauxite Don't Mix". *Wikileaks*, 29 April 2009*c* <https://wikileaks.org/cable/2009/04/09HANOI413.html> (accessed 9 July 2014).

Valencia, M.J., J.M. Van Dyke and N.A. Ludwig. *Sharing the Resources of the South China Sea*. Honolulu: University of Hawaii Press, 1999.

Van Fossen, A. "The Struggle for Recognition: Diplomatic Competition between China and Taiwan in Oceania". *Journal of Chinese Political Science* 12, no. 2 (2007): 125–46.

Ve Dinh. "Vi dang cua chat luong mang ten nha thau Trung Quoc" [The quality bitterness named "Chinese contractor"]. *Vietnamnet*, 31 August 2011 <http://vietnamnet.vn/vn/chinh-tri/37402/vi-dang-cua-chat-luong-mang-ten-nha-thau-trung-quoc.html> (accessed 8 December 2012).

Vergano, P.R., D. Linotte, D.V. An, L.Q. Lan, N.H. Thanh and N.T.L. Huong. *Qualitative and Quantitative Analysis and Impact Assessment of the ASEAN-China FTA: A Critical Review of the Agreement and Issues for Further Reflection and Future Negotiation*. Ha Noi: EU-Vietnam Multilateral Trade Assistance Project, 2010.

Vien, N.K. *Vietnam: A Long History*. Ha Noi: The Gioi Publishers, 1993.

Vietnam Academy of Social Sciences. *Poverty Reduction in Vietnam: Achievements and Challenges*. Ha Noi: The Gioi Publishers, 2011.

Vietnam Electricity. *Corporate Profile 2010–2011*. Ha Noi: Vietnam Electricity, 2011.

Vietnam National Assembly. "Luat Bien Viet Nam" [Sea Law of Vietnam]. *Government of Vietnam Portal*, 2012 <http://www.chinhphu.vn/portal/page/portal/chinhphu/hethongvanban?class_id=1&mode=detail&document_id=163056> (accessed 28 October 2014).

Vietnam News Agency. "Thoa thuan 5 phuong an hop tac Viet–Trung' [Agreement on five measures to promote Vietnam–China cooperation]. 12 April 2003 <http://vnexpress.net/gl/xa-hoi/2003/04/3b9c6c99/> (accessed 25 November 2012).

———. "Lap duong day nong giua lanh dao Viet Nam–Trung Quoc" [Hot line to be established between leaders of Vietnam and China]. 2 June 2008 <http://vnexpress.net/gl/the-gioi/tu-lieu/2008/06/3ba02e9e/> (accessed 24 June 2013).

———. "Trung Quoc vien tro xay Cung huu nghi Viet–Trung" [China funds the construction of Vietnam–China Friendship Palace]. 30 November 2009 <http://www.vietnamplus.vn/Home/Trung-Quoc-vien-tro-xay-Cung-huu-nghi-VietTrung/200911/25817.vnplus> (accessed 1 December 2012).

———. "Tuyen bo chung hai nuoc Viet nam va Trung Quoc" [Vietnam–China Joint Statement]. 21 June 2013a <http://www.vietnamplus.vn/Home/Tuyen-bo-chung-hai-nuoc-Viet-Nam-va-Trung-Quoc/20136/203252.vnplus> (accessed 6 August 2013).

———. "Viet Nam–Trung Quoc ra tuyen bo chung thoi ky moi" [Vietnam and China issue joint statement for new era of relations]. *VnExpress*, 16 October 2013b <http://vnexpress.net/tin-tuc/the-gioi/tu-lieu/vie-t-nam-trung-quo-c-ra-tuyen-bo-chung-tho-i-ky-mo-i-2895706.html> (accessed 22 December 2013).

Vietnamnet. "Lao dong Trung Quoc 'quay' o cong truong Nghi Son" [Chinese workers cause trouble in Nghi Son]. 22 June 2009 <http://vnn.vietnamnet.vn/xahoi/2009/06/854202/> (accessed 9 December 2013).

———. "Bon doi tong thong voi binh thuong hoa bang giao Viet–My" [Four Presidencies and the Normalization of US–Vietnam Relations]. 2011 <http://tuanvietnam.vietnamnet.vn/2011-12-13-4-doi-tong-thong-voi-binh-thuong-hoa-bang-giao-viet-my> (accessed 4 January 2012).

Vinh, D.N. "Tinh hinh hop tac kinh te thuong mai Viet–Trung 1991–1999 va trien vong [Economic and trade cooperation between Vietnam and China in the period of 1991–1999 and prospects]". In *Quan he kinh te - van hoa Viet Nam–Trung Quoc: Hien trang va Trien vong* [Vietnam–China Economic and Cultural Relations: Current Conditions and Prospects], edited by National Center of Social Sciences and Humanity, pp. 71–83. Ha Noi: Social Sciences Publishing House, 2001.

VnEconomy. "Viet–Trung lap duong dien thoai noi thang giua hai bo quoc phong" [Vietnam, China to set up direct hot line between defence ministries]. 7 June 2013 <http://vneconomy.vn/thoi-su/viet-trung-lap-duong-dien-thoai-noi-thang-giua-hai-bo-quoc-phong-20130607095849127.htm> (accessed 29 October 2014).

VnExpress. "Suc manh 'la chan thep' Bastion tran giu bien Dong" [The strength of the Bastion "steel shield" in the Eastern Sea]. 20 February 2013 <http://

vnexpress.net/tin-tuc/xa-hoi/suc-manh-la-chan-thep-bastion-tran-giu-bien-dong-2426826.html> (accessed 19 August 2013).

Voice of Vietnam. "Thanh lap Uy ban chi dao hop tac song phuong Viet Nam–Trung Quoc" [Steering Committee on Vietnam–China Bilateral Cooperation established]. 12 November 2006 <http://vovnews.vn:2011/Home/Thanh-lap-Uy-ban-chi-dao-hop-tac-song-phuong-Viet-Nam--Trung-Quoc/200611/46970.vov> (accessed 1 November 2012).

Vu, T. "The Persistence of Single-Party Dictatorships: The Case of Vietnam". *Southeast Asia Research Centre Working Paper Series*, No. 121, 2012.

Vu, T.B., B. Gangnes and I. Noy. "Is foreign direct investment good for growth? Evidence from sectoral analysis of China and Vietnam". *Journal of the Asia Pacific Economy* 13, no. 4 (2008): 542–62 <doi: 10.1080/13547860802364976>.

Vuving, A.L. "Strategy and Evolution of Vietnam's China Policy: A Changing Mixture of Pathways". *Asian Survey* 46, no. 6 (2006): 805–24.

———. "Vietnam: A Tale of Four Players". In *Southeast Asian Affairs 2010*, edited by D. Singh, pp. 366–91. Singapore: Institute of Southeast Asian Studies, 2010.

———. "Vietnam in 2012: A Rent-seeking State on the Verge of a Crisis". In *Southeast Asian Affairs 2013*, edited by D. Singh, pp. 325–47. Singapore: Institute of Southeast Asian Studies, 2013.

Walt, S.M. "Alliance Formation and the Balance of World Power". *International Security* 9, no. 4 (1985): 3–43.

———. *The Origins of Alliances*. Ithaca, NY: Cornell University Press, 1987.

Waltz, K.N. *Theory of International Politics*. Reading, MA: Addison-Wesley, 1979.

Wantchekon, L. "Why Do Resource Dependent Countries Have Authoritarian Governments?". *Journal of African Finance and Economic Development* 2 (2002): 57–77.

Waterbury, J. "Democracy without Democrats?". In *Democracy without Democrats? The Renewal of Politics in the Muslim World*, edited by Salame. London: I.B. Tauris, 1994.

Weart, S.R. *Never at War: Why Democracies Will Not Fight One Another*. New Haven, CT: Yale University Press, 1998.

White House. "Joint Statement by President Barack Obama of the United States of America and President Truong Tan Sang of the Socialist Republic of Vietnam". 25 July 2013 <http://www.whitehouse.gov/the-press-office/2013/07/25/joint-statement-president-barack-obama-united-states-america-and-preside> (accessed 29 August 2013).

Whitmore, J.K. "Vietnam and the Monetary Flow of Eastern Asia, Thirteenth to Eighteenth Centuries". In *Precious Metals in the Later Medieval and Early Modern Worlds*, edited by J.F. Richards, pp. 363–93. Durham, N.C.: Carolina Academic Press, 1983.

————. "Social Organization and Confucian Thought in Vietnam". *Journal of Southeast Asian Studies* 15, no. 2 (September 1984): 296–306.

————. "'Elephants Can Actually Swim!': Contemporary Chinese Views of Late Ly Dai Viet". In *Southeast Asia in the 9th to 14th Centuries*, edited by D.G. Marr and A.C. Milner, pp. 117–37. Singapore & Canberra: Institute of Southeast Asian Studies & Research School of Pacific Studies, Australian National University, 1986.

Womack, B. "Sino-Vietnamese Border Trade: The Edge of Normalization". *Asian Survey* 34, no. 6 (1994): 495–512.

————. *China and Vietnam: The Politics of Asymmetry*. New York: Cambridge University Press, 2006.

Woodside, A. *Vietnam and the Chinese Model: A Comparative Study of Vietnamese and Chinese Government in the First Half of the Nineteenth Century*. Cambridge, MA: Council on East Asian Studies, Harvard University, 1971.

————. "Central Vietnam's Trading World in the 18th Century as Seen in Le Quy Don's 'Frontier Chronicles'". In *Essays into Vietnamese Pasts*, edited by K.W. Taylor and J.K. Whitmore. Ithaca, NY: Cornell Southeast Asia Program, 1995.

World Bank. "GDP (current US$)". 2015*a* <http://data.worldbank.org/indicator/NY.GDP.MKTP.CD> (accessed 20 October 2015).

————. "Vietnam Country Metadata". 2015*b* <http://databank.worldbank.org/data/reports.aspx?source=2&country=VNM&series=&period=#> (accessed 20 October 2015).

Xiaosong, G. and B. Womack. "Border Cooperation between China and Vietnam in the 1990s". *Asian Survey* 40, no. 6 (2000): 1042–58.

Xinhua. "China's foreign trade up 7.6 pct in 2013". *Global Times*, 2014 <http://www.globaltimes.cn/content/836785.shtml> (accessed 1 August 2015).

Xinhua News Agency. "China-Vietnam trade hits $16.6 bln in first 10 months". 11 December 2008 <http://news.xinhuanet.com/english/2008-12/11/content_10490955.htm> (accessed 12 March 2012).

Xuan, N.T. and Y. Xing. "Foreign direct investment and exports: The experiences of Vietnam". *Economics of Transition* 16, no. 2 (2008): 183–197 <doi: 10.1111/j.1468-0351.2008.00321.x>.

Xuan Tung. "Viet Nam–Ha Lan ki 32 hop dong thuong mai quan su" [Vietnam and the Netherlands concluded 32 military comercial deals]. *Dat Viet*, 17 August 2013 <http://www.baodatviet.vn/chinh-tri-xa-hoi/201308/viet-nam-ha-lan-ki-32-hop-dong-thuong-mai-quan-su-2352748/> (accessed 20 August 2013).

Yee, H.S. and I. Storey. *The China Threat: Perceptions, Myths and Reality*. London: Routledge, 2002.

Yi, R. "Motivation of Chinese investment in Vietnam". *Chinese Geographical Science* 16, no. 1 (2006): 41–47.

Yu, P.K.-H. "The Chinese (Broken) U-shaped Line in the South China Sea: Points, Lines, and Zones". *Contemporary Southeast Asia* 25, no. 3 (2003): 405–30.

Zafar, A. "The Growing Relationship between China and Sub-Saharan Africa: Macroeconomic, Trade, Investment, and Aid Links". *World Bank Research Observer* 22, no. 1 (2007): 103–30.

Zakaria, F. "Islam, Democracy, and Constitutional Liberalism". *Political Science Quarterly* 119, no. 1 (2004): 1–20.

Zhai, Q. "Beijing and the Vietnam Peace Talks, 1965-68: New Evidence from Chinese Sources". *Cold War International History Project, Working Paper No. 18*, 1997.

―――. *China and the Vietnam Wars, 1950–1975*. Chapel Hill: University of North Carolina Press, 2000.

Zhang, X. "China's 1979 War with Vietnam: A Reassessment". *China Quarterly* 184 (2005): 851–74.

―――. "Deng Xiaoping and China's Decision to go to War with Vietnam". *Journal of Cold War Studies* 12, no. 3 (2010): 3–29.

Zhao, S. "China's Global Search for Energy Security: Cooperation and Competition in Asia-Pacific". *Journal of Contemporary China* 17, no. 55 (2008): 207–27 <doi:10.1080/10670560701809460>.

Zou, K. "The Chinese Traditional Maritime Boundary Line in the South China Sea and Its Legal Consequences for the Resolution of the Dispute over the Spratly Islands". *International Journal of Marine and Coastal Law* 14, no. 1 (1999): 27–55.

―――. "Historic Rights in International Law and in China's Practice". *Ocean Development and International Law* 32, no. 2 (2001): 149–68.

―――. "The Sino-Vietnamese Agreement on Maritime Boundary Delimitation in the Gulf of Tonkin". *Ocean Development & International Law* 36 (2005): 13–24.

―――. "Joint Development in the South China Sea: A New Approach". *International Journal of Marine and Coastal Law* 21, no. 1 (2006): 83–109.

Index

Note: Page numbers followed by "n" refer to notes

About the Author

Le Hong Hiep is Fellow at the ISEAS – Yusof Ishak Institute, Singapore, and Lecturer at the Faculty of International Relations, Vietnam National University, Ho Chi Minh City.

Hiep earned his PhD in International and Political Studies from the University of New South Wales, Australian Defence Force Academy, Canberra. Before becoming an academic, he worked for the Ministry of Foreign Affairs of Vietnam from 2004 to 2006.

Hiep's scholarly articles and analyses have been published in *Contemporary Southeast Asia, Asian Politics & Policy, Southeast Asian Affairs, Korean Journal of Defence Analysis, ASPI Strategic Insights, American Review, The Diplomat, East Asia Forum,* and *The National Interest.*

www.ingramcontent.com/pod-product-compliance
Lightning Source LLC
Chambersburg PA
CBHW071848270326
41929CB00013B/2146